THE
EVALUATION OF
COMMON
STOCKS

by Arnold Bernhard

SIMON AND SCHUSTER · NEW YORK
1959

LIBRARY OF CONGRESS CATALOG CARD NUMBER: 59–13148

MANUFACTURED IN THE UNITED STATES OF AMERICA

CONTENTS

PREFACE

THE EVALUATION OF COMMON STOCKS

THIS BOOK *is a transcript of four lectures given by the author during October 1958, at the Bernard M. Baruch School of Business and Public Administration of The City College, New York. The suggestion that the subject first be presented in lecture form before publication came from Professor Jerome Cohen, Assistant Dean, who kindly extended the invitation to appear at the Business School.*

The theme of the lectures was that a disciplined and continuously current standard for determining the value of stocks was essential to rational investing—and especially so during periods when prices moved widely and rapidly in one direction, as had been true during the four years preceding the lecture series. At such a time the confronting question is whether the newly attained price level is right or wrong. Without a standard there is no way to make the determination; and without a determination, the imagination of the investing public, undefended by any rational discipline, falls inevitably under the sway of prevailing sentiment. That way lies the madness of 1929, of 1932, of 1949 and of today.

One of the most eccentric characteristics of the American investment markets is that they have never acknowledged that there should be, or could be, an objective standard for the current evaluation of stocks. In some professional circles there is downright hostility toward the very idea of a standard arrived at by disciplined statistical methods.

Yet the need for such a standard is felt by the great majority of investors. That is demonstrated by the growth, over a period of twenty-one years, of The Value Line Investment Survey, from a mimeographed sheet to one of the most widely circulated investment advisory services in the world. From the beginning, the salient and radical characteristic of this Survey, of which the author is founder and research director, has been its continuous formulation of specific standards of value in respect to the individual stocks covered in the Survey. These standards, by which stocks are rated in the Survey, are based upon correlations over a period of years between prices on the one hand and earnings, dividends and other value factors on the other.

The evolution of the methods of rating has dictated their change from time to time; the reasons for the major changes are explained in these studies. Efforts are constantly being made to improve the Value Line Ratings, to find more significant variables and to reduce the uncertainty of forecasts. It is probable that over the next few years the methods of rating will be further refined. Even in their present form, though, they have proven useful.

Although the production and publication of the Value Line Survey is a competitive and profit-making operation, its methods have always been fully disclosed. The formulas by which prices are equated to earnings, dividends and other variables are set out on the face of the report on each stock. The methods by which the correlations are found have always been revealed.

Because this book is being published some eleven months after the lectures were given, some of the individual stock examples have, at the suggestion of the publisher, been up-dated to January 1, 1959. In most cases the prices which prevailed in January 1959 were even higher than those in October 1958, when the argument was submitted that the then-current prices were too high in relation to objectively determined standards of value.

The standards of value described here were developed over a period of twenty-one years. Literally hundreds of experiments were undertaken. As is ordinarily found to be the case in research, failures far outnumbered successes. Yet it is encouraging that the sum total of these efforts is now contributing something of value not only to the security analyst but also to the economist (since the market will at times exert a powerful influence upon both consumer buying and capital investing, and its aberrations from determinable norms

viii

therefore become a matter of concern to all thoughtful men). The Ratings, even in their still imperfect state, are a profitable refutation, in being and in practice, of the brazen proposition that stocks can be priced without regard to a standard of value. Every period of madness in the stock market grew out of wild, undisciplined variation in the multipliers placed upon the earnings and dividends. Such multipliers cannot be expected to remain constant at all levels of earnings and dividends; but neither can they be permitted to fluctuate irresponsibly to the tune of pure sentiment. The Value Line Ratings give objective indications of what the normal values are in relation to current and foreseeable earnings and dividends.

The contributions of three members of the Value Line research staff have been especially significant in the development of the methods which are discussed in this book. Samuel Eisenstadt, chief statistician, over the past eleven years has been in charge of formulating into statistical method the numerous suggestions as to how value factors might be proved to be significant determinants of future price. And it was he who two years ago finally developed the method presently in use of correlating the prices of a list of stocks grouped according to quality to the average earnings and dividends of that same group over a period of time, and then applying these group equations "cross-sectionally" to the individual stocks of the same Quality Grade. Heinz H. Hutzler, economist, was especially concerned with the development of techniques for measuring growth and stability, the factors which determine the Quality Grade. His method of eliminating year-to-year distortions in measuring those factors may prove of especial interest to students. Nikita D. Roodkowsky, mathematician, has assisted in most of the experiments, bringing to them particularly an inquiry into the validity of the methods.

In the preparation of the lectures, and the production of the book itself, I would particularly acknowledge the assistance of Doris R. Field, on the checking of references and factual data; of Lina T. Swisher, on the preparation of the numerous charts and tables; of Mary Ann J. Feldman, my secretary, in typing the manuscript; and of Alfred Cabrera and his assistant, Brendan McCusker, on the graphic work involved.

To all of them, to Walter C. Boschen, managing editor of The

Value Line Investment Survey, and to the security analysts, statisticians and economists who make up our organization's research staff and who have worked earnestly with me in our effort to develop disciplined methods for evaluating stocks, my thanks. If it all seem like a riddle to which no entirely conclusive answer has yet been found, still it has been a consistent pleasure to share with them the excitement of the search.

ARNOLD BERNHARD

x

CHAPTER

1

THE FIRST of these four chapters is concerned with some widely held but fallacious generalizations about stock evaluation. Much fancy and superstition becloud the subject. Any attempt to get at what is true therefore requires, first of all, clearing away at least part of that which obscures the truth.

Let me start with the popular fallacy that inflation is a factor to be considered in the evaluation of stocks.

At the time this is written, early in 1959, stock prices are high by historical standards. The Standard & Poor's average of industrial stocks is at the highest point in its history. So, too, is the Dow-Jones Industrial Average. The ratio of stock prices to earnings is abnormally high. The Standard & Poor's industrial stock average, for example, is priced at 20 times earnings. We all recognize in retrospect that stocks were too high in 1929 when, at the very peak of the market, they also stood at 20 times earnings. By contrast, in 1949, at the beginning of this bull market, stocks were priced at only 5.4 times earnings. In 1949 the average of stocks yielded 7.6%, whereas today the yield is 3.2%, less than half as much. In 1929 the average of stocks also yielded 3.2% at its peak. Figure 1 shows how the Standard & Poor's average stood in relation

1

to earnings and dividends in the three years of comparison: (1) 1929, when stocks admittedly were high, (2) 1949, when in retrospect we recognize that they were low, and (3) now, when they are at record highs, but not too high in the opinion of most people who buy or hold them. (If most buyers of stocks thought them too high, they would refrain from buying; and if most holders of stocks thought them too high, they would sell. The change in the supply-demand relationship would then bring prices down.)

FIGURE 1

Industrial Stock Price Index, Price/Earnings Ratios and Dividend Yields, 1929, 1949, 1958

	Selected Dates		
	1929	1949	1958
	PEAK	NADIR	PEAK
	(Sept. 7)	(June 13)	(Dec. 31)
Average Price Index *	25.38	13.23	58.97
Price/Earnings Ratio	20	5.4	20
Yield	3.2%	7.6%	3.2%
	Annual Averages		
	1929	1949	1958
Average Price Index *	21.35	15.00	49.36
Price/Earnings Ratio	16	6.2	17
Yield	3.8%	7.6%	3.8%

* (1941–43 = 10)

Source: *Standard & Poor's Trade and Securities Statistics.*

By the criterion of the stock/bond yield ratio, stocks are over-priced today, as can be seen from Figure 2. In terms of the stock/bond yield ratio, stocks are more overvalued now than at *any time of good business* since their 1929 peak.

Yet, despite the apparently gross overvaluation, there is little evidence of the frenetic speculation that characterized 1929. The percentage of stock shares traded per month has been running around 1.3% of the total outstanding. In 1929, by contrast, the monthly

2

FIGURE 2

Stock/Bond Yield Ratios and Level of Business Activity, 1926–1959

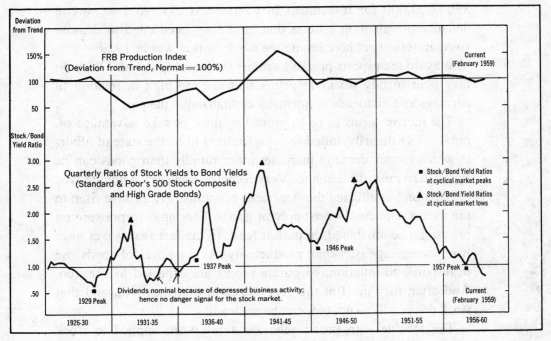

Survey of Current Business.
Computations by The Value Line Investment Survey.

trading volume averaged 9.6% of the shares then outstanding. Obviously, the turnover, or change of ownership, is not on the order of magnitude that could be described as symptomatic of public excitement. Most stocks are firmly lodged in the safe-deposit boxes of their owners. Brokers' loans show no great expansion. In fact, in relation to market values, brokers' loans are small, constituting only .9% of the market value of all stocks as against 8.8% in 1929.

In spite of the historically high prices and apparent overvaluation relative to earnings and yields, an important institutional investor, the American Telephone and Telegraph Company's Pension Fund, announced [1] that it was henceforth going to commit 10% of its

[1] The policy announcement, made in June 1958, became effective August 1, 1958.

3

capital to common stocks instead of bonds. Such redoubtable investment experts as the Lehman Corporation and Lazard Frères have only recently formed open-end mutual funds aggregating over $300,000,000 for investment in common stocks. And all this in defiance of valuation criteria that have long been cited to demonstrate in retrospect how insane the stock market was in 1929!

Why do the experts proceed against the warning signals? Why do they plan to buy stocks at prices that are too high in relation to earnings and dividends as normally capitalized in the past?

The motive seems to be to protect against, or take advantage of, inflation. Ordinarily, inflation is understood to be the state of affairs in which money demand increases more rapidly than goods can be supplied to meet the demand. Very recently, however, a unique type of inflation has afflicted the American economy. Prices have risen in the face of an actual oversupply of goods. This upward pressure on prices can be attributed, in part at least, to the fact that wages have been increasing faster than productivity. As the prices of goods rise in response to inflation, corporate profits are expected to rise, too. And often they do. But the generalization that they will, and that stock prices will go up, too, can be misleading.

The trouble with broad generalizations when applied to stock evaluation is not that they are without some truth, but that too much of the truth has been left out of them. The same, I imagine, may be said of generalizations on other topics.

Let us examine, for example, the comparative price histories of 20 stocks during the postwar inflationary period beginning in 1946 (see Figures 3 to 12 on pp. 5–14). (During this time the Bureau of Labor Statistics' cost-of-living index went up from 77.8 to 123.9, or 59%. Its wholesale price index went up from 69.6 to 119.2, or 71%.) The stocks are paired, two to an industry. The heavy lines depict the course of the annual average prices of the stocks in question. Note that the price movements within the same industry were divergent. In one case, the price went up, as is commonly expected during inflation. In the other case, and within the same industrial classification, the price did not go up, and in some instances actually declined. Obviously inflation did not have a general upward effect on the prices of these stocks.

4

FIGURE 3

Prices, Earnings and Dividends Per Share for Two Printing and Publishing Companies, 1946–1958

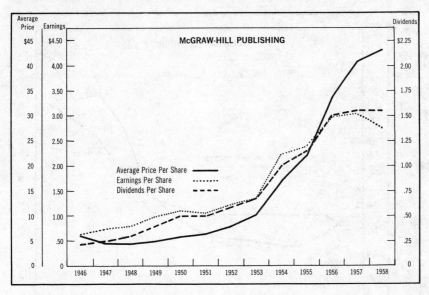

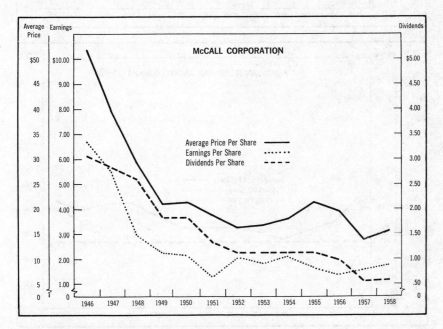

Source: The Value Line Investment Survey.

FIGURE 4

Prices, Earnings and Dividends Per Share for Two Telephone Companies, 1946–1958

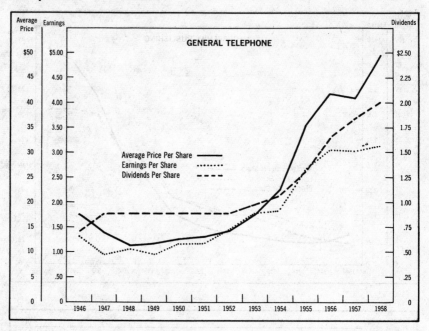

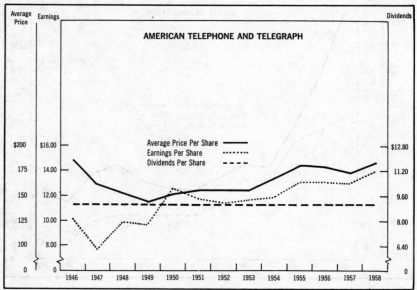

Source: The Value Line Investment Survey.

FIGURE 5

Prices, Earnings and Dividends Per Share for Two Railroad Companies, 1946–1958

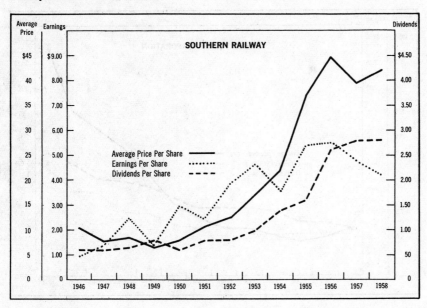

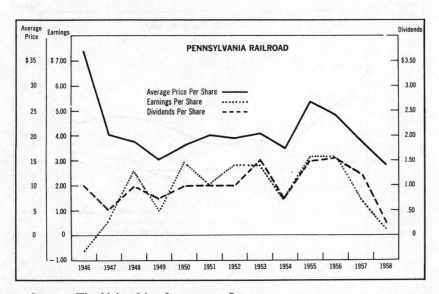

Source: The Value Line Investment Survey.

7

FIGURE 6

Prices, Earnings and Dividends Per Share for Two Electric Utility Companies, 1946–1958

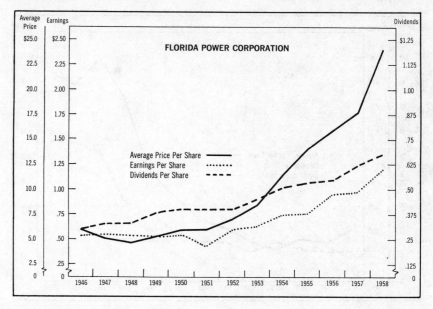

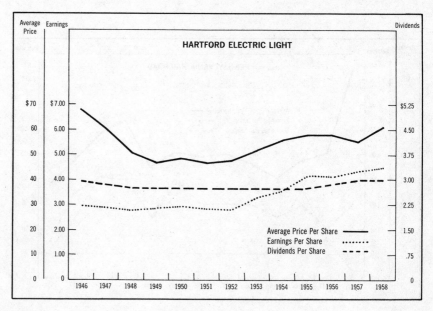

Source: The Value Line Investment Survey.

FIGURE 7

Prices, Earnings and Dividends Per Share for Two Drug Companies, 1946–1958

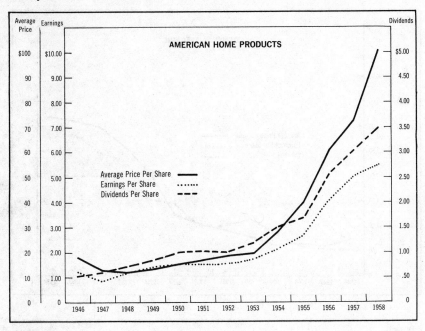

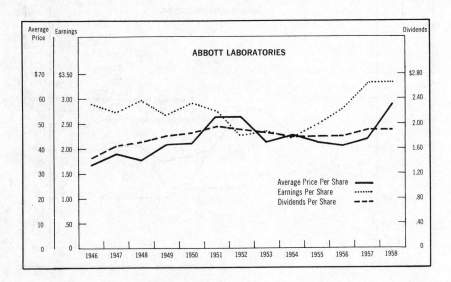

Source: The Value Line Investment Survey.

FIGURE 8

Prices, Earnings and Dividends Per Share for Two Electrical Equipment Companies, 1946–1958

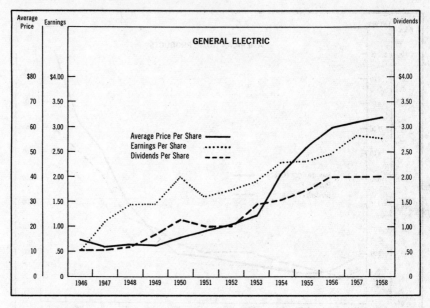

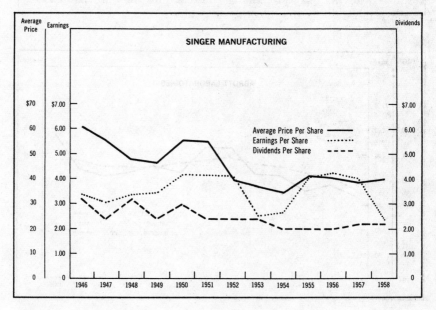

Source: The Value Line Investment Survey.

10

FIGURE 9

Prices, Earnings and Dividends Per Share for Two Nonferrous Metal Companies, 1946–1958

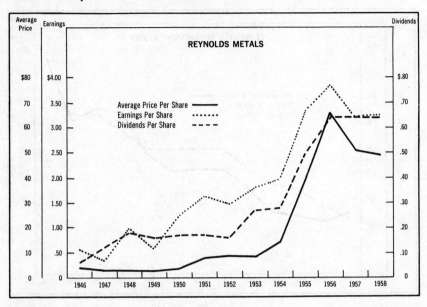

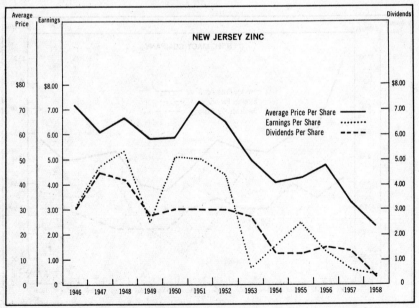

Source: The Value Line Investment Survey.

FIGURE 10

Prices, Earnings and Dividends Per Share for Two Department Stores, 1946–1958

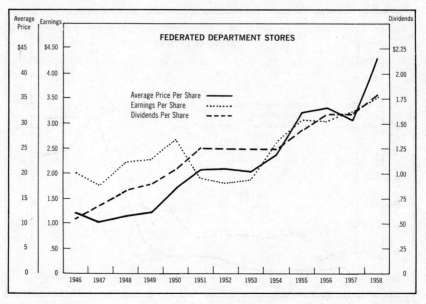

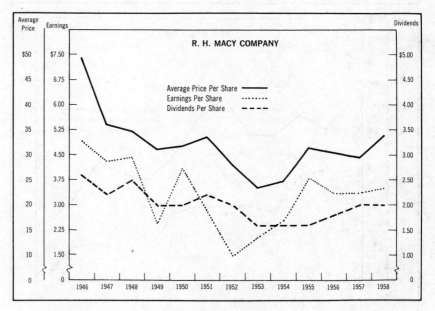

Source: The Value Line Investment Survey.

12

FIGURE 11

Prices, Earnings and Dividends Per Share for Two Chemical Companies, 1946–1958

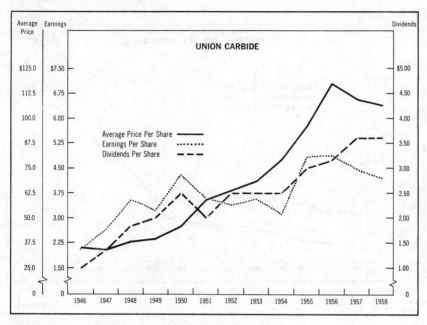

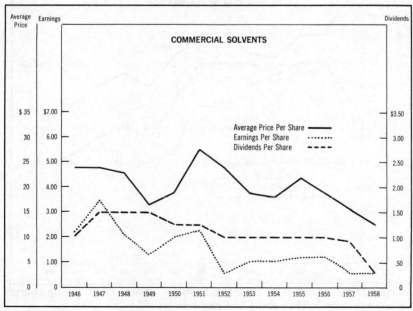

Source: The Value Line Investment Survey.

FIGURE 12

Prices, Earnings and Dividends Per Share for Two Office Equipment Companies, 1946–1958

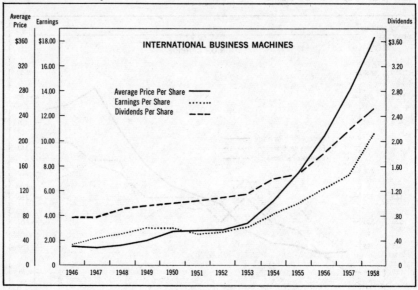

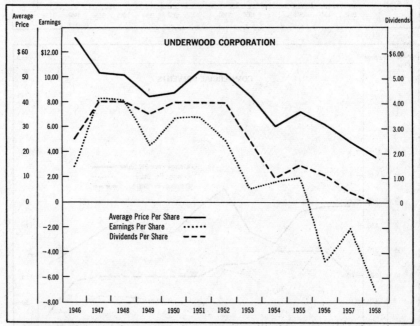

NOTE: Deficit earnings of Underwood stated before non-recurring charges of $6.08 per share in 1956 and $2.14 per share in 1958.

Source: The Value Line Investment Survey.

14

If you will look at the dashed and dotted lines on these charts, which describe the course of cash dividends and earnings, respectively, you will observe that the course of dividends and earnings corresponded in a general way to the course of stock prices. The correlation was not always close, but prices trended in the general direction of dividends and earnings. When the dividend-paying ability (as described by the trend of earnings and dividends) went up, as in the case of McGraw-Hill (Figure 3), the price of the stock went up, too. When the dividend-paying ability went down, as in the case of McCall Corporation, the price went down. And when the dividend-paying ability moved sidewise, as in the case of American Telephone (Figure 4), the price also tended to move out sidewise. At the same time, General Telephone's price went up from 1952 on, when its earnings and dividends turned upward. Similar experiences are cited for two railroad stocks: Southern Railway, which trended upward during the 13-year period, and Pennsylvania Railroad, which moved sidewise (Figure 5); for two electric utilities (Figure 6); two drug stocks (Figure 7); and two electrical-equipment stocks (Figure 8). Additional examples of rising stock prices in reflection of improving dividend-paying ability and declining stock prices in reflection of deteriorating dividend-paying ability are noted for two nonferrous metal stocks (Figure 9); two department-store stocks (Figure 10); two chemical stocks (Figure 11); and two office-equipment stocks (Figure 12). Few exceptions can be found to the rule that the general direction of a stock's price over a period of years corresponds to the direction of its earnings and dividends. It appears then that stock prices are governed, as to general trend, by earnings and dividends over a period of time.

Now please note carefully the negative, as well as the positive, implications of this conclusion. It implies that inflation is not a significant factor in the *evaluation* of stocks. That is not to say that inflation is wholly without significance for the stock market. It *is* to say that the influence of inflation is expressed in the stock market primarily through its effect upon dividend-paying ability. If inflation have the effect of increasing the dividend-paying ability of the stock, the stock goes up in price. But if inflation, or the total of conditions which exist during the period of inflation, have the effect

15

of reducing the dividend-paying ability of the stock, the stock goes down in price. Such movements occur regardless of the purchasing power of the currency. It is important, therefore, to put inflation, like all other environmental factors, in its rightful place. It may be an influence upon dividend-paying ability, but it is not a controlling factor in the *evaluation* of dividend-paying ability. The true equation runs from the dividend-paying ability of the stock to its price, not from the purchasing power of the currency to the stock's price.

To illustrate how misleading generalizations about inflation can be in the stock market, let us refer to the widely circulated discussions of the effect of inflation upon the stock market during the years 1947–1949. In those years, stocks were strikingly cheap relative to earnings and dividends, as well as to bond yields.

In June 1949, the Standard & Poor's industrial stock average sold at 5.4 times earnings to yield 7.6%, in contrast to a price/earnings ratio of 20 and a dividend yield of 3.2% at the beginning of 1959. In 1949 the stock/bond yield ratio was 2.68, compared to a ratio of only .84 in 1959. (This means that stocks then yielded 2.68 times as much as bonds, whereas today they yield less than bonds.)

Now observe what was said about inflation between 1947 and 1949, when stocks were really cheap in relation to dividend-paying ability, and nobody wanted them. The excerpts that I am about to cite are selected, of course; but you can refer to the stock-market letters, the newspaper comments and the magazine articles of the time to satisfy yourself that the following opinions were typical of the thinking of the day and a fair reflection of the popular reasoning.

An article in *Barron's* [2] entitled "Phantom Profits Worry Foresighted Managements," with the subheading, "Stockholders Must Be Taught to See Red Ink Through the Black," stated: "Business executives today, contemplating the black dollar figures that adorn the last lines of their income accounts are giving more . . . thought to informing their shareholders . . . that there is a strong tinge of red in the black . . . The businessman is being hit by the high costs of corporate living just where the bruises don't show. His re-

[2] Arundel Cotter, "Phantom Profits Worry Foresighted Managements," *Barron's,* August 11, 1947, p. 7.

16

ports, if they follow standard corporate accounting, give his stock-holders a false picture of the results of the corporation's current activities . . . *All these evils arise from inflation . . ."* [Italics ours]

The effect of this article was to persuade readers that just because of inflation the valuation of stocks *should be low* relative to reported earnings and dividends.

An article appearing in *The Wall Street Journal* commented on the inadequacy of depreciation charges in a period of rising replacement costs: "Depreciation reserves, necessarily based on the original cost of plants and facilities built or acquired when costs were a fraction of what they are today, are entirely inadequate to meet the needs of business now."

Another writer, in *The Commercial and Financial Chronicle*,[3] expressed the opinion that rising prices could benefit common stocks only in the transition period, and even in this period the benefit might not be general. He felt that in the long-term outlook there was no possible foundation for expecting an increased profit rate on investment capital because of higher capital replacement costs, larger additional plant investment and technological obsolescence of older capital equipment.

"While prices are actively rising, enlarged profits are an unavoidable by-product . . . Two things in particular are favorable, the accidental gains on inventory and the ability to sell all goods produced without exerting any great effort to do so. Both are temporary . . ."

On November 20, 1947, an article appeared in *The Commercial and Financial Chronicle* [4] in which the author stated: *"Inflation is not necessarily bullish for common stocks.* [Italics ours] It is pricing the consumer out of the market. It is impairing the capacity of the consumer to buy durable goods. It is raising the break-even point of industry. It is greatly increasing working-capital requirements of business, depreciating the quality of current assets and diluting

[3] A. T. Ostrander, "Inflation and Common Stock Prices," *The Commercial and Financial Chronicle,* January 1, 1948, p. 4.

[4] Harold E. Aul, "Factors in the Outlook for the Securities Market," *The Commercial and Financial Chronicle,* November 20, 1947, p. 4.

equity earnings through an expansion of commercial debt and capitalization."

Here you have clear examples of the confusion that can result from loose generalization about inflation in the stock market. What the articles said about the effect of inflation upon earnings and dividends was true. But when applied to the valuation of stocks, the truth became falsehood. Stocks were cheap from 1947 to 1949, as we all can see now, with the wisdom of hindsight. They were cheap, too, in terms of price/earnings ratios, dividend yields and the stock/bond yield ratio, as was perfectly plain at the time. But the tendency to evaluate stocks in terms of inflation obscured the values and made the stocks look dear.

Today we have the inflation generalization applied, ironically, to prove that the very same stocks that were dear at 5.4 times earnings at the June 1949 low are cheap at 20 times earnings in 1959. The generalization obviously can be used right side up or upside down, as suits the mood of the time.

Following are some examples of how inflation is being interpreted as a stock market influence now, when price/earnings ratios are as high and yields as low as at the 1929 peak:

Business Week has published several articles concerning inflation and its effect on the market.

> "The Pros Can't Agree on What Holds the Market Up." [5] (Institutional investors' purchases have remained high—a result of their fear of inflation.) The significant point, say brokers, is not what the institutions are buying but that they are still heavily committed to buying stocks. As one broker put it, "My institutional customers believe that equities are still the best bet against a resumption of inflation. And the way they are sticking to stock shows that they are more worried about long-term inflation than this short-term deflation!" [6] . . . Many individuals share the inflation fears of institutions.

[5] Reprinted from the April 5, 1958 issue of *Business Week* (p. 126) by special permission. Copyright 1958 by the McGraw-Hill Publishing Company, Inc.

[6] Apparently "short-term deflation" refers to the 1957–58 business recession, which was not accompanied, however, by a decline in the over-all price level.

18

"A New Faith Bolsters Stocks." [7] This favoritism towards stocks [by institutions] is largely due to the fear of inflation . . . Common stocks have acquired "respectability" . . . and are more popular than ever . . . There [is] widespread acceptance of the notion that inflation is inevitable. That explains the demand for stocks, not only by institutions, but by the public. And with the floating supply of stocks fairly small compared to other investments available—principally bonds and mortgages—the demand has forced prices higher.

An account of a panel discussion by G. M. Loeb, Partner in E. F. Hutton and Company, and Dwight Robinson, Jr., Chairman of the Board of Trustees, Massachusetts Investors Trust, appeared in *The Commercial and Financial Chronicle.*[8]

A prediction of further inflation and its accompanying erosion of the dollar was made by two prominent members of the securities investment field who also agreed on the prospect of higher stock prices a decade from now . . . The spotlight of interest was on the current heights to which the market has risen. Mr. Loeb felt that, barring unexpected world news, the market could go higher since it is essentially discounting an expectation of greater inflation and better earnings . . . He stated that current psychological factors have a great bearing on the price of stocks regardless of the company's earnings.

D. Moreau Barringer, Chairman, Delaware Fund, in an article in *The Commercial and Financial Chronicle,*[9] voiced his views concerning the outlook for the market. He was optimistic concerning the probable course of the stock averages, despite his belief that the market was very high. His appraisal took into consideration the public's eagerness for inflation protection or growth, the presence

[7] Reprinted from the September 20, 1958 issue of *Business Week* (p. 32) by special permission. Copyright 1958 by the McGraw-Hill Publishing Company, Inc.

[8] "Loeb and Robinson Quizzed on Outlook For Stock Market" (at the opening luncheon of the New York Sales Executive Club), *The Commercial and Financial Chronicle*, September 18, 1958, p. 9.

[9] D. Moreau Barringer, "Stock Market Outlook," *The Commercial and Financial Chronicle*, September 25, 1958, p. 11.

of institutional buyers on the demand side, the lack of new stock issues, gradual acceptance of common stocks by conservative managers, and improved plant efficiency.

> The market for those issues particularly identified in the public's mind with inflation-protection or with growth . . . will probably go up from here. As long as business volumes and profits seem to be on the increase, so long will people project the earnings of their favorite growth stock in the same direction—and, irrespective apparently of such things as P/E ratios, do the same with their estimates of future prices.

An article in *Barron's* [10] noted:

> Investment company buying reflects a change in mood . . . The high priority given to . . . natural-resource industries is indicative of the present tendency of fund managers to keep in mind the necessity to protect against the inflationary trend . . . Lawrence A. Sykes, president of the trustees of Massachusetts Life Fund, observes in his semi-annual report: "We are very much concerned with the continued inflationary trends. The cost of living index . . . shows an increase . . . with no end in sight. Recognizing this trend we have . . . [built up the common stock portion of the fund's portfolio] with leaders in the natural resource industries."

On April 2, 1958, *Financial World* [11] stated:

> Recognizing that inflation has become a part of our economy, more people than ever are turning to intelligently selected equities for protection. Common stocks have long been considered an excellent hedge against a deteriorating dollar . . . Companies with large reserves of oil, natural gas, ore or timber possess what constitutes a built-in hedge against inflation . . . Companies with sizable raw material inventories also enjoy a high degree of protection against soaring costs. As prices rise, so does the potential value of their holdings.

[10] Henry Ansbacher Long, "Hedge Against Inflation," *Barron's*, August 5, 1957, p. 5.
[11] "Ten Stocks to Combat Inflation," *Financial World*, April 2, 1958, p. 4.

20

The *U.S. News and World Report* [12] conducted interviews with representatives of leading brokerage firms in the United States. Below are some responses to their queries.

"Hedge Against Inflation"—Interview with Monte J. Gordon, Manager of Research Department, Bache & Co.:

> There [has been] a shift from bonds to stocks based on what has been termed a "flight from the dollar." Much buying is a hedge against inflation. . . . The most important factor [for buying] is an unusual combination of . . . confidence in the future growth of the economy and fear of inflation . . .

"Middle Class Investing"—Interview with Charles M. Thompson, Broker, Pierce, Carrison, Wulbern, Inc.:

> Q. What lies back of the public's interest in the stock market?
> A. Primarily inflation. I think the country is faced with its biggest problem in inflation, and I think a lot of stock buyers are hedging against inflation.

"Investors Fear Inflation"—Interview with Millard F. West, Jr., Partner, Auchincloss, Parker and Redpath:

> Q. What accounts for this increased interest in stocks?
> A. I'd say 9 out of 10 people who come in and you suggest that they buy a municipal bond which is as low in price as it has been for 20 years—they talk about inflation and that's their general thinking.

There is no need to quote further. Such opinions are legion, and they are typical of the thinking, or lack of thinking, that goes on when generalities are substituted for disciplined evaluation.

What is an investment, anyhow, but a body of capital that produces income? The income may be current income, or it may be prospective income, but it is the magnitude of the income, current or prospective, that determines the value of the capital which produces it. The English, with their long tradition of investing, value capital

---

[12] "Who is Buying Stocks Now—and Why," *U. S. News and World Report*, October 31, 1958, pp. 57, 58, 66. (These are excerpts from a series of copyrighted interviews.)

in terms of its income. A man is a millionaire there who has the income that would be produced by a million pounds. The controlling factor remains dividend-paying ability, now and always.

The behavior of stocks during the 1946–1958 inflation, in which it was observed that the prices of stocks moved in various directions but that each stock's price moved, in general, with its individual dividend-paying ability, has been duplicated in other countries at other times. Following are diagrams showing the course of stock prices during the inflation in France after the First World War. Before the First World War the French franc, worth 20¢ in gold, was one of the strongest currencies in the world. Following the World War and the heavy destruction of French property, the franc depreciated from 20¢ to 4¢—or, to put it the other way, the number of francs equivalent to a dollar increased from 5 to 25. The cost of living went up fivefold (Figure 13). Individual stocks then performed as they have during our inflation. As a general rule, the price went up if the dividend rose; if the dividend was stable, the price

FIGURE 13

Inflation in France, 1914–1931: Cost Index of Household Articles and Depreciation of the Franc

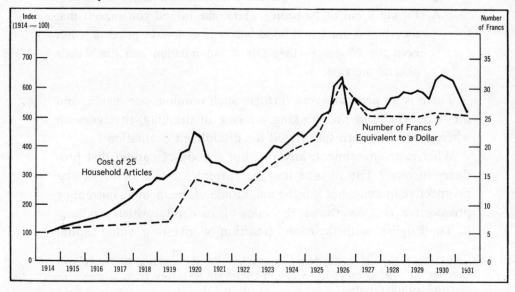

moved sidewise; and if the dividend was cut, the price went down. These various price movements correlated in each case to the respective trend of dividends.

Let us examine the price and earnings trends from 1919 to 1926 of some industrial group averages of stocks on the Bourse in Paris. Note that the utility group went up (Figure 14). It was odd, indeed, that utilities advanced during such a radical inflation as that in France, when the purchasing power of the currency depreciated 80%. But that is what happened. We usually think of utilities as companies that sell their services at fixed prices and buy their commodities in the open market. During an inflation the cost of what they buy goes up, whereas, because of regulation, their rates remain fixed, and their profits consequently are squeezed. But in France it happened differently. There public utilities were, in many cases, owned jointly with the municipalities. The town fathers raised the rates for electric power almost as rapidly as the cost of fuel and other supplies that were purchased by the utilities went up. As a

FIGURE 14

Inflation in France, 1913–1926: Electric Utilities Stock Prices and Earnings

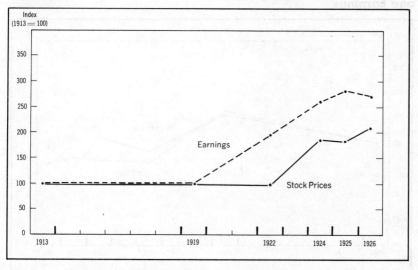

Source: France, Bureau de la Statistique Générale.

23

result, the spread between cost and selling prices was maintained; and with the growth of electric power consumption, the profits of the utilities went up and so did the prices of utility stocks.

Conversely, as a result of the acquisition of Alsace-Lorraine by France after the First World War and the oversupply of iron and steel in world markets, the profits of the French iron and steel companies went down, and their dividends had to be cut. The unfortunate French investor who held iron and steel stocks in France after the First World War, in the expectation that they would be a hedge against inflation, suffered a twofold loss. He not only suffered an 80% depreciation of his francs, but he also suffered a wide shrinkage in the number of francs represented by his stockholdings. For stocks went down in price in step with the decline in dividend-paying ability, as illustrated in Figure 15.

Building stock prices went up, as did their earnings (Figure 16). Railroad stock prices held fairly well, as did their earnings (Figure 17). But the prices at the end of the period, although equal to those at the beginning, were now expressed in depreciated francs.

FIGURE 15

Inflation in France, 1913–1926: Iron and Steel Stock Prices and Earnings

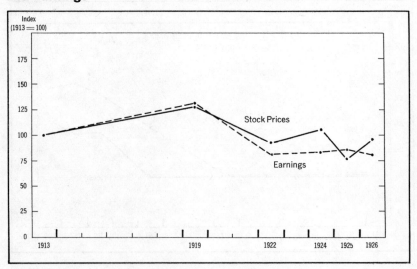

Source: France, Bureau de la Statistique Générale.

24

FIGURE 16
Inflation in France, 1913–1926: Building Stock Prices and Earnings

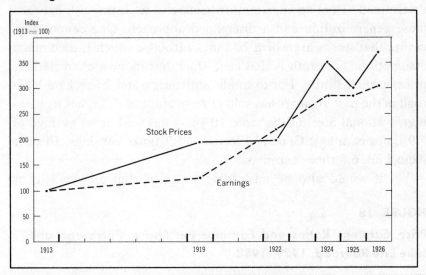

Source: France, Bureau de la Statistique Générale.

FIGURE 17
Inflation in France, 1913–1926: Railroad Stock Prices and Earnings

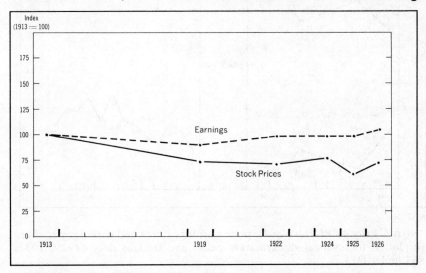

Source: France, Bureau de la Statistique Générale.

It appears, therefore, that dividend-paying ability—earning power, you might call it—is the determinant of stock prices. But how, at a given time, can the right price of the earning power be determined? Here again, we must be careful to distinguish between loose generalization and a disciplined approach. One cannot generalize that stocks are worth 10 times earnings, which is a common assumption. The truth is that each stock has its own characteristic price/earnings ratio. For example, Pittsburgh and Lake Erie Railroad in the past 10 years has sold at an average of 7.2 times its earnings. National Steel in the same 10 years has sold at an average of 8.9 times earnings; General Electric, 17.3 times earnings; Electric Auto-Lite, 6.8 times earnings.

Yet it would also be misleading to assert that an average, or

FIGURE 18

Price/Earnings Ratios and Earnings Per Share, Pittsburgh and Lake Erie Railroad, 1929–1958

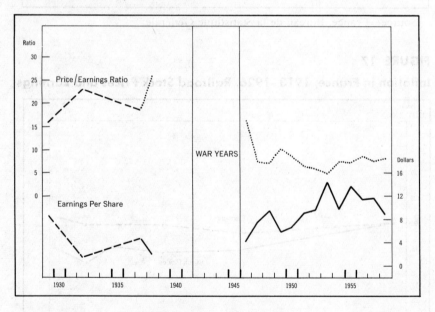

NOTE: Prior to World War II, price/earnings ratios and earnings per share are plotted for cyclical stock market peaks and troughs only (1929, 1932, 1937 and 1938).

Source: The Value Line Investment Survey.

26

typical, price/earnings ratio is a reliable criterion of the value of a stock in all phases of its business cycle. Here are charts of the price/earnings ratios of Pittsburgh and Lake Erie Railroad, Electric Auto-Lite, National Steel, and General Electric over the past 30 years. Note how the price/earnings ratios varied. Pittsburgh and Lake Erie's price/earnings ratio varied from 4.7 to 25.9 (Figure 18); Electric Auto-Lite's varied from 4.3 to 85.6 (Figure 19); National Steel's from 5.1 to 26.5 (Figure 20); and General Electric's from 7.8 to 40.9 (Figure 21). These are variations in the annual average price/earnings ratio. The price/earnings ratio, if taken at the highest and the lowest prices of the year, would fluctuate even more.

The solid line shows the annual earnings per share. The dotted line shows the annual average price/earnings ratio. Note that the

FIGURE 19
Price/Earnings Ratios and Earnings Per Share, Electric Auto-Lite, 1929–1958

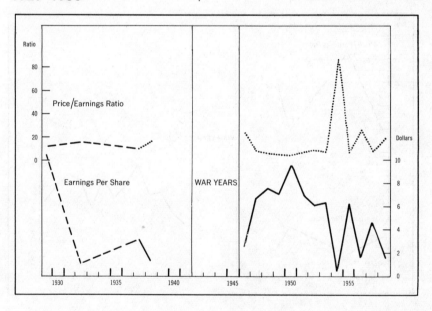

NOTE: Prior to World War II, price/earnings ratios and earnings per share are plotted for cyclical stock market peaks and troughs only (1929, 1932, 1937 and 1938).

Source: The Value Line Investment Survey.

price/earnings ratio tends to move against the earnings. When the earnings rise, the price/earnings ratio tends to fall. But when the earnings fall, the price/earnings ratio tends to rise.

Pittsburgh and Lake Erie's earnings per share fell from $8.75 to $1.58 between 1929 and 1932. The price/earnings ratio rose from 15.8 to 22.9. Earnings per share rose between 1932 and 1937 from $1.58 to $4.68; the price/earnings ratio fell from 22.9 to 18.5. Earnings per share fell between 1937 and 1938 from $4.68 to $1.96; the price/earnings ratio rose from 18.5 to 25.9. For purposes of evaluation it would be best to leave out the war years, when normal operations were distorted and earnings were placed under a fairly rigid ceiling by excess profits taxation and renegotiation. From 1946 to 1948, earnings per share rose from $4.24 to $9.64;

FIGURE 20

Price/Earnings Ratios and Earnings Per Share, National Steel, 1929–1958

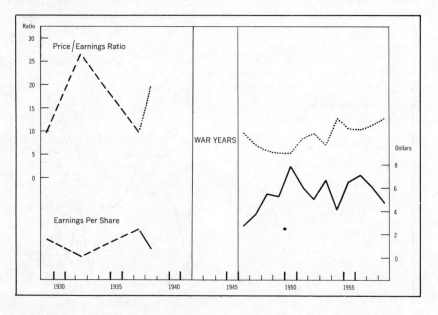

NOTE: Prior to World War II, price/earnings ratios and earnings per share are plotted for cyclical stock market peaks and troughs only (1929, 1932, 1937 and 1938).

Source: The Value Line Investment Survey.

28

the price/earnings ratio fell from 16.3 to 7.0. Between 1948 and 1949, earnings per share fell from $9.64 to $5.86; the price/earnings ratio rose from 7.0 to 10.2. From 1949 to 1953, earnings per share rose from $5.86 to $14.37; the price/earnings ratio fell from 10.2 to 4.7. Between 1953 and 1958, earnings per share fell from $14.37 to $8.90 and the price/earnings ratio rose from 4.7 to 8.0.

The same phenomenon is observable in the case of Electric Auto-Lite and National Steel (Figures 19 and 20).

The usual experience is noted in the case of General Electric (Figure 21) between 1929 and 1952. Between 1952 and 1956, however, General Electric's price/earnings ratio rose as its earnings rose. This runs contrary to normal behavior. It might be argued that a new norm was being established, possibly because General Elec-

FIGURE 21

Price/Earnings Ratios and Earnings Per Share, General Electric, 1929–1958

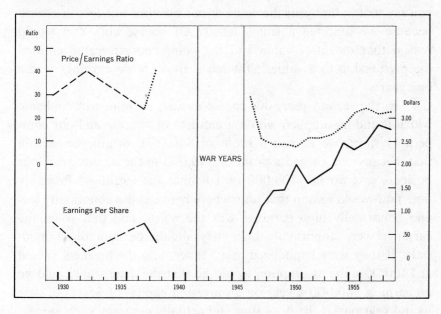

NOTE: Prior to World War II, price/earnings ratios and earnings per share are plotted for cyclical stock market peaks and troughs only (1929, 1932, 1937 and 1938).

Source: The Value Line Investment Survey.

29

tric would no longer be subject to cyclical swings in its earnings, having become a perpetual growth company. But it would be more logical, in view of the long experience of the company and of other cyclical companies, to conclude that the price was out of line with the normal capitalization of earning power.

All too often, the observation is heard that, because a cyclical stock is selling at a price/earnings ratio which is no greater than average, the price may be considered reasonable. This observation ignores the fact that the price/earnings ratio of a cyclical stock normally goes down as the earnings rise. If the price/earnings ratio does not go down when the earnings are very high in relation to asset value, as in the case of General Electric, the stock may be dangerously overpriced.

To illustrate why this is so, imagine, for example, that you and I became partners and bought a small drug store on our block. Let us say that we paid $50,000 for the furniture and fixtures and the stock in trade. In the first year of operation we lost $2,000. Would you say that in that year the value of our business was less than zero because we reported a small deficit? Of course not. You would reason that the asset value and the going-concern value entitled the partnership to a value, although there were no earnings in the one year.

If, in the second year, due to, let us say, an influenza epidemic which found us supplied with a great deal of vaccine and our competitors short, we earned a profit of $40,000, would you reason that, because we earned a profit of $40,000 in the second year, our business was worth $400,000 or 10 times the earnings? Probably not. You would reason that somewhere between the abnormally low and abnormally high earnings was the norm, and that when the earnings were abnormally high they should be capitalized modestly. If they were capitalized at 10 times, and the business valued at $400,000, the assumption would be that the drug store could go on earning $40,000 a year on an invested capital of $50,000, year in and year out. If the drug store did actually earn any such money, it would not be long before the block was full of competing drug stores.

In most competitive businesses, and especially those of a cyclical character, there is a limit to what can be earned in relation to invested capital. If more than that amount is earned, intensive competition is invited and profit margins come under pressure. Where there is not enough competition to bring the profit margin down, governmental regulation will. Hence, reasonable valuation takes account of the fact that very high earnings in relation to invested capital are probably temporary and should be "looked through." By the same token, when earnings are very low, the stock is valued, at least in part, on its assets, without regard to the paucity of earnings.

Therefore, one cannot postulate that a typical price/earnings ratio, or even a moving-average price/earnings ratio, is a reasonable standard for determining what a stock's market price will be, or should be, at all times. *Each stock has its own individual price/earnings ratio, and the price/earnings ratio of the individual stock normally varies at different levels of earnings.*

Williams, in his book *The Theory of Investment Value,*[13] refers to the present value of a common stock as the sum of all its future dividends discounted to the current interest rate. Here indeed is the truth and the whole truth. But it is unfathomable, because nobody knows what the sum of all future dividends will be.

If all this seems frustrating, take some comfort from the fact that you are not alone in your frustration. You may recall that in 1955, after the sharp rise in the stock market had given concern to some thoughtful legislators, the Fulbright Committee called upon Bernard Baruch for his opinion of whether or not stocks were too high. Here is what Mr. Baruch said before the Committee on Banking and Currency of the United States Senate on March 23, 1955:[14]

"At the outset, let me emphasize that no one knows whether stocks are too high today . . . You ask is the market right?

[13] John Burr Williams, *The Theory of Investment Value* (Cambridge, Mass.: Harvard University Press, 1938), p. 55.

Cf., Robert F. Wiese, "Investing for True Values," *Barron's,* September 8, 1930, p. 5. *"The proper price of any security, whether a stock or bond, is the sum of all future income payments discounted at the current rate of interest in order to arrive at the present value."*

[14] "Stock Market Study—Factors Affecting the Buying and Selling of Equity Securities," Hearings Before the Committee on Banking and Currency, United States Senate, 84th Cong., 1st Sess. (Washington: 1955), pp. 983–4.

Senator, I have been in it a good many years, but I have never answered that question, because I do not think anybody is smart enough to know, and I certainly would not want to put myself in that class of demigod . . .

"As your expert witness, I tell you no expert witness is good on that."

Mr. Baruch added the following: "Whether stocks rise or fall is determined by innumerable forces and elements, by economic conditions, the actions of governments, the state of international affairs, the emotions of people, even the vagaries of the weather." I am sure that Mr. Baruch might have included, along with these other generalizations, the influence of inflation. But we are down now to this barren ground: that, in the opinion of such an eminent expert as Mr. Baruch, there is no definable standard of value that governs the price levels of common stocks.

It would be a bold man, indeed, who had the temerity to criticize Mr. Baruch in his judgments of the stock market. Yet, I submit that Mr. Baruch was doing less than full justice to his own reasoning when he made these observations before the Senate Committee on Banking and Currency. If you read his interesting autobiography—and everyone should—you will find there a number of paragraphs that emphasize the importance of painstaking accumulation of all the statistical evidence that can be brought to bear upon the evaluation of stocks. Mr. Baruch was never a lazy man, nor one to rely on tips. He thought, studied and worked things out for himself. His advice has always been that a great deal of profit can be made in the stock market, but not by lazy people. Yet he actually expressed the opinion that nobody can tell whether stocks are dear or cheap, high or low.

The declaration that there is no way to evaluate a common stock is close to the heresy that I sometimes describe as "Winchellism." Let me explain that. Some of you may recall that a few years ago Walter Winchell, on his Sunday-night broadcasts over the radio, always took occasion toward the close of the newscast to mention a particular stock. He would say, for example, "X-Y-Z is going to bring in a big oil well tonight," or "A-B-C is going to announce a merger with D-E-F in the next few weeks." These newscasts had the effect during a bullish market of causing the stock cited by Mr. Winchell to move up substantially in price as soon as trading in it began the next Monday morning. So many people followed these tips that the situation became scandalous. On a few occasions, so many orders to buy flowed in that, for a brief time, would-be buyers so outnumbered willing sellers that it was impossible for trading in the stock to take place at all. Ironically, Wall Street became indignant. But what was it that Walter Winchell said that was untrue or wrong? Whatever we may think of him as a commentator, there is a wide area of agreement that he is a first-class reporter. I may be wrong about this, but it is my belief that every one of his reports turned out to be true. Why, then, was there such general condemnation of Winchell as a "tipster"?

The only objection that could be taken to Winchell's remarks was that the facts he reported were unevaluated. If X-Y-Z did bring in an oil well, that did not prove that the stock was worth more. It might be worth less than it was selling for, in spite of the new oil well, or three new oil wells. If company A-B-C actually did merge with company D-E-F, that would not necessarily mean that the two were worth more together than apart. It might mean that the combination was worth no more than the prices of the stocks at the time; or the truth of the matter might even have been that both companies' stocks were so overvalued at the time that even with a merger their real value was lower than the current quotation. In short, the sin of Walter Winchell was that he presented facts without evaluating them.

Now what is the difference between what Walter Winchell did and what Wall Street in general does when it buys and sells stocks and, at the same time, declares that there is no such thing as a standard of value; that there is no way to tell when a stock is dear or cheap; that generalizations and background influences, such as political developments and the weather, determine what prices should be?

I think I see a trend in Wall Street toward sounder analysis today. But I challenge you to look at the run of market letters and brokers' recommendations up until the middle of 1957 and find any substantial evidence of evaluation. All the evidence that was adduced was background evidence and unevaluated factual material. In most cases, the market-letter writers presented a greater aggregation of facts than Walter Winchell released on his Sunday-night broadcasts. But there still was a virtually brazen absence of any effort to determine what valuation should be placed upon the earnings and dividends or even to estimate what the earnings and dividends would be. Sometimes there were estimates that the earnings and dividends would go up or down. But very seldom was there any effort to estimate how much more, or how much less, the stock would be worth if the higher, or lower, earnings and dividends did materialize. Large brokerage houses undertook big advertising campaigns to acquaint investors with their "research services." Of what did the research consist? Primarily, it was represented as a careful compilation of all the facts deemed relevant to an understanding of the subject company and its stock. That done, the customer was left to his own devices to evaluate the facts. To go beyond that point would probably have appeared irresponsible, or gadgety, to the brokers.

You may have heard the old joke attributed to J. P. Morgan. When asked what the stock market was going to do, he gave it as his considered judgment that the stock market would fluctuate. Now maybe Mr. Morgan, like Mr. Baruch, would argue that nobody can tell whether stocks are too high or too low, and that nobody can determine what they are worth. But the firm of J. P. Morgan attained its great prestige because of a long series of successful flotations, which proved that their evaluation of the securities, before offering them to their customers, was sound.

Nevertheless, Mr. Baruch says nobody can tell when stocks are high or low. Mr. Morgan said that the stock market will fluctuate and he let it go at that. Baron Rothschild was a little more specific, but not much. When asked how he made his fortune in the stock market, he said he made his money by buying stocks when they were cheap and selling them when they were dear. This oracular declaration obviously implied a standard of value somewhere along the line, but it was never disclosed.

Charles H. Dow, a one-time editor of *The Wall Street Journal,* and spiritual father of what has since become known as the Dow theory of stock-market forecasting, came closer to reality. He said, "First of all, know value." If the stock market is to fluctuate, as Mr.

Morgan has assured us it will, and if the way to make money is to buy stocks when they are cheap and sell them when they are dear, as Baron Rothschild has advised, then it would be only rational to conclude with Mr. Dow that one must first of all know value. Yet, to my knowledge, Mr. Dow never enunciated a theory of, or a method for, evaluating stocks. When you press the consistently successful investor to the point, he usually tells you that he has an intuition about these things, or "a feeling." This betrays the fact that he does actually apply a standard of value but has not found a disciplined way to express it.

The most common type of stock forecast in Wall Street is that which is derived from the mind of the chartist. Charts are highly useful. They often indicate the point of time at which a significant price change will get under way. They indicate the trend of price movements. Point-and-figure charts often give an indication, in advance, of the extent of a movement in either direction, once the movement gets under way. Unfortunately, most chartists feel bound by some mystic compulsion to drag in exogenous factors like inflation, politics, the prospect for war and peace, the weather, etc., in order to make what their charts have indicated would happen to prices sound convincing. Thus, good market forecasting is often transfigured into economic nonsense.

Do not take these remarks to mean that charts should be discarded. Every good analyst should have his charts before him, and probably the point-and-figure charts have some advantages over ordinary bar charts. But, if one were to proceed on the basis of charts honestly, one would buy without giving consideration to value. One would buy a "catapult," or a "break-away gap," or a "trend line." In fact, even the name of the stock would be unnecessary. One could point to the chart picture and tell the broker, "Buy that one!" It would then be up to the broker's research department to identify the chart, somewhat in the way that fingerprints are identified, and place the order. Not only would no question of value come up, but the chances are that the results would, on the whole, be superior to those obtained by memorizing a lot of unevaluated facts about a company and using this hodgepodge to confuse the chart interpretation. Do not set charts aside as useless or nonessential. But, do recognize that they have no relevancy to the question of valuation, although they often give clues to the time when prices will readjust to value. I might mention, at this point, that charts have been known to reverse themselves with great rapidity.

Now let me review the conclusions reached in this chapter:

First, background influences or environmental factors like inflation, the future growth of this great country (which, incidentally, has been growing for several hundred years) and the technological break-through (which, incidentally, is only an extension of the Industrial Revolution that has been going on for several hundred years too) are treacherous premises on which to generalize about today's stock values. They may be significant because of their eventual influence upon earnings and dividends, which ultimately determine the value of stocks. But the influence of environmental factors is not always what is commonly assumed. Inflation, for example, may depress earnings as well as inflate them. When inflation has the effect of depressing earnings, it tends to bring about cuts in dividends, and in so doing, depress the prices of stocks. The value of the currency itself bears no direct relationship to the valuation of a stock.

Secondly, in determining how a stock should be valued in relation to earnings, or dividend-paying ability, we must discard the idea of a general price/earnings ratio for all stocks, for we have found that each stock has its individual price/earnings ratio. We must discard the idea of a fixed price/earnings ratio for the individual stock at all levels of its earnings, because we have found that the price/earnings ratio of even the individual stock varies—and *normally* varies— at different levels of its earnings. Yet, we cannot discard the idea that there must be standards that govern men in the purchase and sale of common stocks—Mr. Baruch and Mr. Morgan to the contrary notwithstanding.

Even if we concede that the value of a stock is just a matter of psychology, or, as Lord Keynes once said, "the average man's opinion of what the average man's opinion will be," we still must recognize that there are influences that shape the psychology of the average man over a period of time. Something makes the psychology. That something, in the long run, is the dividend-paying

36

ability of the stock. It determines how anxious the buyer is to demand and how eager the seller is to supply. Here is the true causal relationship. The problem is to express it by rote instead of by ear.

In the next chapter I plan to outline two methods which can be applied to the evaluation of common stocks. One is a method based on the concept of "quality." The other is a method based upon a normal capitalization of average earnings over a three-year period three to five years into the future. In the second method we make the evaluation in terms of a three-year average price for the stock based upon a hypothesis regarding the general economy three to five years ahead. In truth, this projection is not a forecast, but rather a measure of potentiality based on the assumption that the economic hypothesis will be realized. The statistical methods employed to define quality and to measure appreciation potentiality over a three-year period three to five years into the future will be explained.

But let it be said right now that both the concept of quality and the concept of appreciation potentiality during a three-year period three to five years into the future, in a hypothesized economic environment, while valuable and useful aids, do not answer the question, "Is the stock's price right *at this time,* or is it too high or too low *now*?" How that question might be answered will be dealt with in the third chapter.

I propose in the fourth chapter to show how these methods of valuation may be applied to portfolio management and to prove why diversification is a *sine qua non* of any rationally conceived investment program.

II

THE FIRST chapter dwelt upon the dangers, when evaluating stocks, of loose generalizations about environmental factors, such as inflation. The truth about inflation and stock prices is that stocks rise if their dividends increase and go down if their dividends decrease, inflation or no inflation. The purchasing power of money has no direct relationship to the evaluation of stocks, although it may have an indirect effect through its influence on the dividend-paying ability of the stocks.

In 1949, when stocks were cheap relative to their dividend-paying ability, inflation was widely assumed to be a depressant upon stock prices; whereas today, when stocks are dear relative to their dividend-paying ability, inflation is generally assumed to be a great booster of stock prices. The point to emphasize is that the factor of inflation, insofar as it applies to stocks at all, applies through its effect upon the stock's dividend-paying ability, and not through its effect upon the evaluation of the dividend-paying ability. I might remark parenthetically that one exception could be taken to this rule. If the currency were on its way to utter destruction, as was the case in Germany after the First World War, any stock's price might go up, regardless of its dividend-paying ability. What is implied in this observation, of course, is that when the currency becomes worthless, prices expressed in currency become meaningless: any stock is better than any amount of money, and so is almost anything else. Otherwise, the rule holds that, regardless of the purchasing power of the currency, the value of a stock depends upon its dividend-paying ability. The dividends are paid in the same kind of currency that the stocks are bought and sold in, and the purchasing power of the currency washes out of the equation altogether.

Other background factors such as growth of the country and technological "break-through" are equally irrelevant as factors in evaluation. As in the case of inflation, they influence the dividend-paying ability of the stock but not, normally, the capitalization of that dividend-paying ability.

In Chapter I we saw that no general price/earnings ratio was found to be applicable to all stocks. Some stocks sold at typically higher price/earnings ratios than others. Furthermore, it was found that the same stock, especially if a cyclical stock, *normally* sold at varying price/earnings ratios as its earnings fluctuated. *Normally,* very high earnings relative to asset values resulted in low price/earnings ratios, and very low earnings in high price/earnings ratios.

The theoretical definition of the value of a common stock, namely, that the present value of a common stock is equal to the sum of all its future dividends discounted to the current interest rate, is conceded to be the truth and the whole truth; but it is found to be unfathomable, because nobody knows what all the future dividends of a common stock will be.

Prominent investment experts, including Bernard Baruch and John Maynard Keynes, have testified that the value of a common stock cannot be defined. They regard stock evaluation as the product of a congeries of background influences and popular impressions whose net effect can only be intuitively conjectured. So often we hear the expression, "Investment is an art, not a science." Yet it is quite impossible to accept the thesis that consistently successful investors like Baruch and Keynes knew of no way to evaluate stocks. It may be that the mental processes by which they arrived at their correct decisions in such a high percentage of cases were intuitional. If so, that intuitional reasoning must be made understandable.

39

Some way, we reason, must be found to evaluate common stocks according to definable standards. But there is strong reluctance, indeed even hostility, on the part of most analysts toward any formulation of a standard. Leading brokerage firms advertise that they stand ready to submit all the facts to their customers, so that the customers can then make up their minds about what to do regarding stock X-Y-Z. Seldom does one read that the brokerage firm's research department is ready to provide a standard by which the investor can evaluate the facts that are presented to him. "Winchellism," which is a term I apply to the presentation of unevaluated facts, is an occupational delinquency common throughout Wall Street.

It may come as a shock to a thinking man to be told that billions of dollars of trades on the stock market are executed without reference to any definable standard of value. Yet that is the case. I am sure that standards are in use, but they are not defined. They are "intuitional," and they are applied "by ear." What we grope for here is disciplined evaluation. The methods I am about to outline are imperfect. Indeed, my colleagues and I are constantly striving to improve upon them. But they are an attempt, and, unfortunately, the only methodical one I know of, to apply statistical disciplines to the evaluation processes that in today's world of finance are mainly a function of intuition or some other naïve form of apprehension.

What is wrong with an intuitive, or undisciplined, standard? If an undisciplined standard is admitted, the evaluation process inevitably yields to the prevailing mood. Most of the great investment mistakes —the really big ones—were made during periods when nearly everybody was wrong, as in 1929, when speculation was rampant; in 1932, when depression of mood, as well as of business, was so extreme that stocks sold at fractions of their net working capital per share; in 1949, when stocks were extremely undervalued in relation to earnings and dividends; and in the last few years (1955 to the present time), when stocks have been very highly valued, in fact radically overvalued, in relation to the final determinant of their values, which is dividend-paying ability. (In dividend-paying ability we include the financial condition of the company, its sales and its

40

profitability.) In past periods, when, we see in retrospect, the public and the market were wrong, there was a form of reasoning, or specious rationalization, that gave the error of the day its plausibility. 1929 was the time of the "new era"; 1932 was the time of "the inevitable national bankruptcy"; 1949 was the time when "the deflationary impact of inflation" upon stocks was heavily publicized; between 1955 and the present time, the "inflationary impact of inflation" upon stock prices—the upside-down argument of 1949—has been dragged in to justify high stock prices and bring undisciplined evaluation into line with the prevailing emotional state.

Only objective and disciplined evaluation can stand against popular delusion, accompanied as the latter always is by strong and almost universally entertained hopes or fears. Therefore, it is important to develop disciplined standards. That these will disagree with the market for considerable periods of time goes without saying. If it were not so, there would be no need for them. Price would be value, value price, and that is all you would know or need to know. It is precisely when prices deviate from standards of value that the standards have usefulness.

Disciplined evaluation is useful in another way, too. If the investor should disagree with a disciplined standard, for reasons that might seem to him, at the time, to be valid, he at least has a way of knowing what he is disagreeing with. But, when the standard wobbles all over, he can take no issue, because the standard is amenable to any heresy he feels like reading into it.

QUALITY GRADE

One useful disciplined standard is that based on the concept of "quality." The quality of a stock, as The Value Line Investment Survey uses the term, is an index of the stock's general safety. It is a standard based solely upon past experience.

What makes a stock a safe investment? Starting with the premise that dividend-paying ability, in the long run, determines value, the answer obviously is, "First, the growth trend of earnings and dividends; second, the stability of those earnings and dividends."

In the field of enterprise, which is definitely the field in which stock companies function, a good attack is the best defense. That

41

dividend is strongest which is paid by a company whose dividend-paying ability is rising on a secular trend. A company whose dividend-paying ability merely holds stable might be in danger of meeting with adversity that could cause the dividend to be cut below the rate that had been paid for many years in the past. But a company whose dividend-paying ability is increasing, even though it may stub its toe now and then, has a rising trend to brake the dividend against a fall below its earlier level. Therefore, we conclude that the growth of dividend-paying ability is of significance in the determination of a stock's quality, or general safety.

The other, and even more significant, factor is the stability of the dividend, that is to say, the company's ability to avoid stubbing its toe. A stock like American Telephone, for example, whose dividend remained constant for many years, is a high-quality stock not because of a sustained improvement in its dividend-paying ability, but because of the absence of major fluctuations. Notwithstanding the recent 10% hike in the dividend rate—the first in 37 years—and the occasional issuance of rights which could be sold to augment the dividend return, American Telephone's dividend has basically been a stable one, and the high quality of American Telephone derives from the high stability, not from the growth, of the dividend.

Union Carbide, on the other hand, is a stock whose dividend has been somewhat less stable than American Telephone's but has grown persistently over a period of years.

Now, how can we objectively measure the growth and stability of a stock's dividend-paying ability? After we have measured them objectively, how do we combine them into a single index of quality? That is the method that I should like to discuss now. It is only one method, of course, and a better one will probably be found some day. But this method has objectivity, at least.

We measure the growth of a stock's dividend-paying ability in terms of its past dividend record and its earnings. By way of illustration, the computation of a growth number for American Machine and Foundry is shown in Figure 22.

First we note the year-to-year percentage changes in per-share earnings and dividends from 1947 up to and including 1958. In order to avoid distortions caused by extreme fluctuations, the per-

42

FIGURE 22

Computation of Growth Number for American Machine and Foundry

	PER-SHARE EARNINGS		PER-SHARE DIVIDENDS	
	Per Cent Change	Code Number	Per Cent Change	Code Number
	One-Year Period			
1947 to 1948	+ 17.5%	+ 1	0	0
1948 to 1949	− 81.6	− 4	0	0
1949 to 1950	+490.5	+ 4	0	0
1950 to 1951	+ 23.4	+ 1	0	0
1951 to 1952	+ 17.0	+ 1	+ 4.6%	+ 1
1952 to 1953	+ 8.4	+ 1	+ 29.4	+ 2
1953 to 1954	− 20.1	− 2	+ 5.7	+ 1
1954 to 1955	+ 3.2	+ 1	+ 1.1	+ 1
1955 to 1956	+ 89.4	+ 3	+ 7.4	+ 1
1956 to 1957	+ 15.8	+ 1	+ 28.7	+ 2
1957 to 1958	− 9.1	− 1	+ 30.8	+ 2
	Three-Year Period			
1947 to 1950	+ 27.8%	+ 2	0	0
1948 to 1951	+ 34.2	+ 2	0	0
1949 to 1952	+752.4	+ 4	+ 4.6%	+ 1
1950 to 1953	+ 56.5	+ 3	+ 35.4	+ 2
1951 to 1954	+ 1.3	+ 1	+ 43.1	+ 2
1952 to 1955	− 10.6	− 1	+ 38.2	+ 2
1953 to 1956	+ 56.2	+ 3	+ 14.8	+ 1
1954 to 1957	+126.5	+ 4	+ 39.8	+ 2
1955 to 1958	+ 99.4	+ 3	+ 80.8	+ 3
	Five-Year Period			
1947 to 1952	+ 84.5%	+ 3	+ 4.6%	+ 1
1948 to 1953	+ 70.2	+ 3	+ 35.4	+ 2
1949 to 1954	+638.1	+ 4	+ 43.1	+ 2
1950 to 1955	+ 29.0	+ 2	+ 44.6	+ 2
1951 to 1956	+ 98.0	+ 3	+ 55.4	+ 3
1952 to 1957	+ 96.1	+ 3	+ 91.2	+ 3
1953 to 1958	+ 64.4	+ 3	+ 93.2	+ 3
TOTAL		+48		+39

Composite Growth Number: (+48 × 2) + 39 = +135

centage changes are then coded from plus 4 to minus 4, depending upon the magnitude and direction of the change in earnings and dividends.

As shown in Figure 23, the code numbers are applied in accordance with the indicated percentage changes in earnings and dividends. If the increase in earnings from year to year amounts to from 1/10th of 1% to 25%, the code value assigned is +1. If the change is from 25.1% to 50%, the code value is +2, and so on.

FIGURE 23

Code Numbers Applicable to Specific Per Cent Changes in Earnings and Dividends

Change in Earnings and Dividends	Code Number
+ .1% to 25%	+1
+25.1% to 50%	+2
+50.1% to 100%	+3
over 100%	+4
− .1% to −20%	−1
−20.1% to −33.3%	−2
−33.4% to −50%	−3
−50.1% and over	−4
No Change	0

In the case of American Machine and Foundry (Figure 22), the per-share earnings between 1947 and 1948 rose 17.5%. Hence, the code value was +1. Between 1948 and 1949 the earnings dropped 81.6%. The code value then was −4. From 1949 to 1950 they rose 490.5%. The code number then became +4 and so on.

The same method is applied to the computation of changes in dividend rates, and the changes are translated into codes.

This same procedure is followed with the changes that occur during three-year periods and also five-year periods. The reason for using the three different time intervals is that a single year's fluctuation can be erratic and so distort the ratio, whereas the use of the three periods tends to average out wild changes and thus yield a truer indication of the basic trend.

44

The individual code numbers thus derived are then totaled—separately for earnings and dividends—to yield two growth aggregates representing the trend of earnings and dividends over the 1947–58 period. Finally, a composite growth number is obtained for each stock by combining the two growth aggregates, giving twice as much weight to earnings as to dividends. This weighting procedure was deemed appropriate, since a company's earnings experience over a period of years determines, in large measure, the trend of dividend payments, and is, therefore, more important as a growth determinant. For American Machine and Foundry, the growth aggregate of earnings was found to be 48, the growth aggregate of dividends 39, and the composite growth number 135 (that is to say, 48 multiplied by 2 plus 39). (See Figure 22.)

Similar growth numbers are computed for all 804 stocks under our regular review. These numbers are then arranged in order of magnitude into 20 equal groups. The group of stocks with the highest growth numbers is assigned a Growth Index of 100, the next group 95, and so on down to 5 for the group with the lowest growth numbers. The Growth Index applicable to American Machine and Foundry is 95, which means that its growth number of 135 was greater than that of 90% of all stocks and smaller than only 5%.

Next we compute a stability number. We find that stock prices, as a rule, fluctuate in proportion to the variation of their earnings and dividends over a period of time. Hence, we find it practical to substitute price variation as the criterion of dividend stability. The larger the spread (percentagewise) between the high and the low price of a stock in any given year, the less stable the stock was in that year, obviously. By measuring the spread during 11 successive years, we obtain a fairly reliable yardstick of the stability of the stock during the postwar period.

In practice, the calculations are performed as shown in Figure 24 for American Machine and Foundry. We note the high, low and average prices in each year of the 11 from 1947 to 1957. The sum of the highs is 267.9. The sum of the lows is 179.9, and the sum of the average prices is 221.3.

The sum of the annual lows (179.9) is then subtracted from the

45

FIGURE 24

Computation of Stability Index for American Machine and Foundry

| | Annual Price Range | | |
	High	Low	Average Price
1947	21.7	13.9	18.4
1948	17.6	9.9	13.5
1949	12.3	9.3	10.7
1950	13.9	10.4	11.9
1951	16.6	11.5	13.7
1952	20.7	13.9	17.2
1953	21.6	17.2	19.9
1954	26.7	19.7	23.2
1955	32.2	21.8	27.0
1956	40.8	23.2	29.6
1957	43.8	29.1	36.2
	267.9	179.9	221.3

(1) Sum of annual highs 267.9

(2) Sum of annual lows 179.9

(3) Sum of annual price ranges 88.0 (1) − (2)

(4) Secular price trend, 1947–57 * 14.5

(5) Sum of annual price ranges
adjusted for secular price trend 73.5 (3) − (4)

(6) Sum of annual average prices 221.3

$$\text{Price stability ratio} = \frac{73.5}{221.3} = .332 \qquad (5) \div (6)$$

* The secular price trend measures the increase or decrease in price between 1947 and the 1956/57 average.

sum of the annual highs (267.9) to yield the sum of the annual price ranges (88.0). At this stage, the secular price trend, measured by the increase or decrease in price between 1947 and the average of 1956 and 1957 prices, is subtracted from the sum of the annual price ranges. (Without such an adjustment the stock's stability would be penalized for growth, since the annual price range is wider for a growth stock than a non-growth stock, all other things being equal.) In the case of American Machine and Foundry, the stock increased 14.5 dollars per share, and this amount is subtracted from 88 to yield the sum of the annual price ranges adjusted for secular price trend. This sum (73.5) is then divided by the sum of the annual average prices, and the resulting ratio (.332) reflects the degree of price fluctuation around the average price each year.

Similar stability ratios are computed for all stocks under regular review. These ratios are then arranged in order of magnitude, as was true of the growth numbers, into 20 equal groups. The group of stocks with the lowest stability ratios (that is to say, the most stable stocks) is assigned a Stability Index of 100, the next group 95, and so on down to 5 for the group with the highest stability ratio (that is to say, the least stable stocks). The Stability Index applicable to American Machine and Foundry is 30, which means that this stock is less stable than 70% of all stocks and more stable than only 25%.

The 15 most stable stocks among the 804 analyzed by the Value Line Survey organization in accordance with the computation just described are listed in Figure 25. And Figure 26 lists the 15 stocks

FIGURE 25

15 Highest-Ranking Stocks with Respect to Price Stability since 1947

	Stability Ratio
American Telephone & Telegraph	.091
Irving Trust	.098
First National Bank (Chicago)	.099
Northern Indiana Public Service	.102
First National Bank (St. Louis)	.107
Manufacturers Trust	.108
Continental Illinois	.110
Pennsylvania Power & Light	.110
Utah Power & Light	.114
Rochester Gas & Electric	.116
Detroit Edison	.116
Hanover Bank	.120
Sun Oil	.121
South Carolina Electric & Gas	.122
Baltimore Gas & Electric	.122

NOTE: Selected from the 804 stocks under regular supervision by The Value Line Investment Survey.

FIGURE 26

15 Highest-Ranking Stocks with Respect to Earnings and Dividend Growth since 1947

	Growth Number
General Dynamics	207
Winn-Dixie Stores	196
McGraw-Hill Publishing	192
Continental Assurance	191
United Aircraft	189
Boeing Airplane	187
American Home Products	178
Ex-Cell-O	177
Falconbridge Nickel	175
National Lead	175
Reynolds Metals	174
Foremost Dairies	174
Smith, Kline & French	171
Fansteel Metallurgical	170
Lincoln National Life Insurance	168

NOTE: Selected from the 804 stocks under regular supervision by The Value Line Investment Survey.

that score highest with respect to growth of dividend-paying ability over a 12-year period.

Once the Growth and Stability Indexes have been derived, the next problem is to combine them. To what extent is stability the determinant of quality and to what extent growth? Both, it is reasoned, are factors of significance. But which is the more important and how much more? To determine the relative importance of growth and stability, a multiple correlation analysis is used. To those of you who have studied statistics no explanation of multiple correlation analysis is required. But to the others, who have not had statistics, let me explain that multiple correlation analysis is a mathematical method for determining the influence, if any, of two or more fluctuating variables upon a third.

A good explanation of multiple correlation analysis and how it is done can be found in *Statistical Methods*.[15] To understand how a

[15] Frederick C. Mills, *Statistical Methods* (3rd ed., New York: Henry Holt and Company, 1955), Chap. 18.

Quality Grade is derived by the methods here described, it is not necessary to know how to do a multiple correlation analysis. However, it is necessary to know what multiple correlation does for the analysis.

Let me give you a homely illustration. Assume that the problem is to determine what caused the marks received by 20 different youngsters in the eighth grade to vary. Al, for example, received 90, Bob 95, Charles 85, Dan 75, Ed 70, Frank 70 and George 50, etc. Why did their grades differ? The youngsters, all of the same age, were confronted with the same problems in the same classroom by the same teacher. The three variables that caused the differences are assumed to be (1) intelligence, (2) the number of hours of homework each boy put in and (3) the home environment. Do not inquire how we obtained the measures of intelligence, hours of homework and home environment, or whether these were the only and most important determinants. I am only trying to show what function correlation analysis performs. It determines to what degree these variables, in combination, actually influenced the variations in the grades received by the individual boys, and how influential, relatively, each variable was.

To carry out this exercise we set down the names of the boys and alongside each name the grade that each received (Figure 27). The grade is known as the dependent variable. In the next three columns we list the independent variables:

(1) the I.Q. rating of each boy,
(2) the number of hours of homework, on average, that each boy put in every day, and
(3) the home environment factor, which is graded from 100 down to zero according to the findings of social workers.

You will notice that one boy, Ken, who had the highest I.Q. of all, and was naturally the brightest, got a low grade. Note that he did very little homework and that his home environment was unfortunate.

On the other hand, Al got a much higher grade, even though his I.Q. was substantially below Ken's. However, Al's home environ-

49

FIGURE 27
Grades and Related Data for a Group of School Boys

Boy	Grade (Y)	Natural I.Q. (X₁)	Hours Spent on Homework (X₂)	Home Environment (X₃)
Al	90	110	2.5	70
Bob	95	120	2.5	50
Charles	85	120	2.0	30
Dan	75	105	2.0	40
Ed	70	100	2.0	50
Frank	70	110	1.0	30
George	50	90	1.0	70
Harry	65	95	2.5	50
Ike	95	120	2.0	40
John	95	115	3.0	50
Ken	60	140	1.0	10
Larry	40	80	2.0	60
Mike	80	110	1.0	90
Ned	60	90	1.5	80
Oscar	65	90	3.0	30
Paul	70	100	2.5	50
Quentin	75	100	1.0	70
Roy	70	95	2.0	50
Sam	70	95	3.5	30
Tom	80	110	3.0	40

ment was a happy one, and he worked longer hours than the average on his homework.

We find through a solution of this multiple correlation analysis that 72% of the variation in the grades was accounted for by the three independent variables (I.Q., homework, home environment). The analysis also indicated that the I.Q. factor accounted for 45%, the hours of homework for 29% and the home environment for 26% of the total explained variation.

The regression equation was found to be:

$$Y \text{ (grade)} = -71.084$$
$$+ .966\, X_1 \text{ (I.Q. factor)}$$
$$+ 11.308\, X_2 \text{ (hours of homework)}$$
$$+ .399\, X_3 \text{ (home environment)}$$

50

The variation in the boys' grades that is not explained by these three variables is accounted for by some other conditions not measured in the above relationship. Perhaps the eighth-grader fell in love with a girl in senior high school or got himself into some other impossible emotional situation. Or perhaps he was so completely absorbed in football that he could not concentrate on his work. The multiple correlation analysis, as described above, cannot weight the influence of these additional factors, since they have not been included as independent variables, possibly because they could not be measured.

By applying the same correlation procedure to stocks, we derive the weights that should be ascribed to stability and growth respectively. Three lists of stocks are chosen (Figure 28). You will see that List A is a group of 10 stocks recognized everywhere as being the

FIGURE 28

45 Stocks of Well-Defined Quality

List A Highest Quality Stocks	List B Medium Quality Stocks	List C Speculative Quality Stocks
Du Pont	Air Reduction	Avco Manufacturing
General Electric	Allied Stores	Braniff Airways
Hartford Fire Insurance	Allis-Chalmers	Chicago, Milwaukee,
International Business	Armstrong Cork	St. Paul & Pacific
Machines	Bendix Aviation	Continental Motors
Minnesota Mining &	Best & Co.	McCall Corporation
Manufacturing	Burroughs Corporation	Minneapolis-Moline
Penney (J. C.)	Chain Belt	Northwest Airlines
Procter & Gamble	Colgate-Palmolive	Spiegel, Inc.
Scott Paper	General Refractories	U. S. Industries
Standard Oil (New	Great Northern Railway	Virginia-Carolina
Jersey)	Lorillard (P.)	Chemical
Union Carbide	Louisville & Nashville	
	Mallory (P. R.)	
	Maytag	
	McKesson & Robbins	
	Phelps Dodge	
	Radio Corp. of America	
	Republic Steel	
	Ruberoid	
	Sylvania Electric	
	U. S. Pipe & Foundry	
	Westinghouse Electric	
	Wheeling Steel	
	Yale & Towne	

bluest of the blue chips. Concededly, this selection is an *a priori* judgment. What we are trying to find is the weight that belongs to growth and stability respectively in the determination of quality. And since we know that these stocks are the bluest of the blue, and since we have reasoned that growth and stability are the determinants of quality, we can say, "Here is a group of stocks in which stability is combined with growth to produce the highest quality." List B is a group of which it can be said that the combination of growth and stability has produced medium quality. And you will note List C, which comprises stocks that are concededly very speculative and that any investment expert would describe as being of relatively poor quality.

A number is then substituted for each of the three quality groups selected on an *a priori* basis—7.50 for the group of A quality stocks, 4.50 for the B quality stocks and 1.50 for the C quality stocks. The choice of these particular numbers can be explained in terms of the desired objective: the division of all 804 stocks under study into nine quality groups with equal class intervals ranging from 0 to 9.

Quality Grade	Class Interval	Quality Number
A+	8.01 to 9.00	
A	7.01 to 8.00	Average: *7.50*
A−	6.01 to 7.00	
B+	5.01 to 6.00	
B	4.01 to 5.00	Average: *4.50*
B−	3.01 to 4.00	
C+	2.01 to 3.00	
C	1.01 to 2.00	Average: *1.50*
C−	0 to 1.00	

In Figure 29, selected stocks are lined up just as the boys were. Alongside the name of each of the stocks in the three quality groups you will find the number which is substituted for its Quality Grade. Then the stock's growth number and its stability ratio are set down. The solution of the equation then indicates the degree to which the variations in quality from A to B to C are influenced by the variations in the growth and stability of the stocks.

52

FIGURE 29

Quality Numbers, Growth Numbers and Stability Ratios for Selected Stocks by Quality Groups

	Quality Number	Growth Number	Stability Ratio
A			
HIGH QUALITY			
Du Pont	7.50	127	.187
General Electric	7.50	125	.141
.	.	.	.
.	.	.	.
.	.	.	.
Standard Oil (New Jersey)	7.50	132	.177
Union Carbide	7.50	67	.171
B			
MEDIUM QUALITY			
Air Reduction	4.50	77	.290
Allied Stores	4.50	−20	.257
.	.	.	.
.	.	.	.
.	.	.	.
Wheeling Steel	4.50	39	.337
Yale & Towne	4.50	69	.257
C			
LOW QUALITY			
Avco Manufacturing	1.50	−53	.401
Braniff Airways	1.50	16	.519
.	.	.	.
.	.	.	.
.	.	.	.
U.S. Industries	1.50	22	.467
Virginia-Carolina Chem.	1.50	−105	.560

NOTE: This is only a partial listing for purposes of illustration. The quality numbers, growth numbers and stability ratios for *all 45 stocks* listed in Figure 28 are incorporated in the correlation analysis that yields the Quality equation.

The correlation analysis yields this conclusion: stability takes about three times the weight that growth does in the determination of the Quality Grade. The resulting equation, when applied to the growth number and stability ratio of a specific stock, yields a figure representing the quality of the stock. A quality number between 5.01 and 6.00, for example, would correspond to a B+ Grade.

Now, in truth, we cannot in sensible practice cut off at precise points. We cannot say that any stock that has a combined growth and stability score of 5.99 is in one category, whereas another stock with a combined number of 6.00 falls into another, and there is nothing that can be done about this Procrustean standard except to let it cut where it falls. Instead, we assume that stocks in the upper half of the 5.01 to 6.00 range could be either B+ or A— and the stocks in the lower half of that range could be either B+ or B. Letters are used to describe Quality Grades instead of numbers in order to distinguish the combined Quality Grade from the Growth and Stability Indexes, which are numerically expressed. (Besides, quality by long usage has come to be associated with letters rather than numbers.)

Not only is some leeway allowed in choosing between groups in graduated brackets, but leeway of one grade, in deference to the yield history, is also granted. Stocks that have traditionally sold on a low-yield basis may be assumed to be of higher quality generally than stocks that have traditionally sold on a high-yield basis, just as low-yielding bonds are generally of better quality than high-yielding bonds. The yield factor cannot be mathematically weighted because there are groups of stocks, like the airlines, whose yields have been traditionally low, for reasons not related to their security but rather to their inability to pay dividends commensurate with their earnings.

What we have done then is, first, to "take a fix" on quality by measuring the stock according to its growth and stability during the postwar period. Next, we combine these measurements into a composite index of quality in such a way as to give three times as much weight to stability as to growth (the distribution of weights having been determined by the correlation analysis relating quality to growth and stability). We then assign a Quality Grade by letter to each of the nine numerical brackets and allow ourselves leeway of one grade in borderline cases and, in exceptional circumstances, an additional grade for stocks whose yield experience is found to be

54

clearly inconsistent with the quality index derived from the growth and stability measurements.

Now, what we have worked up here is a measure of past growth and past stability confirmed by typical yield. All this, however, refers to past experience. What has it to do with the future?

Let it be said at the outset that most of the money that has been made in stocks has accrued to those who bought stocks of good quality and just sat on them. As one boardroom habitué remarked, his grandfather made more money by the seat of his pants than he, the grandson, had made by the use of his agile brain. Merely sitting on the trend of a sound stock will get most people farther in the long run than almost any other method.

For the conservative investor, the Quality Grade comes first. Your typical conservative is a man who distrusts all forecasts of the future. He reasons that nobody knows what is going to happen tomorrow—and, of course, he is right. On the other hand, there are methods for determining future probability. Still, the typical conservative does not like to venture forth into the unknown in any way at all if he can avoid doing so. He reasons that the visibility into the future is poor. Therefore, he would be guided by the course of events past, where the visibility is better. Perhaps you have heard of the bird that flies backward. It has been said of this bird that he does not care where he is going but is interested in knowing where he has been. A moment's reflection will prove that this is nonsense. If the bird did not care where he was going, he would not bother to fly at all. He does care where he is going, and he intends to get there. But he prefers to be guided on his course by the experience of flight known rather than flight foreseen. And let me tell you that this bird, in the stock market, has done very well in the last 25 years.

What good is this method for the future? For one thing, it helps to avoid risk. Many investors, and especially speculators, are inclined to take a flippant attitude toward risk. If a risk has been avoided which never materialized, the superficial thinker is apt to conclude that it was foolish to have taken pains to avoid that risk. This is the kind of reasoning that goes on in the mind of the man who crosses the street against the traffic light. He sees that a lot of

55

slowpokes stand on the corner waiting for the light to change. He, however, looks in both directions and crosses in the middle of the street, getting to the other side far ahead of everybody else. And nothing happens to him. Superficially, therefore, he concludes that he took the better course. But you know that such conduct, if incorporated into policy, would sooner or later result in an increase in accidents.

Investment in a good, strong company, a company of high quality, avoids many major risks. Management of a high-grade company is almost sure to be sound. Financial condition is usually strong. The company has proved its ability to hold its own or gain on its competition. A high-quality company can usually keep up with, or exceed, the growth of its industry.

In companies whose stocks are of lower quality, these characteristics may or may not be found. The management of an unseasoned company may be of far greater ability than that of the seasoned company, but, until proved, it represents a risk.

If you had to go away to a desert island for 10 years and had to invest your money for that period of time without any way of keeping abreast of what was going to happen, you would do best to buy only the stocks of highest quality—those graded A or better. Of course, it would be even better if you bought only the highest-grade stocks and then watched developments throughout the years to be sure that the quality was holding—that no developments of long-term significance were occurring to undermine the company's position. In any event, restricting investments to stocks of the highest quality certainly avoids a great many unforeseeable risks.

It does not follow, however, that the best results will be obtained simply by buying high-quality stocks at any time. Suppose you had invested $1,000 in Scott Paper at a price of 15 (on an adjusted price basis) in 1946; you would, as of January 1959, have had an investment worth $5,000, and you would have received dividends totaling $1,000. Had you waited a few months longer in 1946 and bought Scott at $10, instead of at $15, your $1,000 investment would, as of January 1959, have been worth $7,500, and you would have received dividends totaling $1,500.

Here then is a difference of $3,000 to an investor who com-

56

mitted $1,000 to a high-grade (A quality stock) and held for the 13-year pull. Buying at a low price, rather than at a high price, is important for the long-pull investor, as well as for the short-term speculator.

Quality, in truth, is a highly useful measure of defense against unforeseeable contingencies. But it is not a measure of whether a stock is cheap, or dear, *at the time*.

A method for determining whether a stock is currently cheap or dear will be described in Chapter III.

RANK FOR APPRECIATION POTENTIALITY IN THE NEXT THREE TO FIVE YEARS

Let me now go to another method of evaluation, that of determining the appreciation potentiality of a stock three to five years hence. The visibility looking ahead three to five years is low. Nobody knows whether there will be a revolution between 1962 and 1964, or whether we shall have total war, or peace, or partial peace. Nobody knows whether 1962 will be a better year than 1963, or 1963 a better year than 1964, or vice versa. Nobody knows whether we shall have a cyclical recession in which the business index will drop between 1962 and 1963 and then recover between 1963 and 1964, or whether we shall have a business boom in 1963 followed by a drop in 1964, or whether the whole period will be one of gradually rising prosperity or gradually declining prosperity. In 1959, these questions, it must be conceded, are unanswerable.

However, just because the future is unknown does not mean that one can afford to ignore it. The way to adjust for the unknowable future is to determine what is probable. It is conceded that the determination of economic conditions three to five years from now involves a speculation which is risky in terms of the probability of its attainment. Note, though, that what we are solving for here is not a forecast of what the price of the subject stock will be, but of what it might be in given circumstances. Those given circumstances, in view of the fact that we cannot forecast them, are based upon a hypothesis. The most realistic hypothesis is that the population will continue to grow at its recent rate in accordance with the demographic projections prepared by experts. The curve in Figure 30 shows how

FIGURE 30
Economic Series Determining Long-Term Projection of Gross National Product

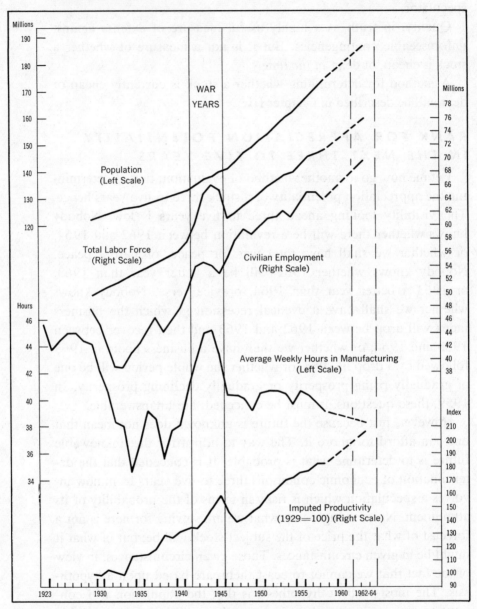

Sources: *Survey of Current Business*, U.S. Department of Commerce. Projections by The Value Line Investment Survey.

the population growth may be expected to persist into the period of our hypothesis.

With that population growth will go an increase in the labor force from 71.3 million in 1958 to over 76 million three to five years hence. Unemployment will average 5% of the civilian labor force, compared to 6.8% in 1958. The productivity of labor has been increasing at an average annual rate of 2% for many years. Projecting that trend into the future and making allowance for acceleration in technological advances which have marked the recent past, we come up with an annual productivity increase in the next five years of 2½ %.

The number of hours worked per week by each worker in manufacturing has been declining steadily and the decline persists. Here you recognize the chief blessing of the industrial revolution. Projecting the persistence of that trend, we come out with 38.3 as the average number of hours of work per week in the hypothesized economy of 1962–64.

On the assumption that prices will increase at an annual rate of 1%, slightly less than the trend of price inflation over the past 10 years, we arrive at a sum which indicates a gross national product of $555 billion (Figure 31). The $555 billion GNP, then, is the master index of the economic environment that we hypothesize for the years 1962–1964.

Please note that what we are solving for is not the stock's highest price potentiality, or its lowest price potentiality, during the period 1962–64, but its average price potentiality for the whole three-year period. By aiming for an average price for three years, we avoid the necessity of forecasting cyclical highs and lows during that period.

By hypothesizing an economic environment, even if we cannot forecast it, we set up a common index of prosperity that is applicable to all stocks. Even if the hypothesis should be exceeded, or the actual events fall short of it, we still would have a basis for determining the relative potentialities of all stocks *in the same environment*.

Having determined what the economic environment might plausibly be, and relating all other national income figures such as disposable income, consumer expenditures and discretionary income to the gross national product figure, we come up with a set of

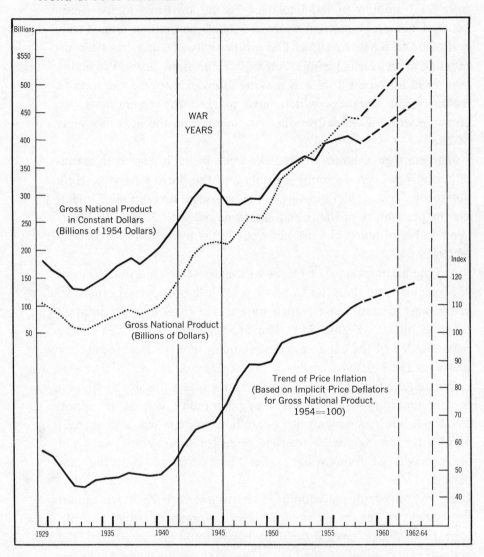

Sources: *Survey of Current Business,* U.S. Department of Commerce. Projections by The Value Line Investment Survey.

60

indexes to which we may correlate the sales of the subject company.

In Figure 32, you will see how the sales of General Motors correlate to disposable income. The company's sales are plotted on the vertical co-ordinate and disposable income is plotted on the horizontal one. You see there is a fairly straight-line fit, so that if we hypothesize what the disposable income will be during 1962–64, we can read the company's projected sales ($15.0 billion) from the graph.

FIGURE 32

General Motors—Sales to Disposable Income, 1937 to 1958, and Projection for 1962–64

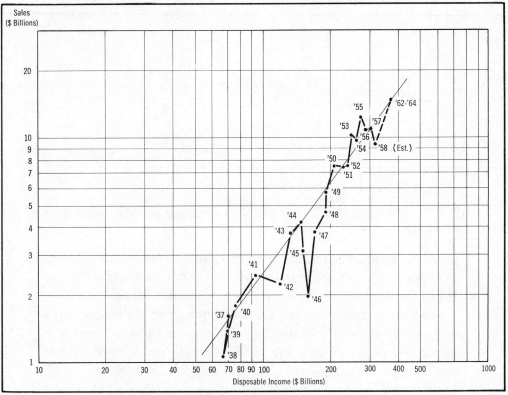

Sources: *Survey of Current Business.*
General Motors' Annual Reports.
1958 estimate and 1962–64 projection by The Value Line Investment Survey.

Another way of getting at the same thing is to plot the sales as a percentage of disposable income, or if the sales of the company happen to correlate more closely to consumer expenditures than to disposable income, then as a percentage of consumer expenditures. Or we could use discretionary income, or whatever series best fitted the pattern of the company's sales fluctuations in the past.

You see in Figure 33 that this company's share of disposable income has been growing at a fairly consistent rate. We project the percentage out to a probable point in line with past experience ad-

FIGURE 33

General Motors—Sales as a Per Cent of Disposable Income, 1937 to 1958, and Projection for 1962–64

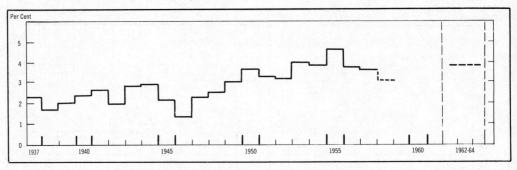

Sources: *Survey of Current Business.*
General Motors' Annual Reports.
1958 estimate and 1962–64 projection by The Value Line Investment Survey.

justed for trend. The result is then compared to the scatter diagram as a check. The two are found to come out approximately the same. If not, a reconciliation is made—a compromise between the two.

We then compare the sales curve with the trend of the company's gross plant account (Figure 34). This gross plant account can usually be projected into the future because management, in its annual report, outlines the capital expenditures it has in mind. Some companies have a policy of devoting a certain part of surplus every year to expansion or modernization. Thus, when the analyst studies the annual reports and determines each company's policies, he is in a position to project the curve of the gross plant account into the future, and he can then run his sales curve at about the same slope as the plant curve. That will give him another "fix" on the sales outlook in the three- to five-year period we are hypothesizing.

A more sophisticated technique would require evaluation of the sales prospects for each of General Motors' divisions and the profit

FIGURE 34

General Motors—Sales and Gross Plant Account, 1937 to 1958, and Projections for 1962–64

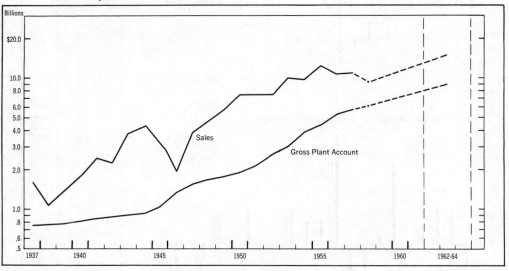

Sources: General Motors' Annual Reports.
        1958 estimates and 1962–64 projections by The Value Line Investment Survey.

margin of each. "Field research"—discussions with management—could be highly useful in this function.

Now, having determined approximately what the sales will be during the three- to five-year period, the analyst must then estimate what the earnings and dividends will be. To do that, he must next determine the profit margin. Figure 35 shows the profit margin (of the same company for which we are estimating sales) and the year-to-year changes in sales and profit margin. You see that the profit margin normally fluctuates with the sales volume. In a year of

FIGURE 35

General Motors—Profit Margin and Annual Changes in Sales and Profit Margin, 1937 to 1958, and Projection for 1962–64

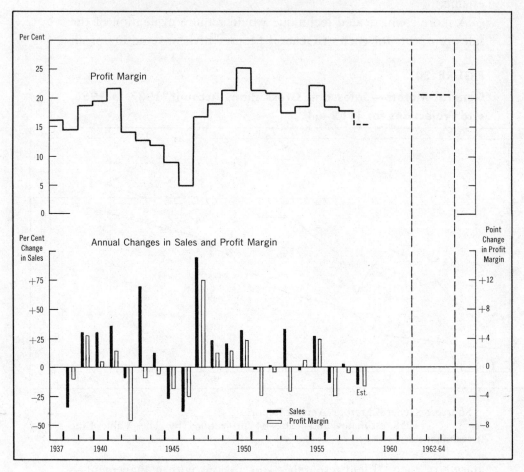

Sources: General Motors' Annual Reports.
1958 estimates and 1962–64 projection by The Value Line Investment Survey.

expanding sales volume, the profit margin rises, as a rule, and when the sales volume goes down, the profit margin also declines.

Now, in the matter of determining the profit margin, other factors than the fluctuation of sales volume must be considered too, as, for example, the price structure in the company's market and political

64

influences upon the company's fortunes, such as tariff adjustments. The determination of the profit margin by simply drawing out a line that is in the general neighborhood of the margins of former years, adjusted for changes in sales volume, is not enough. But it is a good way to start. If the profit margin has fluctuated between 13% and 18%, then 15% is a good working hypothesis to go on; and it may be refined by knowledge of other circumstances, such as those to which I have just referred. Here, though, is a judgment that the analyst must make.

There are three primary speculations that a stock-market analyst must engage in to estimate the dividend declarations of a company. The first is the speculation on sales, for which a method has just been described. The second is the speculation on the profit margin, which was also described. The third is the pay-out ratio. This is the ratio that indicates what percentage of the earnings the management will see fit to distribute as dividends.

In respect to the pay-out ratio, the analyst can start with the assumption that a dividend rate that has held for a long time will tend to be maintained. Much can be said for a dividend forecast based on mere inertia. However, dividends do change. They change in relation to earnings. But they also change in relation to the company's need of working capital.

The ratio of the company's working capital to its sales and the accompanying fluctuations in the pay-out ratio are illustrated in Figure 36. When the ratio of the working capital to sales goes up, it means that the company is in an easy current position. When the ratio of working capital to sales goes down, it means that the company is in a tight financial position. Now note that a tight financial condition may reflect nothing worse than an excellent volume of business. When all the machines and lathes are running at top speed, the company requires materials, fuels and labor to the maximum. Such a situation may be bullish on a company's prospects, but it is not necessarily indicative of an increase in the dividend in the near future. Companies that are growing very rapidly, you may have observed, are nearly always conservative in their dividend policies. They are conservative in that respect because they need their cash to finance their increasing volume.

FIGURE 36

General Motors—Dividend Pay-Out Ratio and Working Capital/ Sales Ratio, 1937 to 1958, and Projections for 1962–64

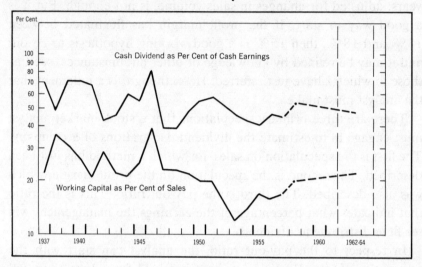

Sources: General Motors' Annual Reports.
        1958 estimates and 1962–64 projections by The Value Line Investment Survey.

On the other hand, a company whose operating rate is below normal and which has a lot of cash on hand could afford to be generous in its dividend pay-out relative to earnings.

Here are two variables, then, that influence the dividend pay-out. One is the profit earned, and the other is the company's ability to pay those profits out, or to put it the other way, its need to retain cash to finance its business volume.

As you can see from this illustration, the tendency is for the percentage of earnings paid out to increase when the working capital in relation to sales increases. Conversely, when the working capital in relation to sales falls, and the company finds itself in need of cash, the percentage of earnings paid out in dividends tends to diminish.

In order to determine what the company's working capital position might be three to five years hence, the analyst must now project

66

the earnings into the 1962–64 period. Having projected the sales and profit margin for the average of the three-year period 1962–64, he assumes an even progression up to those figures during the intervening three-year period, modified whenever necessary by his knowledge of conditions in the industry. For example, if the sales go from the estimated 1958 level of $9.4 billion to $15.0 billion, the average of 1962–64, the analyst might assume an equal increase for each of the years between 1958 and 1963 to bring the 1958 sales volume up to the estimated 1963 volume (1963 being the middle year of the 1962–64 band). This, of course, is only an assumption of a trend based upon the realization of the volume. But it will serve as a basis for estimating the company's accumulation of working capital. As shown by the computation in the table on p. 68 (Figure 37), the cash earnings in each year are reduced by the estimated dividend pay-out, which in turn is influenced by the preceding year's working capital/sales ratio. From the cash earnings thus derived, less the dividends paid out in cash, must be subtracted cash outlays for new plant and equipment and cash required to meet debt maturities. The balance, then, plus any money brought in through new financing, is the increment to working capital, and this increment is carried forward from year to year until an estimated working capital position for the period 1962–64 is reached.

On the basis of this projected working capital in relation to the projected sales volume for the period 1962–64, the analyst then estimates the dividend pay-out ratio and determines the cash dividend that may reasonably be expected at the time under the general economic hypothesis.

Having projected the three-year average earnings and dividends three to five years into the future, the analyst must then put a price on these earnings and dividends. This is the function of valuation. Here is the method that we use.

First of all, the average annual yield of the subject stock is plotted for a period of 22 years. General Motors' average annual yield was 3.4% in 1946, 5.1% in 1947, 7.6% in 1948 and so on as shown in Figure 38. The total dividend declarations during each year are divided by the average price of that year to get the yield for the year, and the yields are plotted as an annual series.

FIGURE 37

General Motors—Annual Income Analysis and Projections,

(Millions

	1954	1955	1956	1957
Sales	$9,823.5	$12,443.3	$10,796.4	$10,989.8
Profit Margin	18.4%	22.2%	18.4%	17.8%
Operating Profit	$1,805.3	$2,757.2	$1,985.3	$1,957.3
Less: Depreciation	232.9	293.8	347.2	414.9
Interest	9.7	9.8	9.8	8.7
Plus: Other Income	50.4	43.6	55.9	43.9
Equity in Unconsolidated Subsidiary Earnings	32.0	45.6	57.2	51.3
Bonus Reserve Restored to Income	—	—	—	19.8
Pretax Income	$1,645.0	$2,542.8	$1,741.4	$1,648.7
Per Cent of Sales	16.7%	20.4%	16.1%	15.0%
Income Taxes	$ 839.0	$1,353.4	$ 894.0	$ 805.1
Per Cent of Pretax Income	51.0%	53.2%	51.3%	48.8%
Net Income	$ 806.0	$1,189.5	$ 847.4	$ 843.6
Preferred Dividends	$ 12.9	$ 12.9	$ 12.9	$ 12.9
Available Common	793.0	1,176.5	834.5	830.7
Common Dividends	436.5	592.2	552.9	555.5
Number of Shares Outstanding	87,343,778	273,512,806	276,374,733	277,732,830
Earnings Per Share	$3.03 [1]	$4.30	$3.02	$2.99
Dividends Per Share	1.67 [1]	2.17	2.00	2.00
Cash Earnings	$1,038.9	$1,483.3	$1,194.6	$1,258.5
Plus: Working Capital (Beginning of Year)	1,236.1	1,350.6	2,058.3	1,746.0
Sale of Properties	—	—	—	—
New Financing	298.5	332.1	44.9	48.3
Other	24.0 [2]	105.5	35.8	—
Total Funds IN	$2,597.4	$3,271.5	$3,333.6	$3,052.8
Total Dividends Paid	$ 449.4	$ 605.2	$ 565.8	$ 568.4
Plus: Plant & Equipment	737.0	608.0	891.0	474.0
Other Investment	—	—	25.7	—
Tooling Expense (Net of Amortization)	60.5	—	91.0	108.0
Capital Retired	—	—	—	13.8
Other	—	—	14.1	27.2
Total Funds OUT	$1,246.9	$1,213.2	$1,587.6	$1,191.4
Working Capital (End of Year)	$1,350.6	$2,058.3	$1,746.0	$1,861.4
Pay-Out Ratio	43.3%	40.8%	47.4%	45.2%
Working Capital/Sales Ratio	13.7%	16.5%	16.2%	16.9%

[1] Per share figures are adjusted for the 3-for-1 stock split which occurred in 1955.
[2] Working capital of foreign subsidiaries consolidated for the first time in 1954.
[3] The projection for 1963 represents the average of the period 1962–64.

68

of dollars)

1958	1959	1960	1961	1962	1963[3]
$9,400	$12,300	$13,000	$13,700	$14,400	$15,000
15.4%	19.5%	20.0%	20.2%	20.4%	20.5%
$1,447.6	$2,400	$2,600	$2,767	$2,938	$3,075
420	420	425	437.5	455	475
8.6	9	9	8.5	8	8
25	35	40	44	48	52
60	64	67	70	73	75
—	—	—	—	—	—
$1,104	$2,070	$2,273	$2,435	$2,596	$2,719
11.7%	16.8%	17.5%	17.8%	18.0%	18.1%
$489	$1,040	$1,147	$1,193	$1,272	$1,332
44.3%	50.2%	50.5%	49.0%	49.0%	49.0%
$615	$1,030	$1,126	$1,242	$1,324	$1,387
$ 12.9	$ 13	$ 13	$ 13	$ 13	$ 13
602	1,017	1,113	1,229	1,311	1,374
559	635	710	787	850	899
280,000,000	282,000,000	284,000,000	286,000,000	288,000,000	290,000,000
$2.15	$3.60	$3.90	$4.30	$4.55	$4.75
2.00	2.25	2.50	2.75	2.95	3.10
$1,035	$1,450	$1,551	$1,680	$1,779	$1,862
1,861	1,859	2,281	2,584	2,844	3,095
—	—	—	—	—	—
45	80	85	90	95	100
—	—	—	—	—	—
$2,941	$3,389	$3,917	$4,354	$4,718	$5,057
$ 572	$ 648	$ 723	$ 800	$ 863	$ 912
350	400	500	600	650	700
—	—	—	—	—	—
150	50	100	100	100	100
10	10	10	10	10	10
—	—	—	—	—	—
$1,082	$1,108	$1,333	$1,510	$1,623	$1,722
$1,859	$2,281	$2,584	$2,844	$3,095	$3,335
55.3%	44.7%	46.6%	47.6%	48.5%	49.0%
19.8%	18.5%	19.9%	20.8%	21.5%	22.2%

Sources: General Motors' Annual Reports.
   1958 estimates and 1959 through 1963 projections by The Value Line Investment Survey.

FIGURE 38

General Motors' Dividend Yield Related to the Average Dividend Yield of 45 Selected Stocks, 1937 to 1958, and Projections for 1962–64

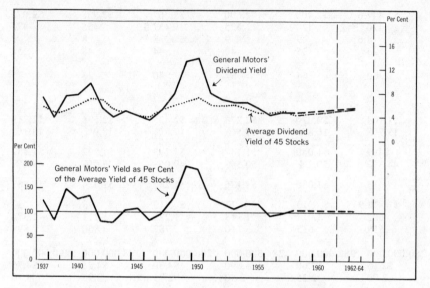

Source: The Value Line Investment Survey.

Because the dividend is divided by the price, the yield will fluctuate, even if the dividend remains the same, according to the fluctuations of the price. And the price of the individual stock will fluctuate, to a degree, in sympathy with general market sentiment. Therefore, in order to take general market sentiment out of the yield curve of the stock, the average annual yield of the stock is divided by the average annual yield of the market in general. To determine the average yield of the market, an average was constructed of 45 stocks (Figure 39) that have paid rather substantial dividends in every year from 1929 to the present, including the depression years. Between 1932 and 1935, you may recall, dividend payments were generally very small or nonexistent, and stocks sold on the basis of their asset values rather than their dividends. In such a situation, naturally, low yields do not truly reflect sentiment, but merely an abnormally low level of dividends. In order to minimize such distortion,

70

FIGURE 39

45 Representative Stocks and Their Average Annual Dividend Yields, 1929–1958

45 Stocks

ASR Products	Columbian Carbon	Myers (F. E.)
Allied Chemical	Combustion Engi-	National Steel
American Brake Shoe	neering	Otis Elevator
American Can	Corn Products	Procter & Gamble
American Chicle	Dome Mines	Pullman, Inc.
American Home	Du Pont	Raybestos-Manhattan
Products	Eastman Kodak	Ruberoid
American Machine &	Eaton Manufacturing	Safeway Stores
Foundry	Electric Storage	Singer Manufacturing
American Tobacco	Battery	Standard Oil
Anchor Hocking Glass	General Electric	(California)
Archer-Daniels-	General Foods	Standard Oil (New
Midland	General Motors	Jersey)
Atlantic Refining	Ingersoll-Rand	Timken Roller
Caterpillar Tractor	International Har-	Bearing
Chain Belt	vester	Union Carbide
Chrysler Corporation	Kresge (S. S.)	U. S. Gypsum
Coca-Cola	Loew's Inc.	Woolworth (F. W.)

Average Annual Dividend Yields of 45 Stocks

1929	4.1%	*1939*	5.0%	*1949*	6.6%
1930	5.7	*1940*	6.0	*1950*	7.2
1931	7.3	*1941*	7.0	*1951*	6.0
1932	8.8	*1942*	6.7	*1952*	5.8
1933	4.7	*1943*	5.1	*1953*	6.0
1934	4.8	*1944*	4.7	*1954*	5.4
1935	4.9	*1945*	4.0	*1955*	4.7
1936	4.8	*1946*	4.0	*1956*	4.7
1937	5.7	*1947*	5.2	*1957*	5.0
1938	4.6	*1948*	5.9	*1958*	4.5

Source: The Value Line Investment Survey.

the 45-stock average was deliberately composed of stocks which paid dividends throughout the depression years.

When the yield of General Motors is divided by the average yield of the 45 stocks, the influence of market sentiment is removed and an indication of the ratio at which this stock will sell in relation to the market as a whole becomes evident (see Figure 38).

Suppose a stock tends to sell at a price which returns a yield equal to about 115% of the yield of the market as a whole. If the average market yield is projected to 5.0% in the hypothesized environment of 1962–64, this stock would be expected to yield 5.75%.

Many stocks have a yield which, when divided by the yield of the 45-stock average, reveals a definite secular trend. For example, if a stock is of improving quality, the tendency will be for its yield relative to the market yield to go down. (This is the same experience as in the bond market where, if a bond is improving in quality, it tends to sell on a lower yield basis relative to other bonds than before.) Conversely, if the quality of the stock is deteriorating, the tendency is for the yield to increase relative to the market, in which case the trend of the stock's yield to the market is upward.

Minnesota Mining and Manufacturing (Figure 40), for example, is an illustration of a stock whose yield relative to the market has been on a steadily declining trend since 1946, indicating steady improvement in its quality. On the other hand, Canada Dry is an example of a stock whose yield has been rising relative to the market, indicating deterioration of quality over a period of years.

Where a secular trend is in evidence, the projection three to five years into the future should take account of that trend. It need not be projected on a straight-line basis. No trend in yield relationships can persist indefinitely. But, within the limits of practical judgment, the trend of the individual stock's yield relative to that of the market should be taken account of.

The average market yield three to five years hence can only be hypothesized. A reasonable yield to extrapolate is that which has been typical of the post-war years, namely 5.5%. During the years 1962–64, therefore, the 45-stock average is projected to yield 5.5%, which is equivalent to the average yield since 1946.

FIGURE 40

Dividend Yields of Minnesota Mining and Manufacturing and Canada Dry as Per Cent of the Average Yield of 45 Selected Stocks, 1937–1958

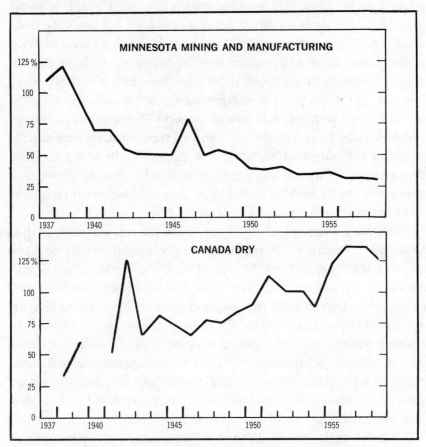

NOTE: Canada Dry did not pay a dividend in 1937 and 1940.

Source: The Value Line Investment Survey.

Since it is estimated that the dividend of General Motors during the period 1962 to 1964 will be $3.10 a share on average, General Motors' indicated yield of 5.7% (104% of the average yield of the 45 stocks) is divided into the estimated dividend to get the estimated price. That is to say, if General Motors is to yield 5.7%, it is going to sell for 17.5 times the dividend; if it sells for 17.5 times the dividend of $3.10, then the price will be about 54. Thus a potential price is determined three to five years into the future on the basis of estimated dividends in a hypothesized economy. This obviously is no forecast. But it is a plausible determination of potentiality. (If anyone disagreed with this estimate of General Motors' sales, earnings and dividends, he still could apply this method, making such adjustments as his judgment dictated with respect to both the forecast dividend-paying ability and capitalization rates that he considered reasonable. In the end, he would know precisely where his judgment conflicted with trend and past experience.)

The same exercise generally is applied to the price/earnings ratio, as shown in Figure 41. A normal price potentiality is derived from the price/earnings ratio of the individual stock relative to the price/earnings ratio of 45 stocks. The price thus determined is reconciled to the price derived from the dividend-yield relationship to give an approximate average price for the three-year period 1962–64.

Once that is done, the measure of Appreciation Potentiality from current price to a projected 1962–64 price is computed and compared with the Appreciation Potentiality of all the other 803 stocks similarly computed. The magnitudes are then tabulated and divided into five equal sections of approximately 160 stocks each.

All those stocks that are in the top 20-percentile group are ranked I (Highest) for 3- to 5-year Appreciation Potentiality. All the stocks in the percentile group between 61 and 80 are ranked II, those between 41 and 60 ranked III (Average), those between 21 and 40 are ranked IV (Below Average) and those from 20 down are ranked V (Lowest).

Thus, we now have two standards to guide investors: (1) Quality, expressed as grades — A+, A, A−, B+, B, B−, C+, C or C−, and (2) Rank according to Appreciation Potentiality three to five years hence, expressed in terms of five groups— I (Highest), II

FIGURE 41

General Motors' Price/Earnings Ratio Related to the Average Price/Earnings Ratio of 45 Selected Stocks, 1937 to 1958, and Projections for 1962–64

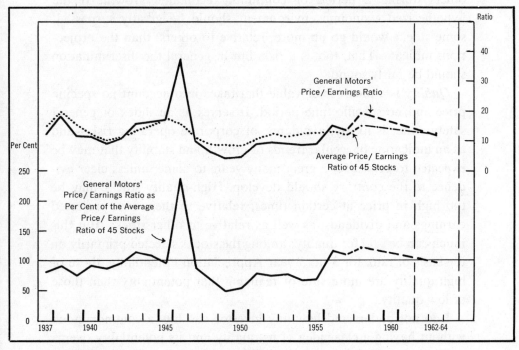

Source: 1958 estimates and 1962–64 projections by The Value Line Investment Survey.

(Above Average), III (Average), IV (Below Average) and V (Lowest). Both are objective in that they rely upon statistical methods for determination.

The rank according to Appreciation Potentiality is of greatest interest to forward-looking investors who seek stocks capable of relatively wide appreciation since they are currently priced favorably in relation to other stocks with regard to their earning potentiality over a three- to five-year pull. But the investor who uses this measure of Appreciation Potentiality must bear in mind that it is a potentiality, not a forecast, and that it is based upon a hypothesis, and not knowledge, of the future.

75

If the hypothesized economic environment should fail of realization or exceed the projection, the rank according to Appreciation Potentiality would still be of some value, because it would give a general indication of which stocks are likely to do better than others during a period of continuing economic growth. If the hypothesized economic environment should be greatly surpassed, some stocks would go up more, relative to others, than the projections indicate. That, too, is a risk, but in general the discrimination should be fairly sound.

Quality is a measure of value that takes into account no specific price and no specific time period. It serves as an index of general safety—that is to say, avoidance of corporate operating risk—and as an indication of secular trends of growth and stability that may be expected to persist for a great many years to come, unless clear evidence to the contrary should develop. High-quality stocks may be too high in price at certain times, relative to their own projected earnings and dividends, as well as relative to other stocks. But this much can be said for quality: among the stocks selected primarily on the basis of rank for 3- to 5-year Appreciation Potentiality, those of high quality are more sure of realizing that potentiality than those of low quality.

I do not understand how any investor can buy a common stock without having a clear idea of its quality and its potentiality over a period of three to five years. Here, then, are two methods for determining both the Quality Grade and the Appreciation Potentiality rank over a three- to five-year period. They are not perfect methods; and, in Chapters III and IV, I intend to show the extent to which they have failed of perfect performance in our experience. But I can report that they have proven useful and successful on the whole. Yet, neither of these standards of value indicates whether a stock is currently too high or too low, or whether the price is just right, now. The determination of the price position of a stock currently will be the subject of Chapter III. That determination, by our method, is made according to a standard called the Value Line Rating, which represents the intrinsic value of the stock during a period of 12 months, based upon a normal capitalization of its earnings and dividends.

76

CHAPTER

I N THE previous chapter, two methods of evaluating common stocks were explained. One was based upon the concept of Quality, or long-term security, the other upon the magnitude of Appreciation Potentiality three to five years in the future in a plausibly hypothesized economic environment.

Quality was determined on the basis of (1) earnings and dividend growth and (2) price stability. A Stability Index and a Growth Index were statistically derived for each stock and then combined, the Stability Index being given about three times the weight of the Growth Index. The quality numbers were arranged in order of magnitude and according to nine groups which were alphabetically designated: A+, A, A—, B+, B, B—, C+, C, C—. A leeway of one grade was allowed for borderline cases, and the final classification was modified in some instances by the yield history of the stock in question. A traditionally low yield was considered to be evidence of high quality, and a traditionally high yield, of low quality. But, it was noted that the yield relationship alone was not reliable because some stocks, airlines for example, were customarily priced on a very low yield basis, not because of the great safety of their dividends, but because of the very low pay-out ratios that resulted from

77

the companies' persistent and urgent need to accumulate cash to replace rapidly obsolescing equipment.

The meaning of the Quality Grade can best be described in terms of safety. Stocks of high quality—in the A+, A, A— or B+ categories—offer greater-than-average assurance against unforeseeable contingencies. In the case of such stocks, there is little doubt about the soundness of the management, the financial condition or the competitive position of the company.

The usefulness of the Quality Grade in evaluation was illustrated by the hypothetical case of an individual who found that he would have to go away to a desert island for 10 years. He had no way of knowing what was going to happen to investments in the 10 years following his exile, but he was under the necessity of investing his money in stocks before leaving. The best stocks he could buy for such a long period of time were the stocks of high quality. Nobody could tell what would happen in 10 years. But, it could reasonably be concluded that, in the absence of knowledge of the future, those companies that had proved their strength and competitive ability in the past would do best over a very long period of time.

What the Quality Grade cannot do is indicate whether the stock is relatively high, or low, compared to all other stocks now, or compared to its own intrinsic value *now*. The importance of determining whether the stock is *currently* overvalued or undervalued was illustrated in the case of Scott Paper. A $1,000 investment in "A" quality Scott Paper in March 1946, when it was overvalued, would have resulted in a capital gain and dividend income total of $5,000 as of January 1959. But the same $1,000 investment would have resulted in a capital gain and dividend income total of $8,000, had Scott been purchased in October or November of 1946, when it was undervalued.

The Quality Grade is based entirely upon a backward look. It includes no estimate of future earnings and dividends, nor forecast of future economic environment. The logic of the Quality Grade is based upon the assumption that long-held trends will persist into the future. The assumption is valid on the pragmatic test of experience in the stock market. Most of the great fortunes built in the stock market have developed through patient retention of stocks of high quality. This is not to say that speculative stocks may not, in certain periods, far outpace the advance of high-quality stocks. But, if one had to take a position for a decade to come, he could probably do no better than select stocks on the basis of quality. While it is true that long-held trends can change, it is logical to assume the persistence of any long-held trend until evidence of change appears. In short, if Du Pont is a stock of high quality, as it is, and its Quality Grade derives from the proof of its competitive, financial and earnings strength over a long period of years past, as expressed in the growth of its earnings and dividends and relative price stability, it is logical to assume that that strength relative to other companies will be maintained until clear evidence develops to the contrary.

The Quality Grade, then, is regarded as one of the most useful standards of selection. While other criteria are also useful, it can be postulated that high quality is always desirable, for high quality implies the avoidance of many risks to which low-quality securities are exposed. The acceptance of these risks, such as unseasoned management, untested markets, experimental design and merchandising, and weak financial condition may, in the end, prove exceptionally rewarding. But such commitments involve risks greater than in the case of higher quality stocks, and to the extent that they do, they detract from the safety of the investment.

Another method of evaluating stocks was based upon a quite different concept, namely, Appreciation Potentiality in a hypothesized environment three to five years into the future. This was the method by which the analyst looked ahead three to five years. He projected his value into a three-year-long period. The reason for estimating over a three-year period three to five years in the future was that the analyst thus avoided the necessity of forecasting so far in advance what the cyclical pattern of the economy would be in the forecast period. Were he to attempt a forecast for any one year in the three-year period, he would be faced with the need to predict the trend of the business cycle in each particular year, three to five years hence. But by estimating for an entire three-year period, he averages out the short cyclical changes in business and the dividend-paying ability of his stock.

79

The projected economic environment is not a forecast. It is a plausible hypothesis based upon an extrapolation of the growth of the labor force, its productivity, the number of hours worked per week and the price trend of goods and services.

Once the economic environment is determined in terms of gross national product, the other key series such as disposable income, consumer expenditures and discretionary income are correlated to the gross national product figure to give the reference points that can most effectively be used to estimate the sales volume of the individual company in the hypothesized economy.

After the future sales are projected, profit margins are estimated. Illustrations were provided to show how such estimates might be made. True, they would have to stand as approximations at best, but they would be approximations based on past experience, adjusted for trend, and they could be regarded as useful bench marks.

Having estimated sales and profit margins in a hypothetical economy, the analyst then computes the probable per-share earnings by going down through the income report. He estimates the dividends paid out of cash earnings on the basis of the traditional policy of the company and the projected working capital/sales ratio, and he comes up with the per-share dividends that might reasonably be expected during the three-year period three to five years hence.

It was pointed out that even if this method failed to give an accurate forecast of the economic environment, and consequently of the average earnings and dividends three to five years ahead, it still had the virtue of providing a common background against which to project the potentiality of a great many stocks relative to one another. 804 stocks are surveyed by our organization. It is, of course, necessary that the large group of analysts who work on so large a number of stocks base their estimates upon a single assumption regarding the economic environment. Otherwise the relative evaluations would become meaningless, since the individual analysts might project earnings according to varying concepts of general prosperity. Hypothesizing a single economic environment gives a common base for measuring the relative potentiality for earnings

80

and dividend improvement of all companies during the period three to five years into the future.

Once the earnings and dividends are projected, it is then necessary to evaluate them. That is done by finding the ratio of the yield of the subject stock to the yield of the market in general. It was found that General Motors, for example, over a period of years sold on a typical annual yield basis that was 104% of the average annual yield of a representative average of stocks. Therefore, General Motors' potential dividend three to five years hence was capitalized at 104% of the projected average market yield of 5.5%, which was determined to be the average norm on the basis of past experience. In determining the potential price of General Motors, the estimated dividend was divided by 5.7%, which is just another way of saying that the potential price would be capitalized at 17.5 times the dividend. Since the dividend was projected to $3.10, the potential value of the stock was projected to 54 in the hypothesized economic environment of 1962–64.

The same method was applied to the price/earnings ratio of the stock. The two values, the one obtained by capitalizing the expected dividend, and the other by capitalizing the expected earnings per share, were reconciled by simple averaging.

This same method was applied to all 804 stocks. The Appreciation Potentiality from current price to the potential price was computed for each and set down in order of magnitude. Those stocks whose Appreciation Potentiality was found to be in the top 20% bracket were ranked I (Highest) for potential appreciation three to five years hence; those whose Appreciation Potentiality was found to be in the bracket higher than 60% of all stocks but lower than the top 20% were ranked II (Above Average); those were ranked III (Average) that fell in the percentiles between 41 and 60; those were ranked IV (Below Average) that were in the percentiles between 21 and 40; and those were ranked V (Lowest) that were in the lowest 20 percentiles.

The rank for 3- to 5-year Appreciation Potentiality is found to be useful because it indicates the relative appreciation that may reasonably be expected over a period of three to five years. The Quality Grade, on the other hand, while it gives an indication of the safety

81

of a stock and its probable relative strength over a very long period of years, cannot be expected to discriminate as to the extent of the appreciation potentiality in a specific period of three years three to five years hence. A stock of the highest quality might not have as great an appreciation potentiality over a three- to five-year pull as a stock of lower quality. In short, the 3- to 5-year Appreciation Potentiality gives specific consideration to the difference between the current price and the projected price. The Quality Grade ignores price altogether and assumes only that the subject stock will continue in its position relative to the economy over a very long period of time, or until evidence to the contrary appears. The Quality Grade is a measure of risk avoided and of secular growth, rather than a measure of the appreciation potentiality to be expected in a definite time period. This distinction is of significance. For example, in October 1958 machine-tool stocks were still depressed in market price because the machine-tool industry was near the bottom of its business cycle. In the event of a sustained cyclical recovery, these stocks, in the relatively short period of three years, could probably cover more ground on the upside than many a less depressed stock with a far better long-term growth trend.

The rank according to 3- to 5-year Appreciation Potentiality is not based upon a forecast. It is a projection based upon a hypothesis. If the hypothesized economic environment should fail to materialize, the Appreciation Potentiality probably would also. But even so, the method would give an indication of the *relative* Appreciation Potentiality of many stocks, whether their actual potentiality is realized or not. Of course, the most reasonable assumption is that the economic hypothesis will in fact be realized.

In considering Appreciation Potentiality, the analyst will wish to bear in mind that there are some potentialities that are more sure of realization than others, even though inferior in point of magnitude. For example, the Appreciation Potentiality projected for a good utility stock is far more likely to be realized than the Appreciation Potentiality of a good machinery manufacturer. The latter is subject to many risks and uncertainties that are not present in the case of the utility, whose growth can be forecast with greater assurance.

82

In general, stocks of high quality are more certain to realize their Appreciation Potentiality than stocks of low quality. On the other hand, the latter—the stocks of low quality—may have the greater Appreciation Potentiality over a three- to five-year period because their earnings and dividends, which are often cyclical, are capable of expanding very rapidly for a few years.

The projected earnings and dividends must be evaluated to find the projected price potentiality. Again, it is a safer operation to project the capitalization of a high-quality stock than of a low-quality stock. Thus, even where the investor chooses to emphasize the standard of Appreciation Potentiality three to five years into the future, the Quality Grade plays a useful ancillary role.

RANK FOR PROBABLE MARKET PERFORMANCE IN THE NEXT 12 MONTHS

Now for the most difficult problem of all, namely, the determination of whether the stock, at its current price, is undervalued or overvalued, or "right." The standard that I will discuss here is best known as the Value Line Rating. It is the average price during a period of 12 months that is statistically determined to be normal or "right" for that 12-month period. The extent to which the current price deviates from the Rating is a measure of overvaluation, or undervaluation, during the year of forecast.

The first attempt to evaluate systematically, according to current standards of value, was made in a book of charts called *The Value Line Ratings*, which was published in 1937. Later the charts were incorporated into a monthly service, to which were added reports on developments in the companies' affairs, estimates of their current year's earnings and other significant data.

Figures 42 and 43 are samples of the early Value Line Ratings. They were a visual "fit" of the price of the stock on the one hand to its earnings and book value on the other. It was found, experimentally, that if a constant multiplier of earnings was added to a percentage of the book value, the resultant curve would fit the fluctuations in the price of the stock closely. That, at any rate, was the experience between 1925 and 1939.

FIGURE 42

Sample of Earliest Value Line Rating, 1925–1942, with

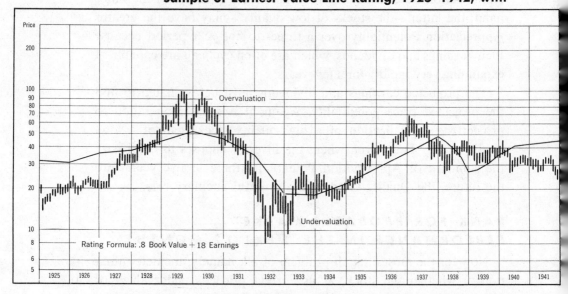

NOTE: Prices and Ratings as shown are not adjusted for the 1954 stock
Rating is 62. From 1943 on, the high and low prices are given for the year

Source: The Value Line Investment Survey. For the years 1925 through

FIGURE 43

Sample of Earliest Value Line Rating, 1925–1942, with

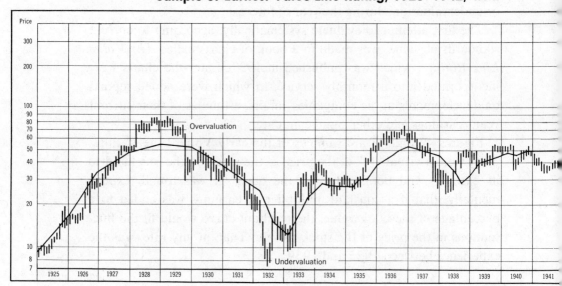

NOTE: Prices and Ratings as shown are not adjusted for the 1950 and 1955
justed Rating is 30. From 1943 on, the high and low prices are given for the

Source: The Value Line Investment Survey. For the years 1925 through

Extrapolations through 1958: General Electric

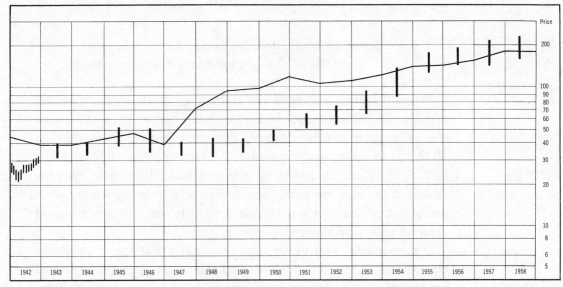

split. Adjusted prices for 1958 range from 57.0 to 79.4 and the adjusted rather than for the month.

1942 the graph is reproduced from the January 11, 1943, publication.

Extrapolations through 1958: General Motors

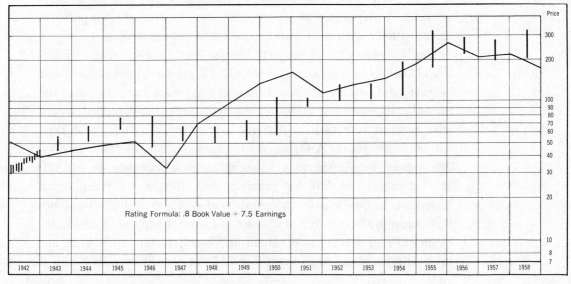

Rating Formula: .8 Book Value + 7.5 Earnings

stock splits. Adjusted prices for 1958 range from 33.8 to 52.0 and the adjusted year rather than for the month.

1942 the graph is reproduced from the January 4, 1943, publication.

Figure 43, for example, is the Value Line Rating of General Motors. The formula that related the price to the book value and the earnings was:

$$\text{Price per share} = .8 \text{ (book value per share)} + 7.5 \text{ (12 months' earnings per share)}$$

When the price exceeded the Rating, as in 1928–29, that was evidence of overvaluation, and when it fell below, as in 1932, that was evidence of undervaluation. The stock became overvalued in 1933 and in 1936, undervalued in the latter part of 1937 and first half of 1938 and in 1941–42. But you will notice that, with the advent of the war, the price moved far away from the Rating for a prolonged period of time. Not only that, but it sometimes moved in an opposite direction to the Rating.

It may interest you to see how those early Ratings, if projected out to 1958 on the same formula that was in use at that time, would have worked. You see that they did give solid indications of overvaluation or undervaluation *in the very long run.* The trouble with the Ratings was that they did not discriminate sufficiently *within the year in which the earnings and dividends could be forecast.* It is of little practical value, under *a method based upon yearly evaluation of earnings and dividends,* to determine that a stock is overvalued or undervalued in a particular year, if prices do not perform in accordance with the recommendation within that year.

Had we been able to project General Motors' and General Electric's earnings and dividends out 10 to 15 years into the future, year by year, and had we projected their normal values according to the formula that we used in the original Ratings, the standard would have worked very well in the end. But it would not have worked within single years. And, since our forecast of earnings and dividends must be limited to a 12-month period, because we are not able at present to forecast earnings and dividends further ahead than that, the eventual conformance of price to Rating could not have been predicted. We could say of General Motors in 1941, for example, that it was undervalued at 37 (equivalent to 6⅛ on the price shown after adjustment for a 2-for-1 split in 1950 and a

3-for-1 split in 1955), and indeed we did, but we were not justified in the assumption we made that, because the stock was undervalued, it would move toward its Rating *in that year*.

Bear in mind that what we are trying to solve for is whether the stock is *currently* right in price, or too high, or too low. The forecast period is *one year*. To be meaningful, therefore, the price, if it is indeed controlled by consideration of value, should adjust to value, at least relative to other stocks, within the year of forecast. This did not happen. We were driven, therefore, to seek other ratings that would discriminate more successfully within one year.

I should like to point out, though, that the old—the very first—Ratings were based upon sound fundamentals of stock evaluation. First of all, they rested on the premise that earnings (dividend-paying ability) determine the price of the stock. Second, they were based on the premise that each stock has its own individual price/earnings ratio. Third, they were based on the premise that the price/earnings ratio normally declines as the earnings rise, relative to asset value, and rises as the earnings fall, relative to asset value. By putting in a book-value factor, we got a fairly constant number which, when added to a fixed multiplier of earnings, did, in effect, give a varying price/earnings ratio. When General Motors' earnings in 1934 went down to $2, the normal, or "right," price/earnings ratio indicated by our Rating was actually 13.5 times those earnings. (Our Rating, it will be recalled, was based on .8 times the book value plus 7.5 times earnings.) Although the earnings were very small, and 7.5 times those small earnings gave a number of only 15, the addition of .8 of the book value brought the normal value up to 27, which was 13.5 times the small earnings. On the other hand, when the earnings rose to $4.40 in 1937, the normal, or "right," price/earnings ratio indicated by the Rating declined to 11. That Rating was still derived by multiplying the earnings by 7.5 and adding 80% of the book value, which had not changed very much since 1934.

Thus, the old visual-fit Ratings were sound as standards of value, and it may interest you to see that, had we projected those formulas out to 1958, they would have approximated the 1958 market price. But during too many individual years and in too many stocks, the deviation between the market price and the Value Line Rating was so large as to preclude successful discrimination.

In searching for a better method, we discovered that the dividend of a stock was a factor of even greater importance than its earnings in determining normal price within one year. To combine earnings and dividends with book value in a correlation with price required use of multiple correlation analysis.

But before going on to this second evolution in the Value Line Rating, I should like to discuss briefly the Graham and Dodd "theory of central value." This method of valuation was first published, to my knowledge, in 1940 in Graham and Dodd's book, *Security Analysis*.[16] This was two years after the Value Line Ratings had been published as a weekly service. The Graham and Dodd method is similar to the Value Line method in respect to certain principles. Basically it is an exercise in the capitalization of future earnings and dividends, as is the Value Line method. But the Graham and Dodd method does not attempt to establish a standard for a stock in any one year, nor, for that matter, in any particular time period. Furthermore, the Graham and Dodd method, as it applies to individual stocks, lacks what we postulate to be the very first requirement of a standard—namely, objectivity. The Graham and Dodd method holds that the multiplier to be placed upon the earnings of a particular stock is a matter of subjective determination. It can be 8 times, 10 times or 12 times, depending upon what the individual investor thinks would be appropriate.

Graham and Dodd, in fact, postulate two methods. First, there is the method of evaluating the stock market as a whole. Here a true discipline is introduced. The multiplier on the Dow-Jones Industrial Average is, first of all, related to the interest rate. This is an economically sound concept, for common stocks are obviously in competition with bonds for the investor's money at all times, and the interest rate should, therefore, be a determinant of value. I might say parenthetically, however, that we have not been able to find any correlation between the interest rate and stock yields in the past 30 years. On the other hand, we concede that there *should* be a rela-

16 Benjamin Graham and David L. Dodd, *Security Analysis* (2nd ed., New York: McGraw-Hill Book Company, Inc., 1940), pp. 685–6.

tionship, and that our failure to discover it may have been due to defective analysis on our part. At any rate, the Graham and Dodd method, as applied to the Dow-Jones Industrial Average, starts with the proposition that one half the reciprocal of the interest rate (as measured by Moody's AAA bond yields) is the correct multiplier to put on the earnings of the Dow-Jones Average of stocks. If the interest rate were 5%, the reciprocal of 5% would be 20. Half of that is 10, and that would be the multiplier to apply to the past 10-year average earnings of the Dow-Jones Industrial Average. If, on the other hand, the interest rate were 4%, the reciprocal would be 25, and the multiplier on the 10-year average earnings would then be 12½ times. One flaw is that no evidence is adduced to prove that the multiplier should be half the reciprocal of the interest rate. Why not a third, or a quarter, or three quarters? The multiplier, thus arbitrarily derived, is then applied to the 10-year moving average of past earnings to determine value. Here then, whether you agree with it or not, or whether the market agrees with it or not, is a partially disciplined determination of the normal value of the Dow-Jones Industrial Average.

But when it comes to individual stocks, the Graham and Dodd method gives up the partially disciplined approach and relies upon subjective determination. It says that the analyst should project any given level of earnings and multiply it by any number that he thinks appropriate, although it is said that the multiplier should in no case exceed 20 or be less than 8. *The multiplier should take account of the future growth of earnings,* although the method does not specify how or by what means. A multiplier of 12 is suggested for stocks with "neutral prospects."

Having approximated the central value of a stock by these rather vague methods, the Graham and Dodd procedure then calls for a 20% margin of error on either side of the derived "central value" line. This reduces the evaluation process to a purely subjective judgment, for where the multiplier can deviate as widely as from 8 to 20 and the resultant value can become the middle of a band with a 20% margin on either side, a case could be made for almost any price.

In fairness to Messrs. Graham and Dodd, it should be observed that they probably had no thought of evolving a specific rating according to a disciplined method. They were probably trying only to force the student of investment values to seek out for himself the proper multiplier to place upon earnings or earnings plus dividends. Since their Central Value Theory required the use of a multiplier, the student had to find one. In short, the Graham and Dodd method is a discipline that forces the student to look for a discipline. It seeks to be nothing more.

In the evaluation of the Dow-Jones Average, however, the Graham and Dodd method is objective. It may be of interest to show how the Graham and Dodd method of evaluating the Dow-Jones Industrial Average, as published in *The Intelligent Investor*,[17] would look if carried out to 1958. You see (Figures 44 and 45) that the central value would indicate a level of 400 for the Dow-Jones Industrial Average. Twenty per cent above that, which is the maximum deviation allowed under the theory, would indicate that the price of the Dow-Jones Average should be no higher than 480. It actually averaged 492 and went as high as 584 in 1958.

The glaring defect of the old Value Line Rating—the visual-fit rating—was that its power to discriminate in single years was inadequate. Of what use was it to say that a stock was 40% undervalued in a particular year, if in that particular year it did not perform better than other stocks that were less undervalued? The answer might be, "Well, eventually it will." That is true, provided the earnings and the dividends stick. But who can say where the earnings and dividends will be five years hence?

How then to find such close correlation that one can be reasonably sure of discrimination within a single year? Starting from the premise that the value of a stock is determined by its dividend-paying ability, one would not find it hard to decide on logical grounds that the determinants of value should be the net worth of the stock (its book value, which is the capital that produces the earnings), its per-share earnings and its per-share dividends. In addition, and this is significant, price trends of individual stocks usually exhibit some degree of persistence which partly measures the subtle changes that

[17] Benjamin Graham, *The Intelligent Investor* (1st ed., New York: Harper & Brothers, 1949), pp. 264–8.

90

FIGURE 44

The Graham and Dodd Central Value Theory Applied to the Dow-Jones Industrial Average, 1924–1958

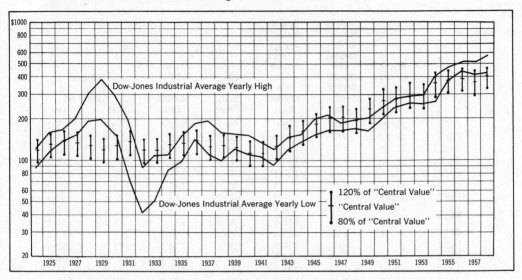

NOTE: For the years 1924 through 1953 the graph is reproduced as it appeared in *The Intelligent Investor,* 1953 edition. For the years 1954 through 1958 the graph was extended by The Value Line Investment Survey using the same method which was employed for 1924–1953 and which was outlined by Mr. Graham.

Source: Benjamin Graham, *The Intelligent Investor* (2nd ed., New York: Harper & Brothers, 1953).

take place in a company's character over a period of time. This being so, it is not surprising that a substantial improvement in forecasting value was obtained by adding the "lagged price" of the stock to the other independent variables. The independent variables that we finally decided upon were the book value, the per-share earnings, the per-share dividends and the previous year's average price. The dependent variable was the annual average price. The use of the price lag tends to introduce a trend factor into the evaluation of stocks, and to that extent it deviates from a pure value concept. But in view of the complexity of the evaluation process, especially with respect to the subtle change that usually goes on in the character of any company, we have found through many tests that the introduc-

FIGURE 45

Calculations of the Graham and Dodd Central Value of the Dow-Jones Industrial Average, 1924–1958

YEAR	Average Earnings of 10 Previous Years	Yield of Moody's All Corporation AAA Bonds April of Same Year	Central Value: Average Earnings Divided by Twice Interest Rates	80% of Central Value	120% of Central Value	Range of D.-J. I. A. Same Year	
						High	Low
1924	11.99	5.08	118.0	94.4	141.6	120.5	88.3
1925	12.62	4.87	129.6	103.7	155.5	159.4	115.0
1926	12.86	4.74	135.7	108.5	162.8	167.0	136.0
1927	12.36	4.58	133.8	107.1	160.6	201.5	152.0
1928	11.28	4.46	126.5	101.2	151.8	300.0	193.0
1929	11.21	4.69	119.5	95.6	143.4	381.2	199.0
1930	11.75	4.60	127.7	102.2	153.3	294.1	160.0
1931	11.98	4.40	136.1	108.9	163.4	193.0	74.6
1932	12.28	5.17	118.8	95.0	142.5	88.2	41.2
1933	11.41	4.78	119.4	95.5	143.2	108.5	50.2
1934	10.59	4.07	130.1	104.1	156.1	111.0	85.6
1935	9.86	3.66	134.7	107.8	161.6	149.9	96.7
1936	9.09	3.29	138.2	110.5	165.8	185.0	143.0
1937	8.60	3.42	125.7	100.6	150.9	194.4	113.0
1938	8.51	3.30	128.9	103.2	154.7	158.4	99.0
1939	7.45	3.02	123.3	98.7	148.0	155.9	121.5
1940	6.36	2.82	112.8	90.2	135.2	152.8	111.8
1941	6.35	2.82	112.6	90.1	135.1	133.6	106.3
1942	7.11	2.83	125.6	100.5	150.7	119.7	92.9
1943	8.08	2.76	146.4	117.1	175.7	145.8	119.3
1944	8.85	2.74	161.5	129.2	193.8	152.5	134.2
1945	9.46	2.61	181.2	145.0	217.5	195.8	151.4
1946	9.88	2.46	200.8	160.7	241.0	212.5	163.1
1947	10.24	2.53	202.4	161.9	242.8	186.9	163.2
1948	10.97	2.78	197.3	157.8	236.8	193.2	165.4
1949	12.58	2.70	233.0	186.4	279.6	200.5	161.6
1950	14.02	2.60	270.0	216.0	324.0	235.5	196.8
1951	15.97	2.87	278.0	222.0	334.0	276.4	239.0
1952	17.58	2.93	300.0	240.0	360.0	292.0	256.4
1953	19.14	3.23	306.0	244.8	367.2	293.8	255.5
1954	20.90	2.85	366.7	293.4	440.0	404.4	279.9
1955	22.73	3.01	377.6	302.1	453.1	488.4	388.2
1956	25.25	3.24	389.7	311.8	467.6	521.0	462.4
1957	27.22	3.67	370.8	296.6	445.0	520.8	419.8
1958	28.95	3.60	402.1	321.7	482.5	583.7	436.9

NOTE: For the years 1924 through 1953 the table is reproduced as it appeared in *The Intelligent Investor,* 1953 edition. For the years 1954 through 1958 the table was extended by The Value Line Investment Survey using the same method which was employed for 1924–1953 and which was outlined by Mr. Graham.

Source: Benjamin Graham, *The Intelligent Investor* (2nd ed., New York: Harper & Brothers, 1953).

92

tion of a price lag corrects, without significantly distorting, the evaluation process in terms of earnings, dividends and book value.

In Figure 46 you will see a Value Line Rating of General Electric as published in 1949. This Value Line Rating is based upon earnings, dividends and price lag. (Book value proved to be an insignificant variable for General Electric and fell out of the equation.) The formula was: $8.83 + (12.65 \times \text{dividends}) + (3.11 \times \text{earnings}) + (.14 \times \text{price lag})$. It was in April of that year that I gave a talk to the New York Society of Security Analysts and presented this Rating of General Electric as evidence of undervaluation in a particular stock, and as just one example of the general undervaluation then prevailing in the market. It made very little impression at the time, I'm sorry to say, because

FIGURE 46

Sample of Early Value Line Rating Based on Multiple Correlation Analysis in Time Series, 1927–1948, with Extrapolations through 1958: General Electric

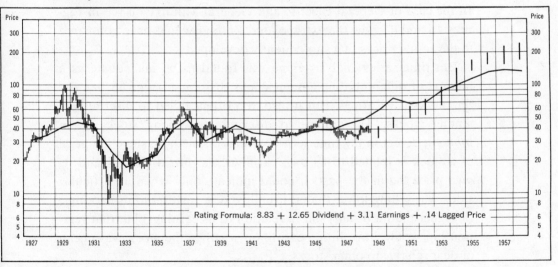

NOTE: Prices and Ratings as shown are not adjusted for the 1954 stock split. Adjusted prices for 1958 range from 57.0 to 79.4 and the adjusted Rating is 46. From 1949 on, the high and low prices are given for the year rather than for the month.

Source: The Value Line Investment Survey. For the years 1927 through 1948 the graph is reproduced from the May 16, 1949, publication.

most people were preoccupied with the thinking that was called to your attention in the first chapter, that is to say, the *deflationary impact of inflation upon stock values*. The mere fact that stocks were selling lower in relation to values as determined by correlation analysis meant nothing at the time, because it was reasoned that inflation *should* cause stocks to sell at abnormally low price/earnings ratios, since the earnings were actually overstated because of inflation. This is the argument, upside down, that you recognize as being applied to justify the extremely high price/earnings ratios and low yields on stocks today. My observations about the significance of current overvaluation will fail equally, I am sure, to make any impression today. These delusions in the field of valuation follow their own authority until shattered by greater events than a book by a security analyst.

Incidentally, you may be interested to see how this Value Line Rating, based upon a multiple correlation analysis in time series, would look if the same formulas that applied in 1949 were extrapolated into 1958 on the basis of 1958 earnings and dividends.[18] In the case of General Electric and General Motors you see in Figures 46 and 47 how the extrapolated Ratings would have compared to the actual prices that subsequently developed.

But time series analysis alone was found to be inadequate as a method of differentiating among stocks. It gave a better fit than did the old visual Ratings. But it also, too often, failed to discriminate among stocks. The failure to discriminate among stocks is an *inherent* defect in the time series correlation method, since the price of a stock is related to its *own* earnings, its *own* dividends and its *own* price lag in the past. It could indicate only when a particular stock was selling lower than it usually did in relation to its earnings, or higher than it usually did in relation to its earnings; but that relationship would have little bearing on whether the stock was cheap or dear relative to other stocks.

Another defect of the time series correlation was that in order to anchor four independent variables—earnings, dividends, price lag and book value—it was necessary to have a large number of

---

[18] The extrapolation, in this case, assumes no annual recomputation of the equation to take account of the intervening years' experience.

FIGURE 47

Sample of Early Value Line Rating Based on Multiple Correlation Analysis in Time Series, 1927–1948, with Extrapolations through 1958: General Motors

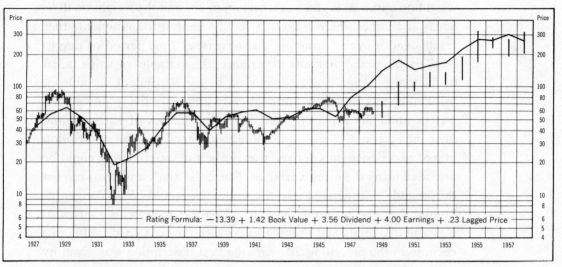

Rating Formula: —13.39 + 1.42 Book Value + 3.56 Dividend + 4.00 Earnings + .23 Lagged Price

NOTE: Prices and Ratings as shown are not adjusted for the 1950 and 1955 stock splits. Adjusted prices for 1958 range from 33.8 to 52.0 and the adjusted Rating is 47. From 1949 on, the high and low prices are given for the year rather than for the month.

Source: The Value Line Investment Survey. For the years 1927 through 1948 the graph is reproduced from the May 2, 1949, publication.

observations—at least 20 annual observations. This in turn had the effect of throwing the period of correlation back to a time when the stock might have been different in character and its economic environment abnormal. A 20-year span included the war years, when earnings and dividends were not valued as in years of peace (during peacetime there was no excess profits tax and fewer restrictive controls). Because of the atypicality of many of the years of correlation, the time series formulas were found to be unstable from year to year. That is to say, when a new year of observation was added to the time series, the weights on earnings, dividends and price lag would shift, sometimes radically.

Because of the atypicality of the years of observation, although not entirely for this reason, other weaknesses developed. Too often

95

in the time period the value factors of earnings and dividends took little weight in the equation. One thing about a multiple correlation analysis that should be remembered is that, once the variables are put into the equation, the answer can come out only one way. If the weight on earnings is given at a certain figure and the weight on dividends at another, there is no way for the analyst to manipulate that result. And if in the equation, due to a freak time period or due to freak earnings and dividend experience, the variables of value failed to fluctuate in significant correlation to the dependent variable of price, then the equation automatically and objectively put all the weight upon the price lag, and the value factors of earnings and dividends fell out of the equation altogether. True, the description of past experience thus derived was the best description that could be provided using the given variables. But if the analyst were to project the formula thus derived into the future, he would be on dangerous ground, because he would have to go on the assumption that earnings and dividends had nothing to do with the next year's value just because in the preceding 20 years the best description was given by the trend (price lag) alone.

Another reason for the instability in the time series correlation was the high interdependence between earnings and dividends. As a result, in many instances, one of the two variables absorbed all the weight, and the other one proved insignificant. As long as the high interrelationship persisted, no harm was done. However, if within a given year the high interrelationship was disturbed, an improbable value would result. As an example, note the divergence between the mathematical rating and the average price of Electric Auto-Lite between 1944 and 1946 (Figure 48). In the rating formula, only earnings and lagged price were included, while dividends dropped out as an insignificant variable. Yet, despite the decline in earnings, the price of the stock advanced sharply from 1944 to 1946 in response to the increased dividends, which did not find reflection in the equation.

As a result of these defects, the Value Line Ratings were revised again. I might say parenthetically that there were several revisions of the time series type of rating, some excluding war years, some leaving out book values, some using different time periods. But,

FIGURE 48

Electric Auto-Lite—Value Line Rating, Average Price, Earnings and Dividends, 1937–1947

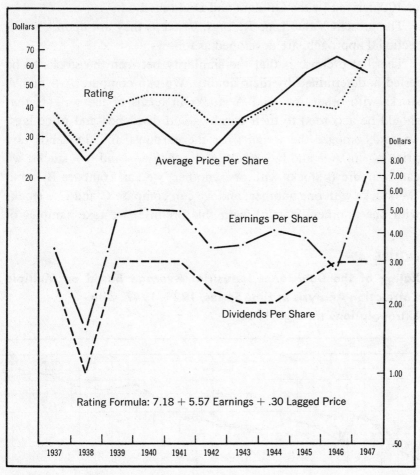

Source: The Value Line Investment Survey, March 7, 1949.

basically, the time series correlation was the correlation which has been described, and its weaknesses were as explained.

Still, you might be interested to see where the old time series correlation would show the normal value of the Dow-Jones Industrial Average to be for 1958. We have projected it on the assumption that the 1948 formula could have been applied to 1958 earnings and dividends without changes reflecting the addition of intervening

97

years of experience. You see (Figure 49) that the time series correlation would have indicated a normal value of 410 for the Dow-Jones Industrial Average today, as compared to the normal value of 400 derived by the Graham and Dodd method.

The present Value Line Ratings, based as they are upon a cross-sectional approach, are developed as follows:

The first premise is that the similarity between the stocks to be tested is determined by their quality. We can compare A+ and A stocks with other A+ and A stocks in terms of the weights that should be accorded to their earnings and dividends and price lags; we can compare the weights for the earnings and dividends and price lags of A— and B+ stocks with other A— and B+ stocks; we can compare B stocks with one another; we can compare B— and C+ stocks with one another; and we can compare C and C— stocks with one another. Starting with this premise, we take samples of

FIGURE 49

Rating of the Dow-Jones Industrial Average Based on Multiple Correlation Analysis in Time Series, 1929–1947, with Extrapolations through 1958

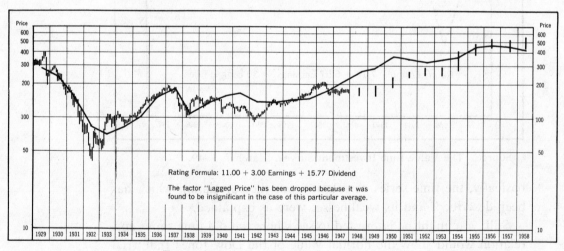

NOTE: From 1948 on, the high and low prices are given for the year rather than for the month.

Source: The Value Line Investment Survey. For the years 1929 through 1947 the graph is reproduced from the September 27, 1948, publication.

98

A+ and A stocks, A— and B+ stocks, B stocks, B— and C+ stocks, C and C— stocks, considering that A+ and A stocks are one group, A— and B+ stocks another group and so forth. Groups of approximately 25 stocks each were used as "guinea pigs."

The earnings, dividends and average price data were obtained for all the "guinea pigs" in all the groups.

The earnings per share, the dividends per share and the average prices per share for all the A+ and A stocks in the sample were then averaged. The same was done for the other quality groups. The result was an average of earnings, dividends and prices for all groups for the years 1937 to 1958 inclusive.

For each of the five quality groups (A+ and A, A— and B+, B, B— and C+, C and C—), earnings and dividends were combined into a single variable by the following method:

The standard deviation of dividends during the period between 1937 and 1958 was divided by the standard deviation of earnings for the same period of time. This ratio, normally less than 1, was applied as the multiplier on earnings, and the product added to the dividends in each single year. This adjustment on the earnings is necessary in order to equalize the variations in the earnings and dividend series. Without the adjustment, the result of combining a volatile earnings series with a relatively stable dividend series would produce a curve primarily representative of earnings.

A time series correlation was then computed for each of the five quality groups. (The weaknesses of time series analysis previously mentioned are minimized by working with a group of stocks rather than with individual stocks.) In these correlations the combined curve of earnings and dividends, weighted as already described, the price lag and the average of 45 stock yields were related to the annual average price of each quality group over the past 21 years. All these factors were expressed in logarithms.

In Figure 50 you will see illustrations of the four variables included in the correlation analysis of each quality group. The A+ and A quality group and the C and C— quality group are used as examples. The heavy solid line is the average price of all the stocks in a quality group by years since 1937. The dashed line is the combined earnings-dividends curve for the same time period. The dotted

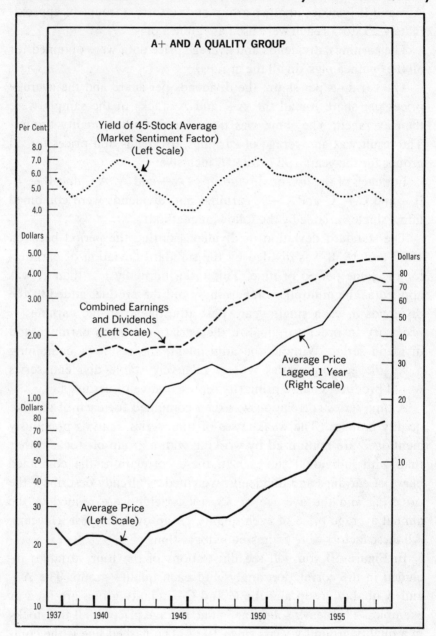

A+ AND A QUALITY GROUP

Per Cent

Yield of 45-Stock Average
(Market Sentiment Factor)
(Left Scale)

8.0
7.0
6.0
5.0
4.0

Dollars

5.00
4.00

3.00

Combined Earnings
and Dividends
(Left Scale)

2.00

Average Price
Lagged 1 Year
(Right Scale)

Dollars

80
70
60
50
40

30

1.00
Dollars

80
70
60
50
40

30

Average Price
(Left Scale)

20

10
1937   1940   1945   1950   1955

100

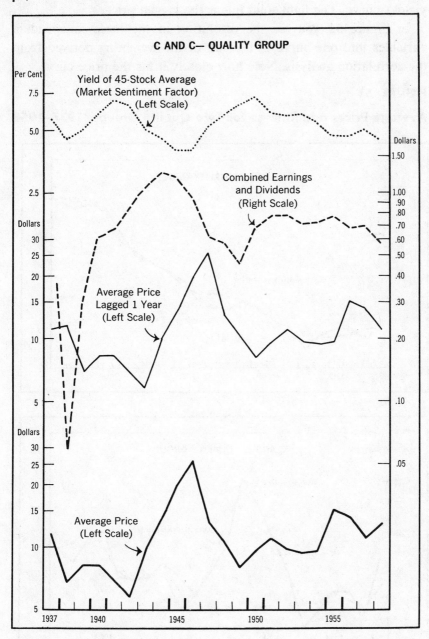

C AND C— QUALITY GROUP

Per Cent

7.5

5.0

Yield of 45-Stock Average
(Market Sentiment Factor)
(Left Scale)

2.5

Dollars

Combined Earnings
and Dividends
(Right Scale)

Dollars

1.50

1.00
.90
.80
.70
.60
.50

.40

.30

.20

30
25
20

15

Average Price
Lagged 1 Year
(Left Scale)

10

5

.10

Dollars

30
25
20

.05

15

Average Price
(Left Scale)

10

5

1937   1940   1945   1950   1955

line is the market sentiment (an average of 45 representative stock yields) curve. The light solid line is the lagged price.

In Figure 51 you see the resolution of the three independent variables into one curve as a result of the weighting derived from the correlation analysis. Note how closely it fits the price curve.

FIGURE 51

Average Prices and Ratings for Two Quality Groups, 1937–1958

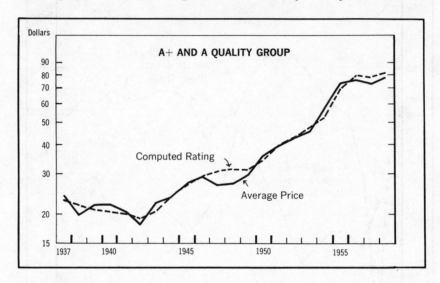

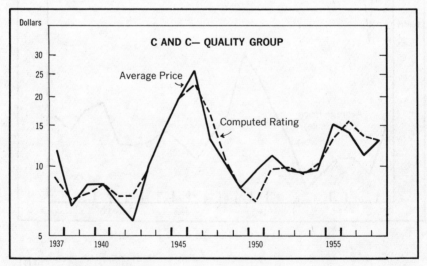

NOTE: Ratings based on correlation of three independent variables: (1) market sentiment factor, (2) combined earnings and dividends, and (3) average price lagged one year.

Figure 52 indicates the combined curve of the three independent series with the market sentiment factor held constant.

The purpose of introducing market sentiment was to avoid forcing the lagged price and the earnings-dividends curve to account for that portion of the price fluctuation that might in fact have been

FIGURE 52

Average Prices and Ratings with Market Sentiment Factor Held Constant for Two Quality Groups, 1937–1958

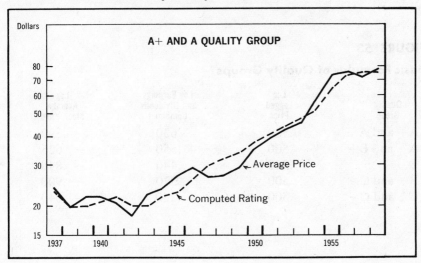

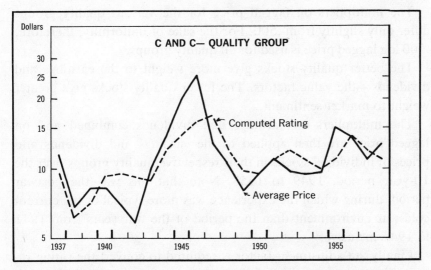

NOTE: Ratings based on correlation of three independent variables: market sentiment factor equivalent to the average market yield for the 22-year period, combined earnings and dividends, and average price lagged.

caused by market sentiment. So we put market sentiment into the equation and then, by holding it "constant," eliminated its influence in the final curve. The final curve then gave true weight to the earnings-dividends influence and the price lag.

The multipliers yielded by the correlation analysis of the five quality groups are indicated in Figure 53. The relative importance of the various factors is indicated in Figure 54.

FIGURE 53

Basic Formulas of Quality Groups

Quality Group	Log Lagged Price	Log Earnings and Dividends Combined	Log Average Stock Yield
A+ and A	.500	.630	− .390
A− and B+	.500	.550	− .625
B	.500	.440	− .840
B− and C+	.500	.370	− .900
C and C−	.500	.250	−1.040

The multipliers on lagged price for the various quality groups differ only slightly from .500. For the sake of uniformity, therefore, .500 log lagged price is used for all quality groups.

The better quality stocks give more weight to the earnings and dividends—the value factors. The lower quality stocks give greater weight to market sentiment.

The multipliers on earnings and dividends combined and on lagged price are then applied to the earnings and dividends and prices of individual stocks in their respective quality groups over the 10-year period, 1949 to 1958. Note that this was the postwar period, during which the experience was more typical of the current cold-war environment than the period of the war years from 1941 to 1945 inclusive.

Finally, an adjustment factor is required to convert the rating re-

FIGURE 54

Relative Importance of the Independent Variables by Quality Groups: Combined Earnings and Dividends, Lagged Prices and Stock Yields

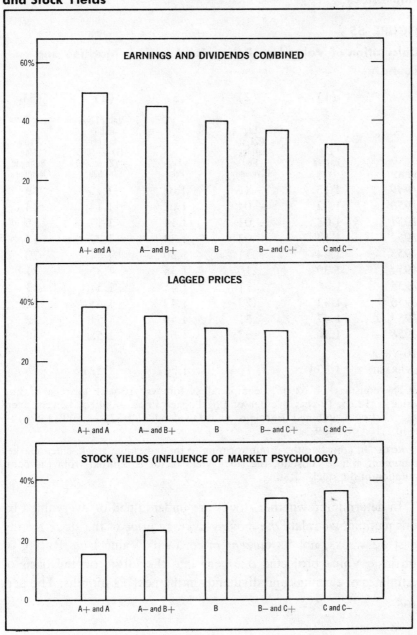

sulting from the group formula to the average price level of the particular stock. Figure 55 illustrates how, in the case of American Machine and Foundry, the group formula was adjusted to the individual stock.

FIGURE 55

Calculation of Value Line Rating for American Machine and Foundry

YEAR	(1) Log Lagged Price	(2) Log (.21 × Earnings + 1.00 × Dividend)	(3) Log Price	(4) Value Line Rating in Logs (1) × .500 + (2) × .440 + .639	(5) Value Line Rating in Numbers
1949	1.13	−.16	1.03	1.13	13
1950	1.03	−.04	1.08	1.14	14
1951	1.08	−.01	1.14	1.17	15
1952	1.14	.03	1.24	1.22	17
1953	1.24	.11	1.30	1.31	20
1954	1.30	.10	1.36	1.33	21
1955	1.36	.11	1.43	1.37	23
1956	1.43	.22	1.47	1.45	28
1957	1.47	.31	1.56	1.51	32
1958	1.56	.37	1.61	1.58	38
10-YEAR AVERAGE	1.274	.104	1.322	1.321	

The constant (+.639) is computed as follows: 10-year average of Log Price − .500 × 10-year average of Log Lagged Price − .440 × 10-year average of Log Combined Earnings and Dividends = 1.322 − .500 (1.274) − .440 (.104) = .639

NOTE: In adjusting the group formula to the individual stock, since market sentiment is held constant, the stock yield factor is omitted from the computation of the stock's Rating.

In determining whether stocks are undervalued or overvalued by this method, we relate *the moving-average price* of the stock for the past 52 weeks, not its *current* price, to its Value Line Rating of Intrinsic Value projected one year into the future on the basis of estimates of earnings and dividends in the next 12 months. The percentage of undervaluation or overvaluation determined by the "average price" relationship is set down in order of magnitude, and a comparison is made with all the other stocks of the 804 under study.

The reason for using a 52-week moving-average price in relation to the Rating, instead of the current price, is that while the difference between the Intrinsic Value as indicated by the Value Line Rating and the actual price is a measure of the extent of price change that will sooner or later take place, in all probability, the "timing" depends to a significant degree upon the immediately preceding trend of the stock's price. Figure 56 depicts, as an example, two different stocks. The price of Stock A is 20. The price of Stock B is 20. The Value Line Rating of Intrinsic Value of Stock A in the next year is 25. So, too, is the Value Line Rating of Stock B. But note from the chart that in the preceding 52 weeks Stock A had fluctuated between 10 and 20 whereas Stock B had fluctuated between 30 and 20. The average price for Stock A during the preceding 52 weeks was 15; the average price of Stock B was around 27.

Obviously, the holders of the two stocks who acquired them within the past year are likely to entertain different attitudes when and if the price should rise to any appreciable extent, say to 25. Those who bought between 10 and 20 would probably be content. Indeed, they might find themselves "locked in" by the capital gain tax liability. Those who had bought closer to 30 than 20 or at an average price of about 27 might be eager to get out whole or with a moderate loss. One group would hold. The other would be inclined to sell. As a rule, it may be said that the stock that has broken sharply below its Value Line Rating tends to require a longer period of stabilization before embarking upon a corrective upward move than the stock that has been rising from a level below its Value Line Rating.

The extent of overvaluation or undervaluation having been determined by the relationship of the moving-average price to the Rating, all those stocks in the top 20%, as far as magnitude of undervaluation or smallness of overvaluation is concerned, are ranked I

107

FIGURE 56

Comparison of Two Hypothetical Stocks with the Same Rating of Intrinsic Value and the Same Recent Price

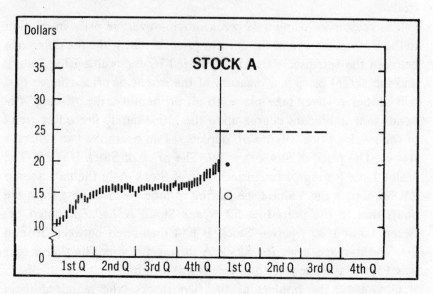

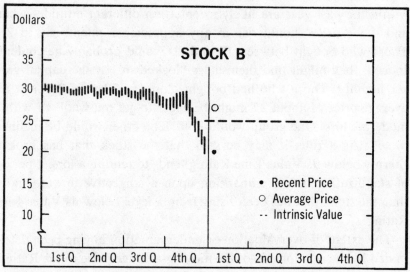

(Highest) for Probable Market Performance in the Next 12 Months. All those stocks whose moving-average price of the past 52 weeks, relative to the Rating projected in the next 12 months, is more favorable than that of 60% of all stocks, but less favorable than the top 20% are ranked II (Above Average) for Probable Market Performance. The third rank, which is marked III (Average), comprises the percentile range between 41 and 60; the group that includes the percentiles between 21 and 40 is ranked IV (Below Average). The group of stocks consisting of the lowest 20 percentiles with regard to the relationship between the moving-average price and the Rating is ranked V (Lowest).

Note that the Rating itself is projected on the basis of estimates of earnings and dividends. The lagged price, of course, is a known variable. The market-climate factor, as previously explained, has been held constant.

The effect of this method is to give two indications: first, an indication of the degree to which the stock's current price stands above or below its own Rating of Intrinsic Value for the 12-month period; second, the relative position of each stock compared to all others, as expressed by the Probable Market Performance rank.

To be effective, these rankings must work out within the period of time forecast, namely, one year.

The method was introduced in November 1957. Of course, it was tested backward through sampling. We are at present engaged in an operations research analysis which will yield a complete performance test for all stocks had this system been in effect since 1946. At present we can report that, for the period from November 1957 to the present, the ranking system did discriminate among stocks. On average the Ratings indicate that stocks are too high now, standing as they do some 18% above their Ratings of Intrinsic Value. But even in a high market, the discrimination between stocks should work out according to the theory, and it has. A detailed analysis of the performance results of this method for the first year it was in operation will be provided in Chapter IV.

So far, then, I have outlined for you three methods of evaluating stocks. These three methods refer to various time periods. The first is the evaluation according to quality. Essentially this is a method

109

for avoiding risk rather than determining value. Its practical application lies in the conclusion that in this growing country of ours the strongest stocks will over a long period of time, say five years or more, do best, and with the greatest degree of assurance.

The second method of evaluation is to determine the specific Appreciation Potentiality of a stock three to five years into the future over a span of three years in that future time, premised upon a hypothetical economic environment. This method is not so much a forecast of what the price of the stock will be as a measure of its potential appreciation if the hypothesized economic environment should be realized.

The third method gives an indication as to whether a stock is cheap or dear now in relation to its own Intrinsic Value this year, and whether it is cheap or dear in relation to all other stocks now.

All these evaluations are based upon probability. The Quality Grade is based on the probability that long-held trends will persist indefinitely into the future. The 3- to 5-year Appreciation Potentiality rank is based upon an estimate of earnings and on the assumption that past capitalization rates will apply to those earnings in a hypothesized economic environment. The rank according to Probable Market Performance in the Next 12 Months is based upon an estimate of earnings and dividends in the next 12 months and the likelihood that the estimated earnings and dividends will command a price capitalization similar to the past.

It has been found that the Quality Grades discriminate as to the stocks that will do best over a very long period of time. The 3- to 5-year Appreciation Potentiality ranks have, in the past five or six years since they were first introduced, found justification in market experience so far as the realization of potential price was concerned, but they have not, in the last two years, proven altogether satisfactory in terms of the *relative* appreciation of the individual stocks. The rank for Probable Market Performance has worked out quite well in terms of the average performance of each group, but it should be noted, and the "score" will be shown to you in Chapter IV, that not all stocks in Group I outperformed those in Group II, and not all those in Group II outperformed those in Group III, even

110

though the average of all stocks in Group I outperformed all those in lower ranks, and so on down.

In Chapter IV, I shall try to outline a method for combining these objective determinations of probability into an investment scheme that is effective in practice.

AN INVESTMENT is a body of capital that yields an income currently or in prospect. In his book *The Theory of Investment Value,*[19] Williams postulates that the present value of a common stock is the sum of all its future dividends discounted to the present interest rate. In our own experience, during periods of inflation as well as at other times, in this country and abroad, it has been found that dividend-paying ability is the final determinant of the price of a common stock. Whenever, over a period of years, the dividend, or the ability to pay dividends, went up, so did the price of the stock. When the dividend-paying ability went down, so too did the price of the stock, inflation or no inflation.

The theory that the present value of a stock can be determined by adding up the sum of all the future dividends and discounting to the prevailing interest rate does not explain how the sum of all the future dividends will be determined, nor over what period of time they will be realized.

Because there is no general agreement upon the single time period

[19] John Burr Williams, *The Theory of Investment Value* (Cambridge, Mass.: Harvard University Press, 1938), p. 55.

in which value should be expressed, and because there is no generally accepted standard of value, the market prices of stocks fluctuate far more widely than their true values. The wide fluctuations have in the past imposed a heavy burden on the general economy and undermined the faith of many people in a free market economy. The need therefore exists for rational and disciplined standards of value that cannot yield to the wildness of periods like 1929 or 1949 or the present.

It must be conceded at the outset that investors differ in temperament and training, and so tend to think differently about stocks. Each seeks the characteristic in his investments that he regards as compatible with his own goals. Therefore, no one standard can be applied exclusively to all stocks, for all time periods and for all investors.

In these chapters I have outlined three standards that may be applied in the evaluation of a stock. Each is different from the others. But each is complementary to the others. There is a fourth standard, too—current yield—to be discussed later.

The first standard was that of quality. Like all other meaningful standards, it refers to the dividend-paying ability of the stock. But the Quality Grade refers to the dividend-paying ability of the subject stock in no specific future time period. The time limit for its validation is left indefinite. The Quality Grade is derived by measuring statistically the growth of the earnings and dividends of the stock over a period of years past, and the stability of its price over the same period of years, and then combining the two numerical indexes—giving three times as much weight to stability as to growth—into a single quality number. Minor modification of this result is permitted, to give weight to the stock's typical yield over a period of years. The quality numbers thus derived for 804 stocks are tabulated according to magnitude and divided into nine segments. Each segment is then expressed as a letter. The top grade is A+, and then, in order, A, A—, B+, B, B—, C+, C and C—. The method of computation was described in detail in Chapter II.

The Quality Grade is based entirely upon past experience. The growth of the dividend-paying ability of the company in the past, plus its price stability in the past, determines its present Quality

113

Grade; and the present Quality Grade indicates the assurance with which the investor may expect dividend-paying ability to be maintained in the indefinite future.

A company may maintain its dividend-paying ability by holding its earnings at a firm and satisfactory level, as in the case of American Telephone, or by increasing its earning power, as in the case of Union Carbide. Even if the growing earning power be somewhat less stable, the very fact of growth gives some assurance that, should the company "stub its toe" in any one or two or three years, the fall in the dividend still need not be expected to carry below the level of one, two or three years earlier. In short, the growth trend is a measure of assurance in the sense that a good attack is the best defense. A high Quality Grade implies that the company can probably maintain its ability to pay dividends indefinitely. This implies growth, or stability, or both. To be of high quality, a stock whose Stability Index is low must have a very high Growth Index to compensate. Or, if growth is low, stability must be high. (Growth and stability were combined through a correlation analysis which gave stability three times the weight of growth.)

Now, in effect, what does the Quality Grade tell the investor about selecting his stocks? It tells him that if he buys a stock of high quality he avoids many risks common to stocks of low quality. A stock that has proved its high quality in the past must be conceded to have good management, proven ability to compete and financial strength.

A company of high quality may in the end turn out to have less success in the coming decade than another company whose present quality is low. But the company of high quality is *proved*. The company of low quality is untested, relatively speaking. It may turn out to be the more brilliant in the end. But the investor does not have the assurance *in the present* that this will be so. The new company may run into a financial crisis. Or its management, seemingly brilliant, may prove erratic and unsound. Or its product base may be narrow and, through failure to develop additional lines, the company may be subjected to a severe profit squeeze. Such risks are largely avoided in stocks of high quality. The illustration was used of a man who was going to live on a desert island for 10 years in-

114

communicado. Before he left, it was necessary for him to invest in common stocks, although he would be unable to follow their fortunes during his absence. The best stocks he could buy for a 10-year holding period would be the stocks of high quality.

But note what high quality does *not* indicate. It does not indicate whether a stock is overpriced or underpriced now, or looking ahead three to five years, or in any other specific period of time. It merely says that in the past 12 years the stock has done relatively well, and because it has, we may assume that it will take care of itself very well for an indefinite period of time in the future, or until evidence appears to the contrary. This ignores the fact that a very high-grade stock could be speculatively priced in the present, or a low-quality stock could be conservatively priced.

In determining how to weight stability and growth in determining the composition of the Quality Grade, we used three lists of stocks selected on an *a priori* judgment of their quality. The first was a list of concededly high-quality stocks, the second a list that was generally recognized as being of medium quality, and the third a list of low-quality stocks. These lists were selected a few years ago and put to the test from 1929 on. You might rightly question whether these would have been the stocks judged to be of high, medium and low quality back in 1929. It is conceded that some might not have fitted their present grades at that time. Minnesota Mining, for example, probably would not have been included in a universally recognized list of the fifteen bluest "blue chip" stocks in 1929. But despite the fact that the selection might have been different then, those whose memories go back to 1929 will concede, I think, that most of the stocks in these three lists would have been accorded approximately the same quality designations then as now. Most Quality Grades change slowly, and only over a period of years.

How did stocks of different Quality Grades perform in the market in the past? Here are two tests: one from the 1929 average price to the 1939 average price; the other from the 1946 average price to the 1958 average price.

It can be seen (Figure 57) that the stocks of highest quality did considerably better in the decade 1929 to 1939 than the stocks of medium quality, and the medium-quality stocks did better than the speculative-quality stocks. The same was true of the period from 1946 to 1958. But note that a small minority of stocks in the speculative category did better than a small minority in the high-grade category during both periods.

For the very long-pull investor the Quality Grade is highly significant. In fact, for every investor quality is significant. Most of the great fortunes in America have been built by people who have held stocks of good quality patiently for many, many years. Capital so committed for the long pull has on average done far better than capital more opportunistically directed.

The second standard is the rank according to Appreciation Potentiality over a period of three to five years hence. You will recall that the Appreciation Potentiality ranks ranged from I (Highest) to II (Above Average), III (Average), IV (Below Average) and V (Lowest). Unlike Quality Grades, which are expressed as letters, these ranks, which are expressed as numbers of I to V, refer to a specific time period, and they refer to specific price goals, too. This measurement says that the subject stock has an appreciation potentiality equal to the percentage difference between today's price and a projected average price three to five years hence. The magnitudes of the potential appreciation are compared for 804 stocks and ranked in percentile groups from I (Highest) down to V (Lowest). A stock whose potentiality is greater than that of 80% of all stocks is ranked I (Highest) for Appreciation Potentiality in the next three to five years. A stock with an Appreciation Potentiality greater than that of 60%, but less than 80% of all stocks, is ranked II (Above Average), etc.

The rank for Appreciation Potentiality over a three- to five-year period is based upon a hypothesis, not a forecast. Nobody can forecast whether there will be war or peace, high-level prosperity or depression, whether we shall have an orderly society or a revolution three to five years from now. But one can assume the most probable set of political and economic conditions and project accordingly. The most probable condition is described by an extrapolation of the trend of the labor force, of productivity, of hours of work per week and of the over-all price level. By such extrapolations, a hypothesized gross national product can be set up, and into that hypothe-

FIGURE 57
Price Performance of Selected Stocks by Quality Groups from 1929 to 1939 and from 1946 to 1958

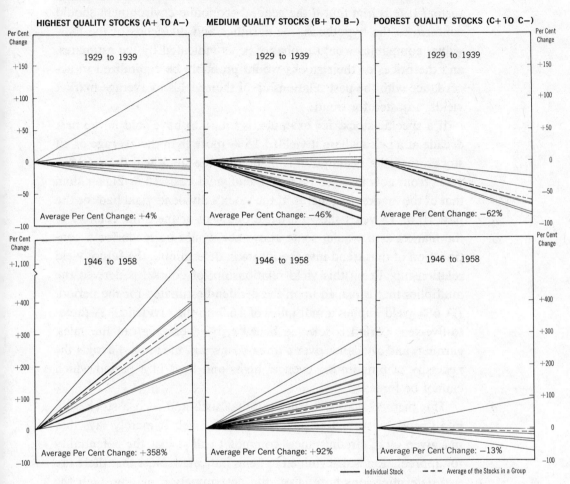

NOTE: In some instances appreciation of individual stocks coincides.

117

sized economy the sales and profit margins of all companies can be projected.

Now what does the Appreciation Potentiality rank tell the investor? It tells him that if the general economic environment should conform to the hypothesis, the earnings and dividends of the individual companies would probably be as indicated by the estimates, and the prices of their stocks would probably be capitalized in accordance with the past relationship of their yields to average market yields, adjusted for trend.

If a specific stock, for example, is found to have sold in the past decade at a price where it yielded 15% more than the average of all stocks, then the assumption is made that the stock will three to five years from now also sell on a dividend yield basis 15% higher than that of the market in general. If the stock's dividend yield had for the past 10 or 15 years shown a trend one way or the other relative to the market as a whole, some allowance would be made for a continuation of that trend into the future in determining the future yield relationship. From this yield relationship, of course, is derived the multiplier that is placed upon the dividend estimated for the period. (A 6% yield implies a multiplier of 16.7 on the dividend.) A three-to five-year period is selected because, by averaging out the sales, earnings and dividends over a three-year span, the analyst avoids the necessity of pinpointing cyclical highs and lows in a period which cannot be forecast.

This method does not truly say that such-and-such a stock will, in all probability, sell at such-and-such a level. It merely says that in a given set of circumstances common to all stocks, the potentiality for appreciation is determined to be as indicated. Note that there are two determinations here: first, the determination of how high the stock may be expected to go in a plausibly hypothesized environment, and second, the determination of how great, relative to all other stocks, such appreciation would be.

If the hypothesized economic environment should fail of realization, the stock's appreciation would probably not correspond to the projected potentiality. On the other hand, useful knowledge would have been gained by measuring the potentiality, whether realized or not. It could be valuable to know that stock X would have an appreciation potentiality of 50% if the most plausible economic environment should materialize in three to five years, whereas stock Y would have only a 10% appreciation potentiality. Assume that the hypothesized environment should not materialize in the three- to five-year period of forecast. It might materialize at some later date. In the absence of knowledge of the future, the only way the investor can adjust to the possibilities is to project the most probable economic environment and apply it commonly to all stocks.

This method was first introduced in the Value Line Survey in 1952. We had previously, in 1944, forecast the postwar years' earnings in a single target year. In 1952 we adopted the more rational procedure of projecting for the average three-year period in order to avoid the distortions that might be caused by a cyclical variation in single years.

The record of results was as follows (see Figure 58).

FIGURE 58

Long-Term Price Appreciation Forecast, Test of Results, July 18, 1952, to 1954–56 Average

Group	Number of Stocks	Expected Price Appreciation	Actual Price Appreciation
I	95	48% & over	57.74%
II	95	32% to 47%	46.15%
III	96	20% to 31%	42.67%
IV	102	9% to 19%	45.27%
V	98	8% & under	32.58%

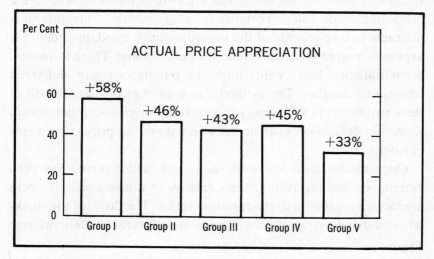

119

It was found in our experience that stocks of high quality are more likely to realize their 3- to 5-year Appreciation Potentiality than stocks of low quality.

Neither Quality Grade nor rank for Appreciation Potentiality three to five years hence indicates whether the stock is too high, too low or "right" in price *now*. To determine what is the "right" price for a stock currently, a Rating of Intrinsic Value for the next 12 months is evolved through two correlation analyses, one a time series and the other a cross-sectional analysis. The method is unorthodox and does not result in any definable standard error. But it has discriminated so far within the time period of its projection. Its construction was explained in the third chapter. The Intrinsic Value is the average price for a 12-month period that is statistically determined to be the normal price in relation to the subject stock's dividend-paying ability in that year.

When the Intrinsic Value for the year has been determined, the degree of undervaluation or overvaluation is computed according to the ratio of the 52-week moving-average price of the stock to its Intrinsic Value projected 12 months ahead. By using the moving-average price of the stock instead of the current price in relation to the projected Rating, we combine the pull of value, which is the tendency for price to move toward Intrinsic Value, with the trend momentum of the stock as expressed through its moving-average price. It has been found that stock prices tend to move *around* their Intrinsic Values, not on them. The price-trend momentum can be a factor of considerable importance for many months. Therefore, it is desirable to take account of the prevailing price trend, provided it is kept in its proper place relative to the pull of value. There is, in fact, a contradiction here. Value might be pulling one way and trend momentum another. The method that is used reconciles the pull of these two forces in such a way as to give a disciplined, if not always a precise, evaluation of their net effect upon the price movements of stocks.

Once the Intrinsic Value of each stock under survey has been determined and the average price relative to it measured, all stocks are ranked according to the resultant ratios. The 20% of the stocks whose moving-average prices stand in most favorable relationship to

120

their projected Ratings of Intrinsic Value are ranked I (Highest), and those 20% of stocks whose moving-average prices stand in least favorable relationship to the projected Ratings of Intrinsic Value are ranked V (Lowest) for Probable Market Performance in the Next 12 Months. The other percentile groups are 80–61 (II—Above Average); 60–41 (III—Average); 40–21 (IV—Below Average).

The rank for Probable Market Performance in the Next 12 Months, which is based upon a relationship of the moving-average price of the stock to its projected Intrinsic Value in the next 12 months, does not measure whether the stock is cheap or dear relative to earnings two years in the future, or three years, or five years, or ten. *It is solely a determination of the price-value relationship of the stock in the next 12 months.*

The importance of such determination was illustrated in the case of Scott Paper. It was observed that had $1,000 been invested in Scott Paper when it was temporarily overvalued at a price of 15 (on an adjusted price basis) in 1946, the result as of January 1959 would have been a profit of $4,000 plus dividends of $1,000 for a total of $5,000. On the other hand, had the stock been purchased when it was undervalued, a few months later in 1946, at a price of 10, the appreciation would have been $6,500 plus dividends of $1,500 for a total of $8,000. Thus, the very same long-term investor who held this high-grade stock for a whole 13-year period would have done 62% better with his capital and 50% better in terms of his income had he made his original commitment when the stock was under-priced rather than overpriced in the year of purchase.

How have the ranks according to Probable Market Performance in the Next 12 Months worked out in practice? It was explained that our rating method has been in use for 21 years, but that changes have been made in it from time to time. First, the visual fit, using a percentage of book value plus a fixed multiplier of earnings, was used to indicate the normal value in a given year. Then a time series correlation was used. Third, and presently, a combination of a cross-sectional and time series analysis is used. The present method has been in use since November 1957.

Shown below is how the stocks ranked I, II, III, IV and V performed during the first 12 months of experience under the present

121

method. Note that this record refers to the average price performance of the five groups of stocks. It does not refer to the performance of every single stock in the group. 804 stocks were ranked. Each of the five groups comprised approximately 160 stocks at all times.

Since the ranking procedure is systematic, it can be readily checked for its effectiveness. The record of our recommendations during the 12 months beginning November 4, 1957, can be evaluated by two different methods.

Test I (Based on ranks in effect on November 4, 1957)

The performance record illustrated in Figures 59 and 60 is based upon the rankings and prices that were published in the Value Line Survey's Weekly Summary-Index of November 4, 1957, when this system of ranking stocks for their Probable Market Performance in the Next 12 Months was first introduced. This test makes no allowance for changes in rank which were made subsequently as a result of market price changes or revisions of earnings and dividend estimates required by developing evidence. An equal amount of money is assumed to have been invested in each of the 804 stocks and held there for a 12-month period.

Note that, over the entire 12-month period (through November 3, 1958) the ranking system discriminated in the expected order, with the exception of Group V, which appreciated slightly more on average than either Group III or Group IV. This record applies to large groups of stocks only and does not imply that every stock in Group I outperformed every stock in Group II, and so on down the line. It is significant, however, that during the 12-month test period about two thirds (65%) of all stocks originally ranked in Group I rose more than the median appreciation,[20] while only 47% of all stocks ranked in Group V matched or exceeded the median appreciation.

Now, it must be borne in mind that the 1957–58 business recession came to an abrupt end in April of 1958 and was immediately superseded by a swift recovery in economic activity which is still

[20] The median is that value which exceeds the values of 50 per cent of all the items included in the distribution (when they are arranged in order of magnitude) and is also exceeded by the values of 50 per cent of all the items.

122

FIGURE 59

Record of All Value Line Recommendations, without Allowance for Changes in Recommendations, November 4, 1957, through November 3, 1958

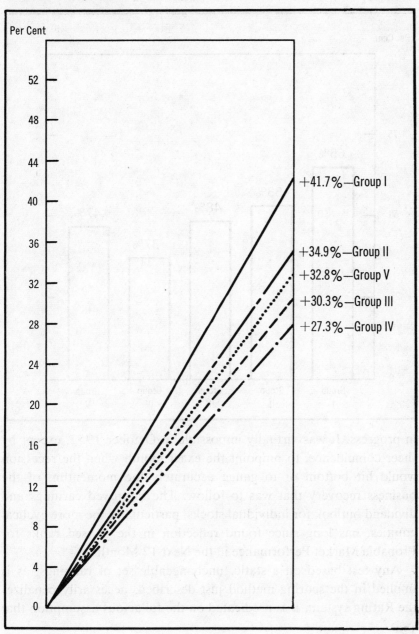

FIGURE 60

Percentage of Each Group That Outperformed the Median Appreciation of All Stocks, without Allowance for Changes in Recommendations, November 4, 1957, through November 3, 1958

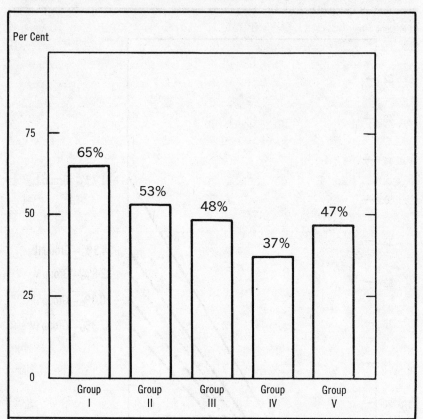

in progress. It was virtually impossible in October 1957, except by sheer coincidence, to pinpoint the exact month when the recession would hit bottom or to gauge accurately the momentum of the business recovery that was to follow. The improved earnings and dividend outlook for individual stocks, particularly the more cyclical equities, has long since found reflection in the revised ranks for Probable Market Performance in the Next 12 Months.

Any test based on a static, unchangeable set of rankings, as is implied in the scoring method just described, necessarily penalizes the Rating system. It is predicated on the fallacious assumption that

124

only original recommendations can be acted upon, and that all subsequent changes in recommendations must be ignored.

Test II (Based on changing ranks)

In practice, of course, the individual investor is not confronted with such a severe handicap. He has the option of altering the composition of his portfolio in conformance with the Value Line Survey's up-to-date recommendations which are summarized in each weekly Summary-Index. A test which allows for revisions in Market Performance ranks, as soon as they occur, is therefore a fairer and far more realistic method of evaluating the efficiency of the Rating system. This is accomplished by crediting an individual stock's performance to Group I only as long as it ranks I (Highest) for Probable Market Performance in the Next 12 Months. If, in a given week, its rank is changed from I to II (Above Average), its subsequent price performance is credited to Group II. The number of stocks (about 160) in each of the five groups remains virtually the same each week. Each group's composition, however, is a perpetually changing one, although normally less than 30 of the 804 stocks under survey are shifted from one group to another in any one week. In effect, the average week-to-week per cent change for each of the five groups is computed at the end of every week and compounded from the original starting date (November 4, 1957). According to this method of computation—without allowance for commissions and taxes, but simply in reflection of the change in prices—the performance test shows discrimination in perfect order from Group I down to Group V, for the full 12-month period. The spread in appreciation between Groups I and V amounted to a highly significant 23.2 percentage points between November 4, 1957, and November 3, 1958 (see Figure 61). As might be expected, the discrimination attained by this test was far better than on the basis of Test I, which made no allowance for interim changes in rankings.

What, then, can we conclude from this detailed record of the performance of 804 stocks ranked according to five groups? The paramount objective—to discriminate successfully among a large group of stocks—was realized in the first 12 months the present Rating system was in operation. Even under the assumption of com-

FIGURE 61

Record of All Value Line Recommendations, with Allowance for Changes in Recommendations, November 4, 1957, through November 3, 1958

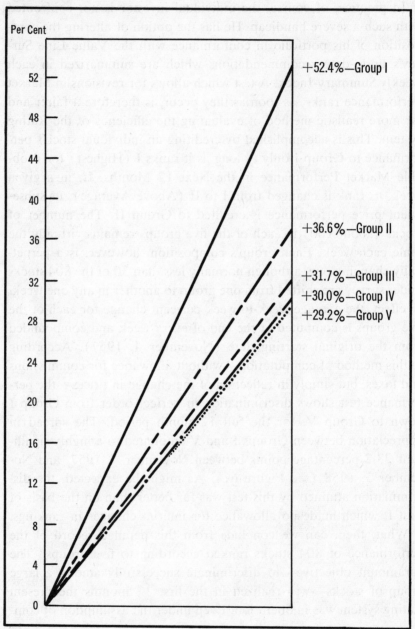

pletely static portfolios—a test which imposes a severe handicap on the system—the stocks ranked in Groups I and II outperformed all others by an appreciable margin. And if the scoring of the results is allowed to reflect interim changes in ranks, the performance record shows to much greater advantage, with perfect discrimination among the five groups and a total spread between Groups I and V in excess of 20 percentage points.

YIELD IN NEXT 12 MONTHS (Estimated)

In addition to Quality Grade, Probable Market Performance in the Next 12 Months and 3- to 5-year Appreciation Potentiality, current yield constitutes a fourth standard of value. The yield of a stock is, of course, its dividend divided by its price. But what dividend? Most published yield figures are based upon the dividends paid in the past 12 months relative to the current price. This method of computing yield has the virtue of being free of any possible error of estimate. The dividends that were paid over the past 12 months are known, and the current price is known. The yield thus derived is simple arithmetic.

But if by yield is meant the income that the investor will receive in the future, the yield computed on the basis of past experience may mean nothing. A stock might have paid dividends quarterly for the past four quarters, yet pass the dividend next week. The only reason for computing yield on the basis of dividends of the past 12 months is the implication that the dividend rate will be maintained in the next 12 months. This, of course, is a forecast.

It would be more realistic, if forecasts are to be made—and they must be made—to base them upon an estimate of the dividend that will be paid in the next 12 months, rather than on the assumption that it will be whatever it was. Dividends can be, and often are, raised or lowered. The changes reflect the earning power of the company, as well as its need for cash.

In determining the yield of a stock, the method that is proposed here is to divide the dividends that are estimated to be paid in the next 12 months by the current price.

Errors in estimating dividends 12 months ahead are generally small, as indicated by the following distribution which compares the

127

Value Line Survey's published dividend projections for 1958 (published at the end of 1957) with actual declarations by 795 companies.

FIGURE 62

Record of Dividend Estimates for 795 Stocks, 1958

Dividend Estimate, Percentage Error	Number of Stocks	Per Cent of Total Stocks
None	378	47%
.1% to 10.0%	189	24
10.1% to 20.0%	85	11
More than 20.0%	143	18
	795	100%

NOTE: Estimates made at the end of 1957 are compared to actual dividends paid in 1958. Test includes stocks which were covered by The Value Line Investment Survey for the entire year.

Note that the 12-month dividend forecast proved exact for 47% of all companies under survey at the end of 1957 (Figure 62). The forecast error was 10% or less for 71% of the supervised stocks. Forecast errors in excess of 20% were encountered for only 18% of all stocks for which dividend projections were made one year in advance.

All objective methods of stock evaluation are based upon probability. The Quality Grade, for example, is based on the probability that because dividend-paying ability was well maintained for a long time in the past, it will be well maintained in the future. This is a probability, not a certainty.

The ranks for Appreciation Potentiality three to five years into the future are based upon the assumption that in the economic environment which it is most plausible to project three to five years into the future, a normal capitalization will be placed upon estimated earnings and dividends, and that the estimates will be close to the mark. Thus, we can gauge the absolute level to which individual stocks might reasonably be expected to rise and, at the same time, we have a measure of discrimination as to the relative appreciation potentiality of stocks one to the other, if the hypothesized environment should be realized. But it is conceded that there can be no assurance that the hypothesized environment will be realized. There is no certainty that the estimates will prove correct. And there is no guarantee that, if the estimates are correct and the hypothesis realized, the capitalization will be as indicated by the ranking method. None of this is certain. But it may be said that all of it has a significant degree of probability.

The record of ranks according to Probable Market Performance in the Next 12 Months indicates ability of this method of valuation to discriminate within the period of one year as to the relative market price movements of each group on average in that year. But it cannot guarantee perfect performance for every stock according to its group ranking.

The yield estimate, based on probable dividend declarations in the next 12 months, is subject to error too. But a yield based upon the past 12 months' experience may also prove misleading. There can be no assurance that the past 12 months' dividend rate will continue in the next 12 months any more than there can be assurance that an estimate of the next 12 months' dividend will be realized. But reasonably good estimates of dividend rates can be made, especially if the estimates are checked periodically throughout the year, both against the company's quarterly reports and by contact with management, and revised if necessary. Incidentally, it can be demonstrated that a high degree of correlation exists between dividend declarations on the one hand, and cash earnings, dividend declarations (lagged one year) and stock price (lagged one year) on the other. This multiple correlation normally provides a good clue as to the coming year's dividend declaration if the future earnings are approximated.

The methods outlined in these chapters have proved in practice to be capable of discriminating among stock values classified into five groups in specific periods of time. But there can be no assurance that the performance of every single stock will conform to every one of its ranks in every forecast time period. Still, it would be virtually impossible for an investor to pick 20 stocks out of the 160 that are included in each of the five groups and have an experience significantly different from that of the group average.

It follows that in order to obtain results corresponding to those

129

of the respective groups, the investor must diversify widely enough to hold a representative sample of each group. All stocks are ranked for Probable Market Performance in the Next 12 Months in five groups from I (Highest), II (Above Average), and so on down to V (Lowest). They are ranked for Appreciation Potentiality over a period of three to five years in five groups also, I (Highest), II (Above Average), III (Average), etc. They are ranked for Quality in nine groups which might be coalesced into a subdivision of only five groups: (1) A+ and A, (2) A— and B+, (3) B, (4) B— and C+, (5) C and C—.

Yield *ranks* may be obtained by relating the yields of individual stocks to the average yield of all dividend-paying stocks. For example, the average yield of all dividend-paying stocks of the 804 under survey at this time is 4.1%. Stocks that yield between 3.6% and 4.6% may be said to be within the average yield bracket. Stocks that yield between 4.7% and 5.5% are in the above-average yield bracket, and those that yield 5.6% or more are in the highest bracket. Those that yield between 2.7% and 3.5% are considered in the below-average yield bracket, and those that yield less than 2.7% are in the lowest bracket (see Figure 63).

FIGURE 63

Yield Ranks for Stocks under Supervision by The Value Line Investment Survey, February 1959

Rank	Estimated Yield in Next 12 Months at Current Price
I (Highest)	5.6% and over
II (Above Average)	4.7% to 5.5%
III (Average)	3.6% to 4.6%
IV (Below Average)	2.7% to 3.5%
V (Lowest)	0 to 2.6%

Now how can these methods be applied in investment practice? Remember that they are based upon determinations of probability and therefore can be relied upon only if the investor *samples* the ranks. He cannot pick a single stock on the basis of rank with the same assurance of success as if he picked 10 or 20. Yet every portfolio is built on selection of individual stocks.

Suppose you hold American Telephone at this time. How good is AT&T for you? That depends, of course, on what you want your portfolio to do for you.

Put yourself in the place of Mrs. Williams. Mrs. Williams is a widow. She has two children away at school, the boy a junior at college, the girl in her second year at a preparatory school. After careful consideration, Mrs. Williams concludes that she wants most of all to conserve her capital. Next, she desires the largest possible current income because, while the children are away at school, every cent will be needed for support. Third, Mrs. Williams would like to see her stocks give a relatively good account of themselves in the market during the next 12 months; and last of all, at this time, Mrs. Williams places her desire for Appreciation Potentiality over a three-to five-year pull. This is not because she doesn't want her capital to grow, but because she needs security and income more at this stage of her life. Once the boy is out of college and on his own—next year in all probability—Mrs. Williams might change the emphasis in her portfolio to give greater weight to capital building. But just now she needs security and income most, and in that order.

A weight is assigned to each of the four attributes of American Telephone. The attribute (Quality) that is most important is weighted four times. The attribute that is next most important (Yield) is weighted three times. The attribute that is third most important (Performance in the Next 12 Months) is weighted two times. And the attribute that is least important (3- to 5-year Appreciation Potentiality) is weighted only once.

In the column below you see how these weights would be assigned to American Telephone's current ranks to accord with Mrs. Williams' scheme.

		Weight
Quality	A	×4
Yield	4.2%	×3
Rank for Market Performance Next 12 Months	III	×2
Rank for 3- to 5-year Appreciation Potentiality	III	×1

In the column below you see how the weights would be assigned to American Telephone's current ranks to accord with the objectives

131

of another investor, a Mr. Forsythe. Mr. Forsythe's objectives are different from Mrs. Williams'. Mr. Forsythe is a salesman, and right now he is making money like mad. The last thing that Mr. Forsythe wants just now is more income on which to pay income tax. No, what Mr. Forsythe wants is to build his capital so that when age creeps up on him he will be in a financial position to retire and hunt, fish, sail or putter around the garden in a manner becoming a man of his ability and former energy.

Mr. Forsythe would assign the following weights to American Telephone's four attributes. They express the difference in his objective compared to Mrs. Williams'.

		Weight
Quality	A	×2
Yield	4.2%	×1
Rank for Market Performance Next 12 Months	III	×4
Rank for 3- to 5-year Appreciation Potentiality	III	×3

Now in order to get all these ranks expressed in terms of a common denominator, we substitute index numbers for the grades and ranks as shown below in the table of substitution.

TABLE OF SUBSTITUTION

Quality	Index Number	Yield	Index Number
A+ and A	10	5.6% and over	10
A− and B+	8	4.7% − 5.5%	8
B	6	3.6% − 4.6%	6
B− and C+	4	2.7% − 3.5%	4
C and C−	2	0 − 2.6%	2

Rank for Market Performance Next 12 Months	Index Number	Rank for 3- to 5-Year Appreciation Potentiality	Index Number
I (Highest)	10	I (Highest)	10
II (Above Average)	8	II (Above Average)	8
III (Average)	6	III (Average)	6
IV (Below Average)	4	IV (Below Average)	4
V (Lowest)	2	V (Lowest)	2

Now it becomes a simple matter to measure how good American Telephone is for Mrs. Williams and how good for Mr. Forsythe.

EFFICIENCY OF AMERICAN TELEPHONE FOR
MRS. WILLIAMS' AND MR. FORSYTHE'S PORTFOLIOS

		Index Numbers	Weight	Efficiency (Index No. × Weight)
MRS. WILLIAMS' PORTFOLIO				
Quality	A	10	×4	40
Yield	4.2%	6	×3	18
Rank for Market Performance Next 12 Months	III	6	×2	12
Rank for 3- to 5-Year Appreciation Potentiality	III	6	×1	6
				76
MR. FORSYTHE'S PORTFOLIO				
Quality	A	10	×2	20
Yield	4.2%	6	×1	6
Rank for Market Performance Next 12 Months	III	6	×4	24
Rank for 3- to 5-Year Appreciation Potentiality	III	6	×3	18
				68

By these objective standards, then, it is determined that in today's market American Telephone is 76% efficient for Mrs. Williams' purposes; only 68% efficient for Mr. Forsythe's.

How Mrs. Williams Could Improve Her Investment Position *

Mrs. Williams' hypothetical portfolio of 10 stocks is reproduced in Figure 64. The over-all 67% efficiency of the portfolio indicates that the individual stocks are fairly well suited for her purposes (an over-all portfolio efficiency of 60% is average). But, the portfolio is still far from ideal and can be substantially improved by proper substitution. Mrs. Williams would first pick out those stocks in her portfolio that are currently least advantageous for her purposes (in Figure 64, circles have been drawn around the efficiencies of these stocks). These stocks would then be replaced by the following, more efficient securities, selected from the Value Line Survey's Weekly Summary-Index.

* Assuming no excessive capital gain tax liability must be taken into consideration.

	Stone & Webster	Bankers Trust	Guaranty Trust
Quality	B+	A	A
Yield	6.5%	4.1%	4.7%
Rank for Market Performance Next 12 Months	I	I	I
Rank for 3- to 5-Year Appreciation Potentiality	III	II	II
Efficiency (computed in Figure 64)	88	86	92

FIGURE 64

Evaluation of "Mrs. Williams' Portfolio," February 4, 1959

No. of Shares	Name of Stock	Market Price Per Share	Market Value	QUALITY Gets Heaviest Weight (×4)	RANK FOR MARKET PERFORMANCE NEXT 12 MONTHS Next to Last in Importance (×2)
20	American Telephone and Telegraph	$232	$4,640	A = (10 × 4) = 40	III = (6 × 2) = 12
120	Boston Insurance	37	4,440	B+ = (8 × 4) = 32	I = (10 × 2) = 20
100	Corn Products Co.	54	5,400	A = (10 × 4) = 40	I = (10 × 2) = 20
100	Detroit Edison	44	4,400	A = (10 × 4) = 40	II = (8 × 2) = 16
90	Douglas Aircraft	56	5,040	B = (6 × 4) = 24	V = (2 × 2) = 4
150	Family Finance	32	4,800	A− = (8 × 4) = 32	V = (2 × 2) = 4
145	Foster Wheeler	35	5,075	C = (2 × 4) = 8	V = (2 × 2) = 4
150	International Shoe	35	5,250	B+ = (8 × 4) = 32	IV = (4 × 2) = 8
75	National Tea	73	5,475	B+ = (8 × 4) = 32	IV = (4 × 2) = 8
100	Standard Oil (New Jersey)	55	5,500	A = (10 × 4) = 40	III = (6 × 2) = 12
			$50,020		

Substitution of 3 Stocks

85	Stone & Webster	$ 58	$4,930	B+ = (8 × 4) = 32	I = (10 × 2) = 20
65	Bankers Trust	78	5,070	A = (10 × 4) = 40	I = (10 × 2) = 20
58	Guaranty Trust	96	5,568	A = (10 × 4) = 40	I = (10 × 2) = 20

Source: The Weekly Summary-Index, The Value Line Investment Survey, February 16, 1959.

134

The three substitutions would raise the over-all efficiency of Mrs. Williams' portfolio from 67% to 80%.

How Mr. Forsythe Could Improve His Investment Position *

In a similar manner, Mr. Forsythe could improve the efficiency of his portfolio from 77% to 84% by eliminating the least efficient stocks (efficiencies circled in Figure 65) and substituting the following three stocks culled from the weekly edition of the Value Line Survey's Summary-Index.

* Assuming no excessive capital gain tax liability must be taken into consideration.

RANK FOR 3- TO 5-YEAR APPRECIATION POTENTIALITY Last in Importance (× 1)	YIELD Second Most Important (× 3)	EFFICIENCY OF EACH STOCK IN THE PORTFOLIO (Sum of the Weighted Indexes)	Per Cent Invested in Each Stock	WEIGHTED EFFICIENCY OF THE STOCKS IN MRS. WILLIAMS' PORTFOLIO (Sum of Weighted Indexes × % Invested in Stock)
III = (6 × 1) = 6	4.2% = (6 × 3) = 18	76	9.28%	7.05%
II = (8 × 1) = 8	4.9% = (8 × 3) = 24	84	8.88	7.46
IV = (4 × 1) = 4	4.1% = (6 × 3) = 18	82	10.80	8.86
IV = (4 × 1) = 4	4.9% = (8 × 3) = 24	84	8.80	7.39
I = (10 × 1) = 10	4.5% = (6 × 3) = 18	(56)	10.08	(5.64)
V = (2 × 1) = 2	5.0% = (8 × 3) = 24	62	9.60	5.95
II = (8 × 1) = 8	Nil = (2 × 3) = 6	(26)	10.14	(2.64)
III = (6 × 1) = 6	5.1% = (8 × 3) = 24	70	10.49	7.34
V = (2 × 1) = 2	3.3% = (4 × 3) = 12	(54)	10.94	(5.91)
III = (6 × 1) = 6	4.1% = (6 × 3) = 18	76	10.99	8.35
			Efficiency of Portfolio	66.59%
III = (6 × 1) = 6	6.5% = (10 × 3) = 30	88	9.86%	8.68%
II = (8 × 1) = 8	4.1% = (6 × 3) = 18	86	10.14	8.72
II = (8 × 1) = 8	4.7% = (8 × 3) = 24	92	11.13	10.24
			Efficiency of Portfolio after Substitution	80.04%

	Warner Bros.	American Machine and Foundry	King-Seeley
Quality	B−	B	B−
Yield	4.8%	3.7%	7.1%
Rank for Market Performance Next 12 Months	I	I	I
Rank for 3- to 5-Year Appreciation Potentiality	I	I	I
Efficiency (computed in Figure 65)	86	88	88

FIGURE 65

Evaluation of "Mr. Forsythe's Portfolio," February 4, 1959

No. of Shares	Name of Stock	Market Price Per Share	Market Value	QUALITY Next to Last in Importance (×2)	RANK FOR MARKET PERFORMANCE NEXT 12 MONTHS Gets Heaviest Weight (×4)
25	American Telephone and Telegraph	$232	$5,800	A = (10 × 2) = 20	III = (6 × 4) = 24
150	Canada Iron Foundries	37	5,550	B− = (4 × 2) = 8	II = (8 × 4) = 32
200	Case (J. I.)	25	5,000	C = (2 × 2) = 4	II = (8 × 4) = 32
75	Creole Petroleum	60	4,500	A− = (8 × 2) = 16	V = (2 × 4) = 8
150	Hooker Chemical	37	5,550	B = (6 × 2) = 12	I = (10 × 4) = 40
300	Howe Sound	15	4,500	C = (2 × 2) = 4	I = (10 × 4) = 40
100	Imperial Oil	46	4,600	B+ = (8 × 2) = 16	I = (10 × 4) = 40
200	Industrial Rayon	23	4,600	C+ = (4 × 2) = 8	I = (10 × 4) = 40
200	Texas Gulf Sulphur	23	4,600	B− = (4 × 2) = 8	I = (10 × 4) = 40
500	U. S. Industries	11	5,500	C = (2 × 2) = 4	I = (10 × 4) = 40
			$50,200		
	Substitution of 3 Stocks				
165	Warner Bros.	$ 29	$4,785	B− = (4 × 2) = 8	I = (10 × 4) = 40
100	American Machine and Foundry	56	5,600	B = (6 × 2) = 12	I = (10 × 4) = 40
175	King-Seeley	28	4,900	B− = (4 × 2) = 8	I = (10 × 4) = 40

Source: The Weekly Summary-Index, The Value Line Investment Survey, February 16, 1959.

I submit to you that probabilities are high that portfolios organized according to ranks weighted this way and adequately diversified will—I say almost assuredly will—perform as indicated. I might say that the way to protect a portfolio against general overvaluation in the stock market is to keep a portion of the capital out of the stock market altogether. If, for example, the 804 stocks that we keep under survey are found to be 18% above Intrinsic Value, as is the case today, the implication is that sooner or later the market will come down and come down sharply. That being the probability, the best defense would be to keep a portion of the capital ordinarily

RANK FOR 3- TO 5-YEAR APPRECIATION POTENTIALITY Second Most Important (× 3)	YIELD Last in Importance (× 1)	EFFICIENCY OF EACH STOCK IN THE PORTFOLIO (Sum of the Weighted Indexes)	Per Cent Invested in Each Stock	WEIGHTED EFFICIENCY OF THE STOCKS IN MR. FORSYTHE'S PORTFOLIO (Sum of Weighted Indexes × % Invested in Stock)
III = (6 × 3) = 18	4.2% = (6 × 1) = 6	68	11.55%	7.85%
I = (10 × 3) = 30	4.1% = (6 × 1) = 6	76	11.06	8.41
II = (8 × 3) = 24	3.2% = (4 × 1) = 4	64	9.96	6.37
II = (8 × 3) = 24	5.7% = (10 × 1) = 10	58	8.97	5.20
I = (10 × 3) = 30	3.1% = (4 × 1) = 4	86	11.06	9.51
I = (10 × 3) = 30	2.7% = (4 × 1) = 4	78	8.96	6.99
I = (10 × 3) = 30	2.9% = (4 × 1) = 4	90	9.16	8.24
I = (10 × 3) = 30	3.3% = (4 × 1) = 4	82	9.16	7.51
I = (10 × 3) = 30	5.2% = (8 × 1) = 8	86	9.16	7.88
I = (10 × 3) = 30	2.7% = (4 × 1) = 4	78	10.96	8.55
			Efficiency of Portfolio	76.51%
I = (10 × 3) = 30	4.8% = (8 × 1) = 8	86	9.53%	8.20%
I = (10 × 3) = 30	3.7% = (6 × 1) = 6	88	11.16	9.82
I = (10 × 3) = 30	7.1% = (10 × 1) = 10	88	9.76	8.59
			Efficiency of Portfolio after Substitution	83.70%

committed to stocks in high-grade bonds. The greatest liquidity would be obtained in bonds of short maturity. The greatest appreciation potentiality, if interest rates should ease again, would be in bonds of the longest maturity. At any rate, high-grade bonds, whether of long or short maturity, are less likely to depreciate at this time of high stock-market prices and the highest interest rates in several decades than are overvalued stocks. But, for a variety of reasons, the investor cannot be out of stocks altogether. Perhaps he must have income greater than can be obtained from bonds. He may find himself frozen in by capital gain taxes, so that, if he were to sell stocks, a portion of his capital would be confiscated. Even though limited to 25%, the amount of capital confiscated on sale increases as the appreciation increases.

The percentage of cash to hold out of the stock market at any given time is a judgment that might be related to the overvaluation in the general market and to the types of stocks held. No stock is entirely insulated against a major change in the general trend of the market. We recommend that the cash reserve at the present time be somewhere between 25% and 50% of the capital ordinarily committed to the stock market. Where the stocks held are of high quality (A+, A, A— or B+) and ranked high for Probable Market Performance in the Next 12 Months (I or II), the cash reserve might be as low as 25%. Where the stocks held are of speculative quality, that is to say, C+ or lower, the cash reserve should be higher. It is extremely dangerous at this time to hold stocks of low quality that are ranked lower than III in terms of Probable Market Performance in the Next 12 Months. A high rank for Probable Market Performance in the Next 12 Months means that, even in a generally overvalued stock market, the chances of depreciation in that particular stock are less than in the list as a whole. But it does not preclude the possibility of depreciation.

When the market as a whole is overvalued as it is today—standing, as 804 stocks do, an average 18% above their Ratings of Intrinsic Value—the investor should be careful to grade up in Quality, or if he does not do that, to be very certain to grade up in rank for Probable Market Performance in the Next 12 Months.

The present market is extraordinary because not only is it

138

radically overvalued, but it is overvalued at a time of strong recovery from a sharp business recession. A situation like this could easily result in some very wide advances in low-quality stocks ranked high for Probable Market Performance in the Next 12 Months. The investor who seeks to take advantage of this state of affairs should be sure to understand that the stocks of low quality ranked high for Probable Market Performance in the Next 12 Months are stocks that might not be suitable for holding over a longer period than one year.

Once a portfolio of stocks has been organized according to disciplined evaluations, it is advisable to watch continuously the subsequent developments that might alter the rankings. This may come about by revisions in earnings and dividend estimates, as well as by extraordinary price movements relative to other stocks. It is not advisable to change stocks around with every change in rank. But if a stock ranked I for Probable Market Performance rises in price to the point where it falls into rank III, consideration should be given to switching if performance in the next 12 months is an important consideration, and if the capital gain tax situation permits.

If stocks are bought primarily for income, and developments during the year indicate that the dividend is falling into jeopardy, the investor should consider a switch to avoid the risk of income loss. Continuous supervision does not imply frequent change, but it does require attention to the current developments that might change the ranks of a stock.

Investments should be regarded not as numbers that go up and down, but as ownership rights selected for specific purposes. If your desire is primarily for income, or for safety, or for relatively strong market performance within a year, you must first decide what you want most and then select according to whether or not the particular stock is strong in the attributes you desire. The perfect stock for anybody, of course, is one whose Quality Grade is A+, whose rank for Probable Market Performance in the Next 12 Months is I (Highest), whose rank for Appreciation Potentiality in the next three to five years is I (Highest) and whose yield in the next 12 months is over 5.5%. There is not a single such paragon in our list of 804 stocks today. But there are A+ stocks, and there are stocks ranked

139

I for Probable Market Performance in the Next 12 Months and I for 3- to 5-year Appreciation Potentiality, and there are stocks that yield over 5.5%. Select the stocks that have the attributes you want.

Here, then, are methods, imperfect but objective, for determining the value of stocks. They work, on balance, but not in the case of every single stock at all times. To experience the degree of success that the methods have actually achieved in discriminating among five groups of stocks, it is necessary to diversify broadly among the favorable ranks.

I do not wish to overstate the case for the Value Line methods. They are objective. They are disciplined. They have worked. But they are far from perfect. We are trying to improve them ourselves. I am sure that in time others will do better. What I hope you will recognize is the need for disciplined evaluation and the possibility of developing it. Once that is done, a long stride forward will have been taken toward eliminating the damaging fluctuations in the stock market which have caused so much grief and loss of faith. I think that if all the deviltry of all the crooked stock-market riggers of all time were raised to the hundredth power, it would count as nothing compared to the desolation wrought by deluded crowds whose imagination knows no discipline.

Go to it then. The field is wide open. The old masters have confessed their inability to determine value objectively. More investors than ever before are committing their capital to stocks. Very little has as yet been done in the field of stock evaluation by statistical organizations—and I say this with full awareness of our own efforts in the past 21 years. Here in the field of stock evaluation you will find a worthy challenge to your intelligence, and exciting adventure too.

TABLE 1

Here in alphabetical order are listed all the stocks in *The Value Line Investment Survey*. A summary such as this is published weekly in order to keep investors posted on up-to-date prices, yield expectancies and Quality Grades of individual stocks, as well as ranks according to Probable Market Performance in the Next 12 Months and Appreciation Potentiality to 1962–64.

804 Stocks Reviewed by
The Value Line Investment Survey,
Weekly Summary-Index, May 11, 1959

NAME OF STOCK	Recent Price (April 30, 1959)	Intrinsic Value Next 12 Mos.	Potential Value 1962-64	RANK according to Probable Market Performance Next 12 Mos.	Appreciation Potentiality to 1962-1964	Quality Grade	Est'd Yield Next 12 Mos. %
ACF Industries	53	44	66	III	II	C+	5.4-6.8
ASR Products	12	11	13	I	IV	C+	4.2-4.8
Abbott Laboratories	80	63	79	II	V	B+	2.5-2.8
Abitibi Power & Paper	37*	31	44	V	II	B	4.6
Adams Express	29	26	33	III	III	A−	3.2
Addressograph	111	68	100	V	V	B+	1.4-1.5
Admiral Corp.	22	18	30	I	I	C	3.4-4.5
Aetna Fire Ins.	75	70	90	IV	II	B+	3.5-3.6
Aetna Life Ins.	254	193	265	V	IV	A−	1.4-1.5
Air Reduction	85	66	89	V	IV	B	2.9-3.3
Alco Products	21	19	25	III	II	C	5.2-6.2
Algoma Steel	37*	35	45	I	II	B	3.0
Alleghany Corp.	13	11	15	I	III	C	Nil
Allegheny Ludlum	46	42	59	IV	I	B−	4.3-4.8
Allied Chemical	112	90	122	II	IV	B+	2.7-2.8‡
Allied Mills	43	37	43	IV	V	B	5.2
Allied Stores	59	49	61	III	IV	B	5.1-5.4
Allis-Chalmers	29	26	40	III	I	B−	5.2
Alpha Portland	35	36	50	III	I	B	4.3-5.0
Aluminium, Ltd.	28	22	48	V	I	B+	1.8

141

NAME OF STOCK	Recent Price (April 30, 1959)	Intrinsic Value Next 12 Mos.	Potential Value 1962-64	RANK according to Probable Market Performance Next 12 Mos.	RANK according to Appreciation Potentiality to 1962-1964	Quality Grade	Est'd Yield Next 12 Mos. %
Aluminum Co.	83	72	107	V	I	B +	1.4-1.6
Amerada Petroleum	92	107	150	I	I	B +	2.2
Amer. Agri. Chem.	106	80	100	IV	V	B	4.5-5.0
Amer. Airlines	30	24	31	III	IV	B	3.3
Amer. Bakeries	47	39	46	IV	V	B	5.1-5.5
Amer. Bank Note	35	32	43	V	II	B −	3.4-3.7
Amer. Bosch Arma	37	25	41	V	III	B −	3.2-3.5
Amer. Brake Shoe	49	43	55	II	I	B	5.4-5.9
Amer. Broadc.-Par't	27	20	35	II	I	B	3.7-4.1
Amer. Can	44	47	58	III	I	A −	4.5
Amer. Chain	57	46	62	IV	IV	B	4.4-4.8
Amer. Chicle	54	45	51	I	V	A −	3.7-3.9
Amer. Crystal Sugar	41	36	48	IV	II	B	3.9-4.9
Amer. Cyanamid	56	47	60	IV	IV	B +	2.9
Amer. Distilling	44	35	50	I	III	B −	3.6-4.5
Amer. Elec. Power	51	48	53	II	IV	A	2.9-3.5
Amer. Export	32	28	36	III	III	B −	6.3
Amer. Home P'd'cts	149	115	137	III	V	A −	2.7
Amer. Insurance	27	27	38	III	I	B +	4.8
Amer. Invest. (Ill.)	20	19	25	III	II	A	5.0
Amer. Mach. & F'dry	88	55	113	I	I	B	2.6-2.8
Amer.-Marietta	55	37	59	V	IV	B +	2.0-2.1
Amer. Metal-Climax	27	25	32	III	II	B −	4.4-5.6
Amer. Metal P'd'cts	30	23	36	IV	II	B −	5.3
Amer. Molasses	15	14	17	IV	III	B	4.7‡
Amer. Motors	38	25	40	II	IV	C +	6.3
Amer. Natural Gas	70	67	78	I	III	A −	3.7
Amer. Optical	45	38	51	III	III	B	4.4-5.3
Amer. Potash	46	41	65	IV	I	B	2.2-2.6
Amer. Seating	40	33	43	II	IV	B	4.0-4.3
Amer. Smelting	47	43	80	V	I	B −	4.3-4.8
Amer. Snuff	60	57	60	II	V	B +	5.0
Amer.-Standard	18	14	21	III	II	C +	4.4-5.0
Amer. Steel Foundries	57	41	65	III	III	B −	5.1-5.9
Amer. Stores	90	76	100	IV	III	A −	2.2-2.7
Amer. Sugar Ref'g	36	32	40	IV	III	B	6.1
Amer. Surety	20	17	26	V	I	B	3.9
Amer. Tel. & Tel.	252	202	265	II	IV	A	3.9
Amer. Tobacco	105	95	120	I	III	B +	5.0-5.1
Amer. Trust	58	49	58	II	V	A	2.8-3.1
Amer. Viscose	50	38	59	I	II	C +	2.0-4.0
Amphenol-Borg	42	28	50	V	II	B	3.3
Anaconda	66	59	75	I	III	B −	6.8
Anchor Hocking	35	28	36	V	IV	B	3.7
Anderson-Prichard	35	31	50	II	I	B −	3.4-4.0
Anheuser-Busch	26	23	30	II	III	B	4.6
Archer-Daniels	46	41	55	II	II	C +	4.3-5.2
Arizona Pub. Ser.	41	35	40	III	V	A	3.1-3.2
Arkansas Fuel Oil	33	37	45	III	I	B	3.0
Arkansas La. Gas	64	52	64	I	V	B +	2.2-2.5
Armco Steel	70	54	65	V	V	B	4.3-4.5
Armour & Co.	24	20	25	II	IV	C +	Nil-3.3
Armstrong Cork	41	31	44	IV	IV	B	3.7-4.0
Arvin Industries	26	22	32	II	II	B	4.8-5.8
Ashland Oil	24	19	26	II	IV	B	4.2-4.8
Assoc. Dry Goods	53	38	53	V	V	B	4.2-4.3

142

NAME OF STOCK	Recent Price (April 30, 1959)	Intrinsic Value Next 12 Mos.	Potential Value 1962-64	RANK according to Probable Market Performance Next 12 Mos.	Appreciation Potentiality to 1962-1964	Quality Grade	Est'd Yield Next 12 Mos. %
Associates Invest.	73	72	80	V	III	A	3.6
Atchison, T. & S. F.	29	25	32	III	III	B +	5.2-5.5
Atlantic City Elec.	45	38	41	III	V	A	3.3●
Atlantic Coast Line	61	43	62	IV	IV	B −	4.1-4.3
Atlantic Refining	50	40	57	IV	III	B +	4.0
Atlas Corp.	7	8.5	11	I	I	B +	Nil
Atlas Powder	84	62	80	V	V	B	2.9-3.2
Atlas Steels	27*	24	37	II	I	C +	4.4
Avco M'f'g	14	8.8	16	V	III	C	2.9-3.2
Babcock & Wilcox	33	28	41	V	II	B	3.0-3.6‡
Baldwin-Lima-Ham.	15	13	20	IV	I	C	4.0-5.0
Balt. Gas & Elec.	46	45	47	I	IV	A	3.9-4.3
Balt. & Ohio	45	42	56	I	II	C +	4.4-6.1
Bank of America	48	45	53	I	III	A	3.8-4.2
Bankers Trust	80	83	100	I	II	A	4.0-4.1
Barker Bros.	8	6.9	10	III	II	C	Nil-5.0
Bath Iron Works	60	49	67	IV	III	C +	5.0-5.4
Bayuk Cigars	38	22	29	V	V	B −	2.6-3.0
Beatrice Foods	50	44	53	III	IV	B +	3.6-4.0
Beech-Life Savers	40	36	45	IV	III	B	4.0-4.3
Bell Aircraft	20	17	27	V	I	B −	4.0-5.0
Bendix Aviation	79	58	81	IV	IV	B +	3.0-3.4
Beneficial Finance	26	24	29	III	III	A −	3.8-4.4
Best & Co.	39	33	36	IV	V	B	5.1-5.5
Bethlehem Steel	51	42	53	V	IV	B +	4.9-5.1
Bigelow-Sanford	17	13	20	I	II	C	Nil-1.5
Black & Decker	64	46	61	V	V	B	3.1-3.6
Blaw-Knox	44	34	48	III	III	B	3.3-3.5‡
Bliss (E. W.)	19	16	21	IV	III	C +	1.6-3.2
Bliss & Laughlin	27	23	31	II	III	B −	5.9-6.7
Boeing	39	36	72	V	I	B	2.7-3.2‡
Bohn Aluminum	30	21	25	II	V	C	3.3
Bond Stores	24	18	22	V	V	B −	5.2
Borden Company	79	73	83	II	IV	A −	3.8-4.1
Borg-Warner	43	34	45	IV	IV	B	4.7
Boston Edison	61	58	61	II	V	A −	4.6-4.9
Boston Insurance	35	39	45	I	I	B +	5.1-4.3
Braniff Airways	15	12	17	II	III	C	4.0
Bridgeport Brass	41	33	43	IV	IV	B −	3.7-4.9
Briggs & Stratton	53	37	49	IV	V	B	3.8-4.2
Bristol-Myers	103	64	81	V	V	B −	2.3-2.7
British Amer. Oil	41	38	58	V	I	B +	2.4
Brooklyn Un. Gas	54	50	59	I	III	A +	4.1-4.4
Brown & Sharpe	31	27	34	II	III	B −	3.9
Brown Shoe	67	56	60	III	V	A −	3.3-3.6
Brunswick-Balke	92	46	105	III	III	B −	2.2-3.0
Buckeye Pipe Line	33	31	33	I	V	A −	4.2-4.8
Bucyrus-Erie	34	23	41	V	II	B −	1.5-2.9
Budd	27	18	29	III	IV	C +	3.7-4.4
Bullard	20	12	22	V	III	C	Nil
Burlington Industries	19	15	21	I	III	C +	5.3
Burroughs	41	34	60	IV	I	B	2.9-3.4
C.I.T. Financial	55	50	54	IV	V	A −	4.7
Calif. Packing	58	46	59	IV	IV	B	3.8-4.5‡

143

NAME OF STOCK	Recent Price (April 30, 1959)	Intrinsic Value Next 12 Mos.	Potential Value 1962-64	RANK according to Probable Market Performance Next 12 Mos.	Appreciation Potentiality to 1962-1964	Quality Grade	Est'd Yield Next 12 Mos. %
Camden Fire Ins.	37	32	37	IV	V	B +	3.2-3.5
Campbell Soup	51	46	55	III	IV	A −	3.1-3.5
Canada Cement	35*	36	42	I	II	B +	2.9-3.6
Canada Dry	21	18	25	IV	II	B	5.0-5.5
Canada Iron Foundries	35*	32	51	III	I	B −	4.3
Canadian Breweries	42	34	46	IV	III	B	3.6-4.5
Canadian Oil Cos.	30*	29	47	I	I	B +	2.7-3.3
Canadian Pacific	30	31	43	I	I	B −	5.0-5.8
Cannon Mills	66	61	72	II	III	B	4.5-5.3
Capital Airlines	20	19	38	I	I	C	Nil
Carborundum	43	38	47	II	III	B −	3.7-4.0
Carnation	65	54	64	IV	V	B +	2.8-3.0
Carolina Power & Light	37	33	38	III	IV	A −	3.9
Carrier	44	42	70	II	I	B	4.1-4.8
Case (J.I.)	23	22	38	II	I	C +	3.5
Caterpillar Tractor	95	74	100	IV	IV	B	2.5
Celanese	32	25	33	I	IV	C	3.1-3.8
Celotex	43	31	48	V	III	C +	4.7-5.6
Cen. Aguirre Sugar	22	20	25	IV	III	B	6.4
Cen. Hudson G. & E.	22	18	22	II	V	A −	4.0-4.1●
Cen. Illinois Light	36	31	35	III	V	A −	3.9-4.2
Cen. Illinois P.S.	46	37	42	IV	V	A −	3.8
Cen. Maine Power	27	27	30	I	III	B +	5.2-5.7●
Cen. & South West	60	53	68	III	III	A	3.0-3.3
Cerro de Pasco	41	40	64	II	I	C +	2.9-3.9
Chain Belt	59	40	54	V	V	B	4.0
Champion Paper	42	36	50	V	II	B +	2.9
Champlin Oil	24	23	36	II	I	B	4.2-4.6
Chase Manhattan Bank	59	63	75	I	II	A	4.3-4.4
Chemetron	31	27	40	V	I	B	3.2
Chemical Corn	62	62	77	I	II	A	4.0-4.2
Chesapeake & Ohio	73	62	80	III	III	B	5.5-5.8
Chic. Great Western	49	44	55	II	III	B −	4.2-4.6
Chic. Milwaukee	26	22	28	III	IV	C	5.8
Chic. & N.W.	27	23	35	IV	I	C	Nil
Chic. Pneu. Tool	29	22	29	V	V	B	4.1
Chic. Rock Island	37	29	38	II	IV	B −	4.9-5.4
Chrysler	65	54	82	II	II	B −	3.1-4.6
Cincinnati G. & Elec.	34	34	38	II	III	A −	4.4
Cincinnati Milling	44	34	45	V	IV	B +	3.6-3.2
Cities Service	58	53	73	IV	II	B	4.1
Clark Equipment	70	45	60	V	V	B −	3.2
Cleveland-Cliffs	52	43	60	IV	III	B −	4.0-5.0
Cleveland Electric	52	49	52	I	V	A	3.5-3.8
Clevite	36	22	34	III	V	B −	3.2-3.5
Cluett, Peabody	58	41	67	V	III	B −	3.9-4.3
Coca-Cola	132	118	145	II	III	B	3.8-4.2
Colgate-Palmolive	121	74	122	IV	IV	B	3.0-3.3
Collins & Aikman	24	23	29	I	II	C	3.8-4.8
Collins Radio	41	18	30	V	V	C +	0.9
Colorado Fuel	26	23	37	II	I	B −	3.9-6.2
Columbia Br'c't'g	46	37	58	I	II	B	2.6-2.7
Columbia Gas	22	21	27	II	II	B +	4.5-5.2
Columbia Pictures	20	17	30	IV	I	C +	1.3-3.8
Columbian Carbon	51	45	55	I	IV	B	4.7
Columbus & S. O. El.	37	34	38	III	IV	B +	4.3-4.7

NAME OF STOCK	Recent Price (April 30, 1959)	Intrinsic Value Next 12 Mos.	Potential Value 1962-64	RANK according to Probable Market Performance Next 12 Mos.	RANK according to Appreciation Potentiality to 1962-1964	Quality Grade	Est'd Yield Next 12 Mos. %
Combustion Eng.	37	25	35	V	V	B+	3.0-3.2
Commercial Credit	60	54	67	IV	III	B+	4.7
Commercial Solvents	17	14	20	II	II	C	1.2-2.9
Commonwealth Ed.	61	53	62	II	IV	A	3.3‡
Community Pub. Ser.	24	22	26	II	IV	A-	4.2-4.4
Conde Nast	9⅝	6.4	8.5	IV	V	C	1.0-3.1
Congoleum-Nairn	14	10	12	V	V	C+	Nil
Conn. General Life	382	321	540	II	I	A+	0.7
Conn. Light & Power	26	24	26	I	V	A-	4.2-4.6•
Consol. Cigar	54	41	60	III	III	B	3.9-4.6
Consol. Edison	64	59	62	II	V	A-	4.4
Consol. Electrodyn.	41	31	52	V	II	C+	1.0-1.2
Consol. Foods	27	19	31	V	III	B-	3.7-4.4‡
Consol. Mining	22	20	30	IV	I	C+	3.6
Consol. Natural Gas	50	49	59	III	II	A-	4.2-4.3
Consolidation Coal	33	31	43	V	I	B	3.6
Consumers Power	54	56	64	II	II	A	4.4-4.8
Container Corp.	28	23	27	V	V	B+	3.6-3.2
Continental Assurance	144	125	160	II	III	A	0.8-0.9
Continental Baking	49	39	56	V	III	B	4.5-4.9
Continental Can	47	51	60	III	II	A-	3.8-4.3
Continental Casualty	136	102	140	III	IV	A	1.4-1.7
Continental Illinois	122	113	124	I	IV	A	3.4-3.5
Continental Insurance	58	60	71	I	II	A-	3.4-3.8
Continental Motors	13	9.8	15	IV	III	C	5.0
Continental Oil	62	53	69	V	III	B+	2.6-2.7
Cooper-Bessemer	42	28	38	V	V	C+	3.8-4.3
Corn Products	55	51	58	I	IV	A	3.6-4.0
Cornell Dubilier	27	19	37	III	I	C+	3.0-4.1
Corning Glass	125	83	109	V	V	A-	1.2-1.3
Crane Company	40	38	44	I	III	C+	3.0-4.5
Creole Petroleum	53	60	60	V	III	A-	6.2-5.3
Crown Cork	32	23	31	V	V	C+	1.3-2.5
Crown Zellerbach	57	47	64	V	III	B+	3.2
Crucible Steel	28	27	38	I	I	C+	5.0-5.7
Cuban-Amer. Sugar	27	25	33	V	II	C	7.8
Cudahy Packing	14	14	17	I	II	C	Nil-3.2
Curtis Publishing	12	12	20	II	I	C+	2.9
Curtiss-Wright	37	28	40	III	IV	C+	6.8-5.4
Cutler-Hammer	84	50	74	V	V	B	3.0
Dana Corp.	68	54	68	III	V	B+	4.4-5.1
Daystrom	43	30	43	V	V	B-	2.8-3.1
Dayton Power & Light	53	50	57	IV	IV	A-	4.5-4.8
Decca Records	19	16	26	III	I	C+	5.3
Deere & Co.	59	44	67	IV	III	B	4.4-4.7
Delaware & Hudson	30	24	34	IV	III	B-	6.7
Delaware, Lack.	11	11	13	I	II	C	Nil
Delaware Power & Light	63	57	67	II	IV	A	3.3-3.5
Delta Airlines	32	24	34	II	IV	C+	3.8
Denver & Rio Grande	20	16	20	III	V	B+	5.0-5.3
Detroit Edison	44	43	48	I	III	A	4.5-4.9•
Diamond Alkali	54	44	60	II	III	B	3.3‡
Diamond Gardner	33	33	46	II	I	B	4.5-5.5
Distillers Corp. -S.	34	30	42	IV	II	B-	5.0
Divco-Wayne	25	16	28	IV	III	C+	4.0-4.6

NAME OF STOCK	Recent Price (April 30, 1959)	Intrinsic Value Next 12 Mos.	Potential Value 1962-64	RANK according to Probable Market Performance Next 12 Mos.	Appreciation Potentiality to 1962-1964	Quality Grade	Est'd Yield Next 12 Mos. %
Dr. Pepper	15	12	15	IV	V	C+	4.0
Dome Mines	18	17	17	II	V	B−	3.9
Domin. F'dries & St.	49*	38	50	II	IV	B+	2.4-2.7
Domin. Steel & Coal	19*	20	30	IV	I	B−	5.3
Dominion Stores	78*	78	96	II	II	A	1.6-1.9
Douglas Aircraft	53	50	88	V	I	B	4.7-1.9
Dow Chemical	88	71	95	II	IV	A−	1.4-1.5‡
Dresser Industries	40	35	44	V	III	B	5.0
Duke Power	47	40	45	II	V	A	3.2-3.4
Dumont Lab's	8⅛	5.5	12	III	I	C−	Nil
Du Pont	242	201	245	II	IV	A	2.5-2.7
Duquesne Light	25	23	24	II	V	A−	4.4-4.7
Eagle-Picher	48	37	60	IV	II	B−	4.8
Eastern Air Lines	41	37	61	I	I	B	2.4‡
Eastern Gas & Fuel	31	26	43	IV	I	C+	5.2‡
Eastman Kodak	88	68	95	I	IV	A	1.9-2.0
Eaton M'f'g	72	53	70	IV	V	B	4.2-4.9
El Paso Nat. Gas	33	33	41	III	II	B+	3.9●
Elec. Auto-Lite	44	39	50	I	III	B−	4.5-5.7
Elec. Storage Bat.	42	35	45	III	IV	B	4.8
Emerson Electric	62	36	60	V	V	B−	2.6‡
Emerson Radio	22	12	17	I	V	C+	2.7
Empire Dist. Elec.	25	23	28	II	III	B+	4.8-5.2
Endicott Johnson	36	32	36	IV	V	B+	4.4
Equitable Gas	38	36	41	II	II	A−	4.6-4.7●
Erie Railroad	13	11	16	I	II	C	Nil
Ex-Cell-O	41	42	50	I	II	B+	3.7
Fairbanks, Morse	34	32	41	V	II	B−	4.1
Fairchild Engine	9	6.6	9.0	V	V	C+	Nil
Falconbridge	27*	31	40	I	I	B	4.4-5.2
Falstaff Brewing	24	20	28	I	II	B	4.2-5.0
Family Finance	32	27	31	V	V	A−	5.0
Fansteel Metal.	57	51	70	II	II	B	1.8-2.1‡
Fedders Corp.	20	17	21	I	IV	C+	5.0-5.8
Federal-Mogul	58	42	52	IV	V	B+	4.1-4.6
Federal Paper B'd	50	42	58	IV	II	B	4.4-4.8
Federated Dep't St.	59	47	59	III	V	A−	3.4-3.6
Fibreboard Paper	52	39	54	IV	IV	C+	2.3-2.7‡
Fidelity-Phenix Ins.	63	62	73	I	III	A−	3.2-3.5
Fireman's Fund	58	62	76	I	I	A−	3.1-3.3
Firestone Tire	143	95	144	V	IV	B+	1.8-2.2
Firstamerica	22	21	26	I	II	A	3.6-4.0
First Nat'l (Bos.)	86	86	100	I	II	A	4.1
First Nat'l (Chi.)	345	334	395	I	III	A	2.3
First Nat'l (St. L.)	78	72	87	I	III	A	4.1
First Nat'l City	78	78	88	I	III	A	3.9-4.1
First Nat'l Stores	65	70	86	III	I	A−	3.8-4.2
Flintkote	40	29	45	V	III	B−	4.5
Florida Power	29	25	32	IV	III	A	2.7
Florida Power & Light	91	74	96	IV	IV	A+	1.8-1.9
Food Fair	38	41	48	I	II	B+	2.6-2.8‡
Food Machinery	45	35	45	IV	V	B	2.8
Ford Motor	64	49	74	I	III	B	3.8-4.7
Ford of Canada	140	109	160	I	III	B	3.6-4.3

146

NAME OF STOCK	Recent Price (April 30, 1959)	Intrinsic Value Next 12 Mos.	Potential Value 1962-64	RANK according to Probable Market Performance Next 12 Mos.	RANK according to Appreciation Potentiality to 1962-1964	Quality Grade	Est'd Yield Next 12 Mos. %
Foremost Dairies	20	20	26	I	I	B+	5.0
Foster Wheeler	42	31	45	V	IV	C	Nil
Freeport Sulphur	35	32	50	II	I	B+	3.4
Fruehauf Trailer	24	15	20	V	V	C+	Nil-2.5
Gardner-Denver	52	39	49	V	V	B	3.8-4.1
General Amer. Invest.	33	31	42	IV	II	B+	1.6
General Amer. Trans.	59	50	70	III	II	A−	3.4-3.6
General Baking	13	13	17	II	I	B	5.8-6.2
General Cable	42	33	50	V	II	B−	4.8-5.2
General Cigar	28	21	30	IV	IV	B	2.9-3.2
General Dynamics	58	60	91	II	I	B+	3.4-3.8
General Electric	84	68	89	III	IV	A	2.5-2.7
General Foods	78	70	80	II	IV	A	3.1-3.2
General Mills	108	85	97	II	V	B+	3.0-3.2
General Motors	49	42	56	IV	III	B+	4.1-4.6
General Portland Cem.	39	37	45	III	III	B+	3.2-3.6
General Precision Eq.	41	28	46	V	III	C+	1.8-2.4•
General Public Util.	51	46	50	III	V	A−	4.2-4.3
General Railway Signal	36	28	38	V	IV	B−	4.2-4.9
General Refractories	52	43	56	III	IV	B+	3.8-4.6
General Tel. & Electro.	71	57	65	II	V	A	2.8-3.0
General Tire	75	32	83	V	III	B	0.9-1.6
Genesco, Inc.	36	26	31	III	V	B	4.2-4.3
Georgia-Pacific	65	38	63	V	V	C+	1.9-2.3
Gerber Products	68	59	74	II	IV	A	2.6-2.8
Getty Oil	24	27	40	II	I	B−	Stk.
Gillette	51	40	57	V	III	B	4.4
Gimbel Bros.	44	33	53	IV	II	C+	4.1-4.4
Girard Trust	56	58	70	I	II	A	4.6
Glen Alden Corp.	14	—	—	—	—	C+	—
Glens Falls Ins.	40	38	45	I	III	A−	2.5-3.0
Glidden	49	39	55	IV	III	B−	4.1-4.6
Goodrich	92	70	97	III	IV	B+	2.4-2.7
Goodyear Tire	144	91	135	V	V	B+	1.7-2.2
Gould-National	37	35	48	III	I	B	5.4-5.5
Grace (W.R.)	45	39	56	V	II	B	3.6
Grand Union	52	46	58	III	III	A−	1.7‡
Granite City Steel	61	45	64	V	IV	B−	3.7-4.9
Grant (W.T.)	45	40	55	II	II	B	4.9
Great American Insur.	42	43	52	II	II	A−	3.6-3.8
Great Atlantic & Pacific	41	36	46	V	III	A−	4.4-2.4
Great Northern Iron	30	29	36	I	II	B	9.2-10.0•
Great Northern Paper	51	39	73	V	I	B−	1.2-2.0
Great Northern Railway	59	43	71	IV	II	B	5.1-5.5
Great Western Sugar	28	26	31	IV	III	B	6.1-5.4
Green (H.L.)	32	30	34	V	IV	B−	5.0-3.8
Greyhound	23	17	25	II	IV	B+	4.3-5.0
Grumman	27	23	36	III	I	C+	5.6
Gulf Mobile & O.	29	25	31	I	IV	C+	6.9
Gulf Oil	114	114	150	II	I	A−	2.4-2.6
Gulf States Utilities	58	52	63	II	IV	A	3.4•
Halliburton Oil	63	58	92	IV	I	B+	3.8
Hammermill	31	28	44	IV	I	B−	3.2-4.8
Hanover Bank	52	54	63	I	II	A	3.9-4.1

NAME OF STOCK	Recent Price (April 30, 1959)	Intrinsic Value Next 12 Mos.	Potential Value 1962-64	RANK according to Probable Market Performance Next 12 Mos.	Appreciation Potentiality to 1962-1964	Quality Grade	Est'd Yield Next 12 Mos. %
Harbison-Walker	49	40	47	III	V	B +	3.7-4.1
Harris-Intertype	49	30	41	III	V	B +	4.1
Harshaw Chemical	30	24	35	IV	II	B −	3.3-3.8
Hartford Electric Light	71	64	65	II	V	A −	4.2-4.4●
Hartford Fire Insurance	187	182	220	I	II	A	1.6-2.0
Heinz (H. J.)	68	58	76	IV	III	B +	3.2-3.4
Hercules Powder	70	47	63	IV	V	B +	1.8-1.9
Hershey Chocolate	76	67	81	II	IV	B +	4.1-4.7
Hoffman Electronics	74	31	46	V	V	B −	1.4-1.8
Holland Furnace	14	13	17	I	II	C	4.3-5.0
Hollinger Consolidated	34	31	37	I	IV	B −	1.8-2.1
Holly Sugar	23	20	32	IV	I	B	5.2
Home Insurance	52	50	58	I	III	B +	3.8-4.2
Homestake Mining	40	41	50	III	II	C +	5.0
Hooker Chemical	40	35	50	II	II	B	2.5-2.8
Houdaille Industries	22	18	30	IV	I	B −	4.7‡
Household Finance	32	32	36	IV	III	A −	3.8‡
Houston Light & Power	72	66	80	II	III	A +	2.2-2.5
Howe Sound	18	14	22	I	II	C	2.2-3.3
Hudson Bay Mining	58	55	80	III	I	B −	5.2-6.9
Idaho Power	45	45	53	II	II	A	3.8●
Illinois Central	47	44	61	II	I	B −	6.4-7.4
Illinois Power	41	36	41	II	V	A −	3.7-3.9
Imperial Oil	45	55	63	I	I	B +	3.0-3.1
Indianapolis P. & L't	40	38	44	I	III	A	4.3
Industrial Acceptance	38*	36	46	III	II	A	4.2-4.5
Industrial Rayon	23	21	32	II	I	C +	Nil-2.6
Ingersoll-Rand	102	83	100	IV	V	B +	3.9
Inland Steel	139	107	135	V	V	B +	3.7-4.1
Inspiration C. Cop'r	44	39	50	II	III	C +	8.5-9.1
Insurance Co. N. Amer.	138	113	144	IV	IV	A	2.2
Interchemical Corp.	33	19	28	V	V	B −	3.4
Interlake Iron	27	24	33	II	II	B −	5.2-7.4
Int'l Business Mach.	392	294	400	II	IV	A +	0.5-0.6
International Harvester	42	38	50	III	II	B	5.5-5.7
International Minerals	35	29	43	II	I	B −	4.6
International Nickel	92	83	126	III	I	B +	3.3-4.1
International Paper	116	92	150	V	I	B +	2.6-2.7
International Salt	147	123	165	III	III	B +	3.2-3.7
International Shoe	36	35	40	II	III	B +	5.0-5.4
International Silver	45	37	48	III	IV	C	3.3-4.4
International Tel. & Tel.	42	24	36	IV	V	B	2.4-2.6
Interprov'c'l Pipe	54*	65	69	I	II	B +	4.2
Interstate Dept.	33	25	39	V	II	B −	3.6-4.2
Interstate Power	19	17	21	IV	III	B +	4.7●
Iowa-Illinois Gas & Elec.	38	35	45	III	II	B +	4.7-5.0
Iowa Power & Light	37	33	40	II	IV	B +	4.9
Irving Trust (N.Y.)	38	39	49	I	II	A	4.3
Island Creek Coal	40	38	56	IV	I	B −	5.0-5.3
Jewel Tea Co.	49	41	46	IV	V	A −	2.4-2.8‡
Johns-Manville	60	46	62	III	IV	B +	3.3-3.8
Johnson & Johnson	50	46	48	II	V	B +	1.6-1.8
Jones & Laughlin	69	49	63	V	V	B −	4.0-4.7
Joy Manufacturing	49	39	63	V	I	B −	4.1-4.5

148

NAME OF STOCK	Recent Price (April 30, 1959)	Intrinsic Value Next 12 Mos.	Potential Value 1962-64	RANK according to Probable Market Performance Next 12 Mos.	Appreciation Potentiality to 1962-1964	Quality Grade	Est'd Yield Next 12 Mos. %
Kaiser Aluminum	43	30	56	V	I	B −	2.1-2.6
Kansas City P. & L't	54	48	52	II	V	A −	4.1
Kansas City Southern	82	75	100	III	II	B +	6.1
Kansas Gas & Electric	43	37	42	III	V	A −	3.7
Kansas Power & Light	32	28	36	III	III	A −	4.3-4.4
Kearney & Trecker	17	11	14	I	V	C +	0.9-1.8
Kellogg	41	31	33	IV	V	A −	2.4-2.8
Kelsey-Hayes Co.	46	34	56	V	II	B −	5.2-5.9
Kennecott Copper	114	100	120	II	IV	B	6.1
Kerr McGee Oil	65	61	80	I	II	B	1.2-1.8
Kimberly-Clark	63	55	70	V	III	B +	3.0-3.2
King-Seeley	34	29	40	I	II	B −	5.9-7.4
Koppers	43	39	60	IV	I	B −	3.7-4.7
Kresge (S. S.)	34	32	40	I	II	B	4.7-5.3
Kress (S. H.)	43	36	52	IV	II	B	4.7
Kroger	29	27	33	IV	III	A −	3.2‡
Laclede Gas	20	21	23	I	III	A	4.5-5.4
Lee Rubber & Tire	29	22	31	IV	IV	B −	4.1-4.8
Lehigh Portland	31	34	50	III	I	B	3.2-4.0
Lehigh Valley R. R.	8¾	9.2	12	I	I	C	Nil
Lehman Corporation	31	28	36	IV	II	A −	2.0
Lehn & Fink	54	32	38	V	V	B −	3.3-3.7
Lerner Stores	21	19	24	II	III	B −	5.7
Libbey-Owens-Ford	57	47	65	II	III	B +	3.5-4.0
Libby, McNeill	13	11	18	IV	I	C	3.1-3.8
Liggett & Myers	97	78	92	II	V	B +	5.2
Lily-Tulip Cup	102	81	100	V	V	A −	2.0-2.2
Lincoln Nat'l Life	221	228	230	I	IV	A +	0.9-1.0
Link-Belt	62	56	75	III	II	B	4.8
Lockheed	36	26	45	V	II	B −	3.3-4.2
Loew's, Inc.	32	28	45	III	I	C +	3.1-4.7
Loew's Theatres	14	11	15	II	IV	C +	Nil-1.4
Lone Star Cement	33	34	45	II	I	B +	3.6-4.2
Lone Star Gas	43	42	46	II	IV	B +	4.2-4.7
Lone Star Steel	33	24	37	IV	III	C +	Nil
Long Island L't'g	35	31	31	I	V	A	3.4-3.7
Lorillard (P.)	40	35	38	IV	V	B	5.0
Louisiana Land	60	52	69	IV	III	B +	2.5-2.9
Louisville Gas & Elec.	42	38	45	II	IV	A	3.3
Louisville & Nash.	84	72	99	III	II	B	6.0-6.3
Lowenstein	17	15	26	IV	I	C +	3.5-4.7
Mack Trucks	42	31	42	III	V	C +	4.3-4.8
Macy (R.H.)	41	36	46	III	III	B	4.9-5.1
Madison Fund, Inc.	19	17	24	III	II	A −	3.4
Magma Copper	63	69	79	I	II	C +	Nil
Magnavox	58	39	55	V	IV	B −	2.6-3.4
Mallory (P.R.)	43	35	43	I	V	B	3.3-3.6
Manhattan Shirt	18	15	23	III	II	B −	3.9-5.6
Manufacturers Trust	54	56	65	I	II	A	4.1-4.3
Marine Midland	25	24	29	I	II	A	4.3-4.4
Marshall Field	46	39	47	IV	IV	B	4.9-5.3
Martin Co.	49	35	64	II	I	C +	3.3-3.7‡
Maryland Casualty	40	40	50	II	II	A −	3.8-4.0
Masonite	44	34	50	IV	III	C +	3.0-3.4

149

NAME OF STOCK	Recent Price (April 30, 1959)	Intrinsic Value Next 12 Mos.	Potential Value 1962-64	RANK according to Probable Market Performance Next 12 Mos.	Appreciation Potentiality to 1962-1964	Quality Grade	Est'd Yield Next 12 Mos. %
Massey-Ferguson	15	11	17	I	III	C+	4.7-5.3
Matson Navigation	45	33	55	V	II	B −	2.7-3.1
May Dept. Stores	49	45	55	II	III	B+	4.5-4.9
Maytag	81	42	64	V	V	B	3.5-4.3
McCall	20	17	30	IV	I	C+	3.3-4.0
McCord Corp.	38	28	45	II	II	B −	5.8-5.9
McCrory-McLellan	15	12	18	IV	II	B −	5.3
McDonnell Aircraft	43	31	60	IV	I	B −	2.3-2.9 ‡
McGraw-Edison	42	36	52	IV	II	B+	3.3-3.6
McGraw-Hill Publ.	59	46	66	V	III	A −	2.8-3.1
McIntyre Porc. Mines	86	80	94	IV	III	B −	3.5
McKesson & Robbins	86	61	75	IV	V	B+	3.3-3.5
McQuay-Norris	22	18	22	IV	V	B −	5.5
Mead Corp.	45	37	53	V	II	B+	3.8-4.0
Mead Johnson	77	50	67	V	V	B+	1.6-1.8
Melville Shoe	28	24	30	III	IV	B	4.6-4.9
Mercantile Stores	33	27	32	III	V	B −	5.0-5.6
Merck & Co.	85	70	75	I	V	B+	1.9-2.1
Mergenthaler	56	38	51	V	V	B −	3.6
Merritt-Chapman	20	19	26	II	I	B −	6.0-7.0
Mesta Machine	59	51	68	IV	II	B −	5.9-5.1
Miami Copper	44	36	40	II	V	C+	9.1
Middle South Util.	48	45	50	II	IV	A	4.0
Midland-Ross	47	38	52	IV	III	B −	6.4
Minneapolis-Honeywell	135	97	144	IV	IV	A −	1.4-1.5
Minneapolis-Moline	22	20	28	I	II	C −	2.7-3.6
Minnesota Mining	147	100	125	III	V	A −	1.0-1.1
Minnesota & Ont. P.	33	29	41	V	II	B	7.0
Minnesota P. & L't	38	33	41	III	IV	A −	4.2-4.6
Mission Corp.	45	47	62	I	I	B	3.1
Mission Development	27	23	36	II	I	B −	Nil
Mississippi R. Fuel	40	35	45	III	III	A −	5.9-4.5
Missouri Pacific	48	39	67	I	I	C+	5.9-9.4
Mohasco Industries	16	12	17	I	IV	C	2.8-4.7
Monarch Mach. Tool	22	19	23	III	IV	B −	5.5-4.5
Monsanto	49	41	55	I	III	B+	2.0 ‡
Montana-Dak. Util.	31	30	40	I	I	B	3.2-3.9
Montana Power	75	62	75	III	V	A	3.2
Montgomery Ward	48	39	53	III	III	B	4.2-4.7
Moore Corp.	112*	84	125	II	III	A	2.0-2.1
Moore-McCormack	22	19	27	IV	II	B −	6.8
Morgan Guaranty Trust	95	93	116	I	II	A	4.2
Morrell (John)	27	22	34	II	II	C+	2.2-3.7
Motor Wheel	17	15	21	III	II	C+	3.5-Nil
Motorola	94	50	75	IV	V	B	1.7-2.0
Mueller Brass	29	27	41	IV	I	B −	4.8-5.9
Murphy (G.C.)	47	46	57	I	II	B+	4.8
Murray Corp.	27	28	32	III	II	C+	2.2-3.0
Myers (F.E.)	40	43	55	IV	I	B	5.3
Nat'l Acme	60	50	68	IV	III	B	4.2-5.0
Nat'l Airlines	24	15	28	V	II	C+	Stk.
Nat'l Bank (Detroit)	59	60	75	I	II	A	3.4
Nat'l Biscuit	52	50	60	II	III	B+	4.6
Nat'l Can	11	12	17	II	I	C+	Stk.-0.9 ‡
Nat'l Cash Register	70	55	85	V	II	B+	1.9-2.0

150

	Recent Price (April 30, 1959)	Intrinsic Value Next 12 Mos.	Potential Value 1962-64	RANK according to		Quality Grade	Est'd Yield Next 12 Mos. %
NAME OF STOCK				Probable Market Performance Next 12 Mos.	Appreciation Potentiality to 1962-1964		
Nat'l Dairy P'd'cts	52	49	52	I	V	A	3.8
Nat'l Distillers	32	26	40	IV	II	B	3.1-3.4
Nat'l Fire Insur.	140	86	140	V	V	B	1.6-2.1
Nat'l Fuel Gas	23	22	26	I	III	A –	4.8-5.2
Nat'l Gypsum	69	47	69	V	V	B	2.9
Nat'l Homes "A"	24	16	24	III	V	C+	Stk.
Nat'l Lead	122	109	140	I	III	A –	2.7-3.1
Nat'l Malleable	37	29	42	II	III	C+	5.4
Nat'l Steel	79	67	83	III	IV	B	3.8-5.1
Nat'l Sugar Refining	38	35	41	IV	IV	B	5.9-6.6
Nat'l Tea	21	19	24	IV	III	B+	3.3-3.8
Nat'l Theatres	11	11	21	I	I	C+	5.9-6.8
Neisner Bros.	14	12	15	IV	IV	B –	5.7
New England Elec.	21	18	21	IV	V	B+	4.8-5.2●
N.J. Zinc	26	30	38	I	I	C+	2.3-3.8
N.Y. Air Brake	29	23	34	I	II	C+	5.5
N.Y. Central	28	25	38	I	I	C+	1.8-3.6
N.Y., Chic. & St. L.	34	29	37	II	IV	B	5.9-6.5
N.Y., N. Haven	8⅝	11	12	I	I	C –	Nil
N.Y. State E. & Gas	57	51	60	II	IV	A –	4.0-4.4
New York Trust	92	96	104	I	III	A	4.5-4.6
Newberry (J.J.)	40	37	47	II	II	B –	5.5
Newmont Mining	89	96	121	II	I	B	2.2-3.4
Newport N. Ship.	43	38	50	V	II	C+	4.7-5.2
Niagara Mohawk	40	36	40	III	V	A –	4.5-5.0●
Noranda Mines	52*	51	70	I	I	B+	3.8-4.2
Norfolk & Western	99	77	95□	III	V	B+	4.0-4.5
No. Amer. Aviation	46	32	58	V	II	B	3.5-4.3
Northern Ind. P. Ser.	51	45	54	III	IV	A	4.2
Northern Nat. Gas	31	31	35	II	III	B+	4.5
Northern Pacific	51	42	71	III	I	B –	4.5-5.4
Northern States P'w' r	25	21	26	III	IV	A –	4.4-4.5
Northrop Corp.	40	26	36	V	V	C+	4.0-4.5
Northwest Airlines	40	21	32	V	V	C	2.0-3.0
Norwich Pharm.	74	46	49	III	V	B+	1.9-2.1
Ohio Edison	65	56	67	III	IV	A –	4.1-4.2
Ohio Oil	40	36	48	V	II	B	4.0-4.3
Oklahoma G. & Elec.	33	27	31	III	V	A	3.0-3.2●
Oklahoma Nat. Gas	29	26	29	III	V	A –	4.3
Olin Mathieson	49	42	60	I	II	B	2.0-2.7
Oliver Corp.	18	13	22	IV	II	C	3.9-4.4
Otis Elevator	71	55	66	V	V	B+	3.4-3.5
Owens-Corning	74	56	85	II	III	B	1.1-1.3
Owens-Ill. Glass	89	78	87	III	V	B+	3.1-3.4
Pabst Brewing	14	11	17	I	II	C	Nil-2.1
Pacific Finance	65	52	64	V	V	B+	3.7-3.8
Pacific G. & Elec.	64	59	66	II	IV	A	4.1-4.2●
Pacific Lighting	52	51	57	II	III	A	4.6
Pacific Tel. & Tel.	164	139	160	III	V	A	4.3-4.9
Page-Hersey Tubes	31*	36	47	I	I	A	2.9-3.9
Pan American Airways	31	20	30	IV	V	B –	2.6
Panhandle Eastern	49	52	74	II	I	A –	3.7
Paramount Pict.	45	39	60	V	I	B –	4.4-5.1
Parke, Davis	44	35	38	I	V	B+	3.0

151

NAME OF STOCK	Recent Price (April 30, 1959)	Intrinsic Value Next 12 Mos.	Potential Value 1962-64	RANK according to Probable Market Performance Next 12 Mos.	Appreciation Potentiality to 1962-1964	Quality Grade	Est'd Yield Next 12 Mos. %
Peabody Coal	14	13	21	III	I	B –	4.3
Penick & Ford	55	44	48	II	V	B +	4.1-4.4
Penn-Dixie Cement	34	33	44	III	I	B	4.1-4.7
Penney (J.C.)	112	105	114	I	IV	A	4.0-4.2
Pennsalt Chem.	89	66	90	IV	IV	B –	2.1-2.5
Penn. Power & Light	58	49	54	III	V	A –	4.3
Pennsylvania R.R.	18	17	24	I	I	C +	4.2
Peoples Drug Stores	49	39	55	IV	III	B	4.1-4.5
Peoples Gas L't & C'ke	58	51	61	I	IV	A –	3.4-3.8
Pepperell M'f'g	65	56	79	IV	II	B	5.4-5.8
Pepsi-Cola	30	26	35	II	II	B –	4.3-4.7
Pet Milk	48	33	45	IV	V	B –	2.7-3.1
Pfizer (Chas.)	130	85	88	IV	V	B +	1.8-2.0
Phelps Dodge	64	58	70	II	III	B	6.3-7.0
Phila. Electric	52	47	52	I	V	A	4.3
Phila. Nat'l Bank	43	43	57	I	I	A	4.4-4.9
Philco	35	26	40	I	III	C +	2.9-4.6
Philip Morris	63	55	65	III	IV	B	4.9-5.1
Phillips Petroleum	51	45	53	III	IV	B +	3.4
Phoenix Insurance	85	82	100	I	II	B +	3.5
Pillsbury Co.	45	30	38	V	V	B	3.1
Pitney-Bowes	39	25	35	V	V	B +	1.5
Pitts. Coke & Chem.	23	22	30	I	I	C +	4.3-5.4
Pitts. & Lake Erie	93	80	94	I	IV	B	4.3-6.5
Pitts. & W. Va.	20	23	27	I	I	C +	6.0-8.0
Pitts. Forgings	16	16	23	II	I	B –	6.6-7.5
Pitts. Plate Glass	76	74	90	III	II	B +	2.9-3.6
Pittston	68	61	126	III	I	B –	1.8-2.4‡
Plymouth Oil	29	28	34	I	II	B –	4.5-5.5
Poor & Co.	28	22	30	III	IV	C +	6.3-7.1
Potomac Elec. P'w'r	29	26	29	II	V	A –	4.3
Procter & Gamble	79	68	79	III	V	A –	2.8-3.0
Public Ser. (Colo.)	51	47	57	II	III	A	3.7-3.8
Public Ser. (Indiana)	46	43	52	II	III	A –	4.7●
Public Ser. (N.H.)	21	19	22	III	IV	B +	4.8-5.0●
Public Ser. Elec. & Gas	41	38	44	II	IV	A –	4.5-4.9
Puget Sound P. & L't	34	34	39	I	III	A –	4.2-4.5
Pullman	61	57	74	III	II	B	5.7-6.6
Pure Oil	45	41	54	II	II	B	3.8-4.4
Quaker Oats	47	46	52	III	III	B +	4.3
Radio Corp. Amer.	62	42	57	II	V	B +	2.4
Ralston Purina	54	39	42	V	V	A –	2.2
Raybestos Manh't'n	62	55	69	II	III	B	5.5-6.0
Rayonier	26	19	30	III	III	C +	1.5-3.8
Raytheon M'f'g	71	47	80	II	III	C +	Nil-2.5
Reading Company	22	24	39	I	I	B –	4.5-6.8
Reed Roller Bit	25	14	32	V	I	B –	Nil
Reliance Insurance	49	47	59	I	II	B	4.5
Republic Aviation	22	21	34	V	I	C +	4.5-6.8
Republic Steel	69	53	67	V	V	B	4.7-5.1
Revere Copper	48	29	55	V	III	B	2.1-2.6
Rexall Drug & Chem.	44	25	42	IV	V	B	1.1-1.6
Reynolds Metals	86	50	81	V	V	B	0.8-1.0‡
Reynolds Tob.	57	45	52	II	V	A –	3.7-3.8

152

NAME OF STOCK	Recent Price (April 30, 1959)	Intrinsic Value Next 12 Mos.	Potential Value 1962-64	RANK according to Probable Market Performance Next 12 Mos.	Appreciation Potentiality to 1962-1964	Quality Grade	Est'd Yield Next 12 Mos. %
Rheem M'f'g	22	18	33	I	I	C+	2.7-3.6
Rhodesian Sel'n Tr.	2⅛	2.1	3.8	V	I	C+	5.6
Richfield Oil	90	84	105	V	II	B	3.9-4.4
Robertshaw-Fulton	46	30	38	IV	V	B−	3.3-3.9
Rochester G. & Elec.	43	38	45	III	IV	A−	4.2-4.7
Rockwell M'f'g	38	31	40	III	IV	B+	4.0-4.3‡
Rockwell-Standard	38	28	36	III	V	B	5.3-5.4‡
Rohm & Haas	623	441	600	II	V	A−	0.3-0.5‡
Royal Crown Cola	20	15	19	IV	V	B−	4.0‡
Royal Dutch Petr.	44	43	68	III	I	B+	3.0-4.3
Royal McBee Corp.	19	15	30	V	I	C+	Nil-1.6
Ruberoid	47	37	47	IV	V	B	4.5-4.7
Safeway Stores	38	34	43	III	III	A−	3.2-3.6
St. Joseph Lead	36	29	48	III	I	C+	3.3-3.6
St. Louis-San Fran. R.R.	23	20	29	I	II	C	4.3-5.4
St. Paul Fire & Marine	60	54	71	III	II	A	2.1-2.2
St. Regis Paper	50	36	53	V	IV	B−	2.8-3.2
San Diego G. & Elec.	29	26	29	II	V	A−	3.6-4.0
Sangamo Electric	49	34	56	II	III	B	3.9-4.3
Schenley Industries	37	28	44	V	II	C+	2.8-3.9
Schering	63	48	51	III	V	B	2.1-2.2
Scott Paper	82	74	88	I	IV	A	2.4-2.7
Scovill M'f'g	25	21	34	V	I	B−	Nil-3.0
Seaboard Air Line R.R.	39	32	40	IV	IV	B	5.1-6.4
Seaboard & Western	12	9.7	15	II	II	C−	Stk.
Seaboard Finance	28	21	32	III	III	A−	3.6-4.3‡
Sealright-Oswego	42	38	42	III	V	B+	3.6-3.8
Sears, Roebuck	43	36	46	II	IV	B+	2.9-3.2
Security-First Nat'l	55	56	67	I	II	A	2.9-3.3
Shamrock Oil	39	37	49	IV	II	B	4.1
Sharon Steel	35	32	50	V	I	C+	5.0-5.7
Shell Oil	85	74	97	IV	III	A−	2.6-2.8
Sheller M'f'g	18	15	23	V	II	B−	4.4-5.5
Sherwin-Williams	224	169	190	V	V	A−	2.6-2.9
Signal Oil "A"	37	40	65	II	I	B	2.2-2.5
Simmons Co.	52	42	63	III	II	B−	6.0
Simonds Saw	91	66	87	III	V	B	4.4-5.2
Sinclair Oil	63	56	75	V	II	B	4.8-4.9
Singer M'f'g	50	43	53	III	IV	B−	4.4-4.0
Skelly Oil	66	64	83	III	II	B+	3.0-3.3
Smith (A.O.)	57	38	50	IV	V	B	2.8-3.5
Smith-Corona March.	17	16	25	V	I	C	5.9
Smith, Kline & French	146	113	117	I	V	A	2.2
Socony Mobil Oil	45	49	65	II	I	A−	4.4-5.6
So. Carolina E. & Gas	36	31	37	II	IV	A−	3.8
So. Puerto Rico Sugar	26	26	43	IV	I	C	3.8-4.8‡
S'th'n Calif. Edison	59	58	65	II	III	A	4.4-4.6
S'th'n Co.	39	33	36	III	V	A	3.5
S'th'n Nat. Gas	40	41	56	II	I	A−	5.0
S'th'n Pacific Co.	68	51	69	V	IV	B−	4.4-5.0
S'th'n Railway	58	44	62	V	IV	B	4.8-5.2
Southwest. Pub. Ser.	44	36	40	III	V	A	3.6●
Spencer Kellogg	19	19	22	I	III	C+	4.2-6.3
Sperry Rand	26	22	35	I	I	B−	3.1
Spiegel, Inc.	39	24	52	I	I	C+	4.6-5.6

153

NAME OF STOCK	Recent Price (April 30, 1959)	Intrinsic Value Next 12 Mos.	Potential Value 1962-64	RANK according to Probable Market Performance Next 12 Mos.	Appreciation Potentiality to 1962-1964	Quality Grade	Est'd Yield Next 12 Mos. %
Springfield Fire & M.	31	31	50	IV	I	B +	3.2
Square D	30	24	34	V	III	B	3.3-3.8
Staley (A.E.)	41	31	38	V	V	B	3.3-3.8 ‡
Standard Brands	66	55	69	IV	IV	B +	3.9-4.2
Standard Oil (Cal.)	55	56	68	I	II	A	3.8-4.4
Standard Oil (Ind.)	51	46	60	III	II	B +	4.1
Standard Oil (Ky.)	68	61	78	III	III	A −	5.1-5.3
Standard Oil (N.J.)	53	52	56	IV	IV	A	4.2-4.0
Standard Oil (Ohio)	64	53	63	IV	V	B	3.9-4.3
Stanley Warner	24	20	34	I	I	B	5.0
Starrett (L.S.)	97	68	92	II	V	B	4.1-4.7
Steel Co. of Canada	77*	74	100	I	I	A	2.5-3.0
Sterling Drug	55	38	45	V	V	B	2.9-3.1
Stevens (J.P.)	29	25	39	III	I	B −	5.2
Stewart-Warner	51	37	52	V	IV	B	4.1-4.5
Stokely-Van Camp	17	14	22	IV	I	C	3.5-4.7 ‡
Stone & Webster	59	57	70	I	II	B +	5.1-6.8
Studebaker-Packard	12	13	12	I	V	C −	Nil
Sun Chemical	13	11	15	III	III	C +	5.4-6.2
Sun Oil	63	68	86	I	I	A −	1.6
Sunbeam	55	53	72	III	I	B +	3.0-3.5
Sunray Mid-Cont.	28	26	36	III	I	B −	5.0-5.2
Sunshine Biscuits	102	88	109	III	IV	B +	4.3
Sutherland Paper	44	38	50	IV	III	B	4.5
Swift & Co.	36	35	48	III	I	B	4.4-5.6
Tampa Electric	50	41	55	III	III	A	2.8
Technicolor	$8\frac{7}{8}$	7.9	14	I	I	C	4.2
Tennessee Corp.	77	52	70	IV	V	B	3.2-3.4
Tenn. Gas Trans.	34	35	42	I	II	A	4.1●
Texaco	85	76	91	II	IV	A	2.8-3.2
Texaco Canada, Ltd.	71*	66	86	I	II	B +	2.3-2.5
Texas Eastern Trans.	32	33	42	I	I	B +	4.4-5.0
Texas Gulf Producing	30	28	44	V	I	B	2.1-2.3
Texas Gulf Sulphur	21	23	34	I	I	B −	5.0-5.7
Texas Pacific Coal & Oil	30	33	45	III	I	B	3.3-4.0
Texas Utilities	67	60	70	I	IV	A	2.8
Thatcher Glass	31	28	34	V	III	B +	4.5-5.2
Thompson Ramo	68	50	77	V	III	B	2.1-2.4
Tidewater Oil	26	21	36	V	I	B −	Stk.
Time, Inc.	71	63	84	IV	II	B	4.9-5.3
Timken Roller	57	41	51	IV	V	B	3.5-3.9
Toledo Edison	17	15	18	III	IV	A −	4.7
Torrington	30	29	40	I	I	B	6.0
Transamerica	29	27	36	II	II	A −	2.8-2.9
Transcont'l Gas Pipe	23	24	28	II	II	A −	4.3-4.8●
Trans World Airlines	20	16	24	I	II	C	Nil
Travelers Insurance	90	88	100	II	III	A −	1.3-1.4
Tri-Continental	42	38	50	II	II	A −	3.9
Truax-Traer Coal	23	21	31	IV	I	C +	7.0
Twentieth Cen.-Fox	39	33	60	IV	I	B −	4.1-4.9
Underwood	27	26	40	I	I	C	Nil
Union Bag-Camp	48	33	47	V	V	B	3.1
Union Carbide	134	117	150	I	III	A −	2.7-2.8
Union Electric	34	33	38	II	III	A −	4.5-4.7●

154

NAME OF STOCK	Recent Price (April 30, 1959)	Intrinsic Value Next 12 Mos.	Potential Value 1962-64	RANK according to Probable Market Performance Next 12 Mos.	Appreciation Potentiality to 1962-1964	Quality Grade	Est'd Yield Next 12 Mos. %
Union Oil (Cal.)	45	41	60	V	I	B+	2.2-3.1
Union Pacific	35	33	40	II	III	B+	4.6-4.9
Union Tank Car	34	34	40	II	II	B+	5.0-5.1
United Air Lines	38	28	51	V	I	C+	1.3‡
United Aircraft	60	63	77	II	I	B+	5.0-4.2
United Biscuit	24	23	37	V	I	B	3.3
United Carbon	84	64	85	III	IV	B+	2.4
United Corp.	9¼	8.9	10	I	IV	A−	2.7
United Elec. Coal	37	29	43	IV	II	C+	4.3-4.7
United Engineering	21	15	22	IV	IV	B−	4.8
United Fruit	39	42	55	IV	I	B−	5.1
United Gas Corp.	42	39	48	I	III	A−	3.6-3.8
United Gas Imp't	58	50	55	I	V	A−	4.1
United-Greenfield	18	14	22	III	II	B−	5.6-6.1
United Merchants	20	16	24	III	II	C+	5.0-6.0
United Shoe Mach.	47	44	58	III	II	B	5.3
U.S. Fidelity & G'ty	86	72	97	III	III	B+	2.3-2.6
U.S. Fire Insurance	32	30	37	I	III	B+	3.1-3.4
U.S. Gypsum	114	82	95	V	V	B+	2.6-2.9
U.S. Industries	13	10	15	II	III	C	Nil-3.1
U.S. Lines	33	28	39	IV	II	B−	6.1
U.S. Pipe & Foundry	26	23	32	IV	II	B	4.6
U.S. Playing Card	97	84	96	III	V	B	5.2
U.S. Plywood	52	42	68	I	I	B−	4.3-4.8
U.S. Rubber	57	39	60	V	IV	B	3.5
U.S. Smelting	34	39	48	I	I	C	Nil-1.5
U.S. Steel	91	78	91	III	V	A−	4.1-4.4
U.S. Tobacco	26	24	24	IV	V	B+	4.6
Universal Leaf Tob.	53	39	44	V	V	B+	4.2
Utah Power & Light	34	31	36	III	IV	A	3.8-3.9●
Van Norman	12	8.9	12	V	V	C	Nil
Vanadium	36	35	53	III	I	B	2.8-3.9
Vick Chemical	134	63	87	V	V	B	1.3-1.5‡
Victor Chemical	38	30	37	IV	V	B	2.6
Va.-Carolina Chem.	31	20	42	III	I	C−	Nil
Va. Elec. & Power	39	33	41	III	IV	A	3.1●
Virginian Railway	48	32	52□	V	IV	B	4.2-5.2
Walgreen Co.	54	39	53	V	V	B+	3.0
Walker (Hiram)	35	29	38	V	IV	B+	4.0-4.6
Walworth	17	12	20	IV	II	C+	3.5-2.6
Warner Bros.	40	27	45	I	III	B−	3.0-3.4
Warner-Lambert	110	68	96	V	V	B	2.8‡
Warner & Swasey	31	24	35	II	III	B−	4.5-4.8
Washington Gas L't	51	48	53	I	IV	A	4.4-4.5
Washington Water	45	43	53	II	II	A−	4.4-4.7●
Wesson Oil	35	32	42	III	II	C+	4.0-5.4
West Indies Sugar	47	50	61	V	I	C	2.1§
West Ky. Coal	18	13	20	V	III	C+	Nil
West Penn Electric	37	32	37	III	V	A−	4.3
West Va. Pulp & Paper	46	38	55	V	II	B	2.6-3.5
Western Airlines	35	20	35	V	V	B−	2.3‡
Western Auto Supply	31	21	27	IV	V	B	3.9-4.2
Western Md. Railway	77	66	82	IV	IV	B−	4.7-5.1
Western Pacific R.R.	79	64	78	II	V	B−	3.8-4.7

155

NAME OF STOCK	Recent Price (April 30, 1959)	Intrinsic Value Next 12 Mos.	Potential Value 1962-64	RANK according to Probable Market Performance Next 12 Mos.	RANK according to Appreciation Potentiality to 1962-1964	Quality Grade	Est'd Yield Next 12 Mos. %
Western Union	36	26	41	IV	III	B −	3.3-**3.9**
Westinghouse Air	36	29	50	II	I	B −	3.3-**4.2**
Westinghouse Elec.	86	67	89	II	IV	B +	2.3-**2.8**
Weyerhaeuser	45	42	50	IV	III	A −	**3.4**
Wheeling Steel	57	48	72	III	II	B −	5.3-**6.0**
Whirlpool Corp.	36	25	37	IV	IV	B −	3.3-**4.2**
White Motor	48	30	45	III	V	B	3.6-**4.2**
Wilson & Co.	35	26	36	V	IV	C +	4.0-**4.6**
Winn-Dixie Stores	41	42	44	I	IV	A	2.6-**2.9**
Wisconsin Elec. P'r.	39	37	42	II	IV	A −	4.5-**4.7**
Wisconsin Pub. Ser.	26	25	29	II	III	B +	4.8-**5.0**
Woolworth (F.W.)	54	51	65	II	II	B +	4.6-**5.0**
Worthington	78	54	77	V	V	B	3.3-**3.5**
Wrigley (Wm.)	88	87	98	II	III	A −	**5.1**
Yale & Towne	33	29	35	III	IV	B	**4.5**
Young Spring & Wire	35	32	42	III	II	C +	**5.7**
Youngstown S. & T.	120	104	154	IV	I	B	4.2-**5.0**
Zenith Radio	107	48	120	III	III	B	1.9-**2.5**

*—Canadian Funds.

☐—Assumes merger between Norfolk & Western and Virginian R.R.'s.

‡—Plus stock.

•—Dividends believed partly exempt from ordinary income tax.

§—Plus possible distribution from sale of properties.

NOTE: Where the dividend estimate is a range, the figures are so presented as to indicate the probable direction of any change. The yield based on the more likely dividend is printed in bold-face type.

Due to mergers and substitutions, the number of stocks appearing in the *Weekly Summary-Index* may vary slightly from week to week, but changes are insignificant.

TABLE 2

Here in terms of Quality Grade is the order of all the stocks in *The Value Line Investment Survey* as of May 11, 1959. Revisions of Quality Grades are infrequent. Investors interested in avoiding risk over the very long term will usually do best in stocks of the highest quality.

804 Stocks Reviewed by The Value Line Investment Survey, May 11, 1959, Ranked According to Quality

Stocks with a Quality Grade of A+

Brooklyn Un. Gas	Florida P'w'r & L't	Lincoln Nat'l Life
Conn. Gen'l Life	Houston L't & P'w'r	Texas Utilities
	Int'l Business Mach.	

Stocks with a Quality Grade of A

Amer. Elec. Power	Eastman Kodak	Manufacturers Trust
Amer. Invest. (Ill.)		Marine Midland
Amer. Tel. & Tel.	Firstamerica	Middle South Util.
Amer. Trust	First Nat'l (Bos.)	Montana Power
Arizona Pub. Ser.	First Nat'l (Chi.)	Moore Corp.
Associates Invest.	First Nat'l (St. L.)	Morgan Guaranty Tr.
Atlantic City Elec.	First Nat'l City	
	Florida Power	Nat'l Bank (Detroit)
Balt. Gas & Elec.		Nat'l Dairy P'd'cts
Bank of America	Gen'l Electric	New York Trust
Bankers Trust	Gen'l Foods	Northern Ind. P. Ser.
	Gen'l Tel. & Electro.	
Cen. & South West	Gerber Products	Oklahoma G. & Elec.
Chase Man. Bank	Girard Trust	
Chemical Corn	Gulf States Util.	Pacific G. & Elec.
Cleveland Electric		Pacific Lighting
Commonwealth Ed.	Hanover Bank	Pacific Tel. & Tel.
Consumers Power	Hartford Fire Ins.	Page-Hersey Tubes
Cont'l Assurance		Penney (J. C.)
Cont'l Casualty	Idaho Power	Phila. Electric
Cont'l Illinois	Indianapolis P. & L't	Phila. Nat'l Bank
Corn Products	Industrial Accept'ce	Public Ser. (Colo.)
	Insurance Co. N. Amer.	
Delaware P'w'r & L't	Irving Trust (N. Y.)	St. Paul Fire & Marine
Detroit Edison		Scott Paper
Dominion Stores	Laclede Gas	Security-First Nat'l
Duke Power	Long Island L't'g	Smith, Kline & French
Du Pont	Louisville G. & Elec.	S'th'n Calif. Edison

157

S'th'n Co.
Southwest. Pub. Ser.
Stand'd Oil (Cal.)
Stand'd Oil (N. J.)
Steel Co. of Canada

Tampa Electric
Tenn. Gas Trans.
Texaco

Utah Power & L't

Va. Elec. & P'w'r

Washington Gas L't
Winn-Dixie Stores

Stocks with a Quality Grade of A—

Adams Express
Aetna Life Ins.
Amer. Can
Amer. Chicle
Amer. Home P'd'cts
Amer. Natural Gas
Amer. Stores

Beneficial Finance
Borden Company
Boston Edison
Brown Shoe
Buckeye Pipe Line

C.I.T. Financial
Campbell Soup
Carolina P'w'r & L't
Cen. Hudson G. & E.
Cen. Illinois Light
Cen. Illinois P. S.
Cincinnati G. & Elec.
Community Pub. Ser.
Conn. L't & P'w'r
Consol. Edison
Consol. Nat. Gas
Cont'l Can
Cont'l Insurance
Corning Glass
Creole Petroleum

Dayton P'w'r & L't
Dow Chemical
Duquesne Light

Equitable Gas

Family Finance
Federated Dep't St.
Fidelity-Phenix Ins.
Fireman's Fund
First Nat'l Stores

Gen'l Amer. Trans.
Gen'l Public Util.
Glens Falls Ins.
Grand Union
G't Amer. Insur.
G't Atl'c & P'c'f'c
Gulf Oil

Hartford Elec. L't
Household Finance

Illinois Power

Jewel Tea Co.

Kansas City P. & L't
Kansas G. & Elec.
Kansas P'w'r & L't
Kellogg
Kroger

Lehman Corp.
Lily-Tulip Cup

Madison Fund, Inc.
Maryland Casualty
McGraw-Hill Publ.
Minneapolis-H'w'll
Minnesota Mining
Minnesota P. & L't
Mississippi R. Fuel

Nat'l Fuel Gas
Nat'l Lead
N. Y. State E. & Gas
Niagara Mohawk
Northern States P'w'r

Ohio Edison
Oklahoma Nat. Gas

Panhandle Eastern

Penn. P'w'r & L't
Peoples Gas L't & C'ke
Potomac Elec. P'w'r
Procter & Gamble
Public Ser. (Indiana)
Public Ser. Elec. & Gas
Puget Sound P. & L't

Ralston Purina
Reynolds Tob.
Rochester G. & Elec.
Rohm & Haas

Safeway Stores
San Diego G. & Elec.
Seaboard Finance
Shell Oil
Sherwin-Williams
Socony Mobil Oil
So. Carolina E. & Gas
S'th'n Nat. Gas
Stand'd Oil (Ky.)
Sun Oil

Toledo Edison
Transamerica
Transcont'l Gas Pipe
Travelers Insurance
Tri-Continental

Union Carbide
Union Electric
United Corp.
United Gas Corp.
United Gas Imp't
U. S. Steel

Washington Water
West Penn Electric
Weyerhaeuser
Wisconsin Elec. P'r
Wrigley (Wm.)

Stocks with a Quality Grade of B+

Abbott Laboratories
Addressograph
Aetna Fire Ins.
Allied Chemical
Aluminium, Ltd.
Aluminum Co.
Amerada Petroleum
Amer. Cyanamid
Amer. Insurance
Amer.-Marietta

Amer. Snuff
Amer. Tobacco
Arkansas La. Gas
Atchison, T. & S. F.
Atlantic Refining
Atlas Corp.

Beatrice Foods
Bendix Aviation
Bethlehem Steel

Boston Insurance
British Amer. Oil

Camden Fire Ins.
Canada Cement
Canadian Oil Cos.
Carnation
Cen. Maine P'w'r
Champion Paper
Cincinnati Milling

158

Columbia Gas
Columbus & S. O. El.
Combustion Eng.
Commercial Credit
Container Corp.
Cont'l Oil
Crown Zellerbach

Dana Corp.
Denver & Rio Grande
Domin. F'dries & St.

El Paso Nat. Gas
Empire Dist. Elec.
Endicott Johnson
Ex-Cell-O

Federal-Mogul
Firestone Tire
Food Fair
Foremost Dairies
Freeport Sulphur

Gen'l Amer. Invest.
Gen'l Dynamics
Gen'l Mills
Gen'l Motors
Gen'l Portland Cem.
Gen'l Refractories
Goodrich
Goodyear Tire
Greyhound

Halliburton Oil
Harbison-Walker
Harris-Intertype
Heinz (H. J.)
Hercules Powder
Hershey Chocolate
Home Insurance

Imperial Oil
Ingersoll-Rand
Inland Steel

Int'l Nickel
Int'l Paper
Int'l Salt
Int'l Shoe
Interprov'c'l Pipe
Interstate Power
Iowa-Ill. G. & Elec.
Iowa P'w'r & L't

Johns-Manville
Johnson & Johnson

Kansas City South'n
Kimberly-Clark

Libbey-Owens-Ford
Liggett & Myers
Lone Star Cement
Lone Star Gas
Louisiana Land

May Dept. Stores
McGraw-Edison
McKesson & Robbins
Mead Corp.
Mead Johnson
Merck & Co.
Monsanto
Murphy (G. C.)

Nat'l Biscuit
Nat'l Cash Register
Nat'l Tea
New England Elec.
Noranda Mines
Norfolk & Western
Northern Nat. Gas
Norwich Pharm.

Otis Elevator
Owens-Ill. Glass

Pacific Finance
Parke, Davis

Penick & Ford
Pfizer (Chas.)
Phillips Petroleum
Phoenix Insurance
Pitney-Bowes
Pitts. Plate Glass
Public Ser. (N. H.)

Quaker Oats

Radio Corp. Amer.
Rockwell M'f'g
Royal Dutch Petr.

Sealright-Oswego
Sears, Roebuck
Skelly Oil
Springfield Fire & M.
Stand'd Brands
Stand'd Oil (Ind.)
Stone & Webster
Sunbeam
Sunshine Biscuits

Texaco Canada, Ltd.
Texas Eastern Trans.

Union Oil (Cal.)
Union Pacific
Union Tank Car
United Aircraft
United Carbon
U. S. Fidelity & G'ty
U. S. Fire Insurance
U. S. Gypsum
U. S. Tobacco
Universal Leaf Tob.

Walgreen Co.
Walker (Hiram)
Westinghouse Elec.
Wisconsin Pub. Ser.
Woolworth (F. W.)

Stocks with a Quality Grade of B

Abitibi Power & Paper
Air Reduction
Algoma Steel
Allied Mills
Allied Stores
Alpha Portland
Amer. Agri. Chem.
Amer. Airlines
Amer. Bakeries
Amer. Brake Shoe
Amer. Broadc.-Par't
Amer. Chain
Amer. Crystal Sugar
Amer. Mach. & F'dry
Amer. Metal-Climax
Amer. Molasses
Amer. Optical

Amer. Potash
Amer. Seating
Amer. Sugar Ref'g
Amer. Surety
Amphenol-Borg
Anchor Hocking
Anheuser-Busch
Arkansas Fuel Oil
Armco Steel
Armstrong Cork
Arvin Industries
Ashland Oil
Assoc. Dry Goods
Atlas Powder

Babcock & Wilcox
Beech-Life Savers

Best & Co.
Black & Decker
Blaw-Knox
Boeing
Borg-Warner
Briggs & Stratton
Burroughs

Calif. Packing
Canada Dry
Canadian Brew's
Cannon Mills
Carrier
Caterpillar Tractor
Cen. Aguirre Sugar
Chain Belt
Champlin Oil

159

Chemetron
Chesapeake & Ohio
Chic. Pneu. Tool
Cities Service
Coca-Cola
Colgate-Palmolive
Columbia Br'c't'g
Columbian Carbon
Consol. Cigar
Consolidation Coal
Cont'l Baking
Cutler-Hammer

Deere & Co.
Diamond Alkali
Diamond Gardner
Douglas Aircraft
Dresser Industries

Eastern Air Lines
Eaton M'f'g
Elec. Storage Bat.

Falconbridge
Falstaff Brewing
Fansteel Metal.
Federal Paper B'd
Food Machinery
Ford Motor
Ford of Canada

Gardner-Denver
Gen'l Baking
Gen'l Cigar
Gen'l Tire
Genesco, Inc.
Gillette
Gould-National
Grace (W. R.)
Grant (W. T.)
G't Northern Iron
G't Northern R'lw'y
G't Western Sugar

Holly Sugar
Hooker Chemical

Int'l Harvester
Int'l Tel. & Tel.

Kennecott Cop'r
Kerr McGee Oil

Kresge (S. S.)
Kress (S. H.)

Lehigh Portland
Link-Belt
Lorillard (P.)
Louisville & Nash.

Macy (R. H.)
Mallory (P. R.)
Marshall Field
Maytag
Melville Shoe
Minnesota & Ont. P.
Mission Corp.
Montana-Dak. Util.
Montgomery Ward
Motorola
Myers (F. E.)

Nat'l Acme
Nat'l Distillers
Nat'l Fire Insur.
Nat'l Gypsum
Nat'l Steel
Nat'l Sugar Refining
N. Y., Chic. & St. L.
Newmont Mining
No. Amer. Aviation

Ohio Oil
Olin Mathieson
Owens-Corning

Penn-Dixie Cement
Peoples Drug Stores
Pepperell M'f'g
Phelps Dodge
Philip Morris
Pillsbury Co.
Pitts. & Lake Erie
Pullman
Pure Oil

Raybestos Manh't'n
Reliance Insurance
Republic Steel
Revere Copper
Rexall Drug & Chem.
Reynolds Metals
Richfield Oil
Rockwell-Standard

Ruberoid

Sangamo Electric
Schering
Seaboard Air Line R. R.
Shamrock Oil
Signal Oil "A"
Simonds Saw
Sinclair Oil
Smith (A. O.)
S'th'n Railway
Square D
Staley (A. E.)
Stand'd Oil (Ohio)
Stanley Warner
Starrett (L. S.)
Sterling Drug
Stewart-Warner
Sutherland Paper
Swift & Co.

Tennessee Corp.
Texas Gulf Pr'd'cing
Texas P'c'f'c C'l & Oil
Thompson Ramo
Time, Inc.
Timken Roller
Torrington

Union Bag-Camp
United Biscuit
United Shoe Mach.
U. S. Pipe & F'dry
U. S. Playing Card
U. S. Rubber

Vanadium
Vick Chemical
Victor Chemical
Virginian R'lw'y

Warner-Lambert
West Va. Pulp & P'p'r
Western Auto S'ply
White Motor
Worthington

Yale & Towne
Youngstown S. & T.

Zenith Radio

Stocks with a Quality Grade of B—

Allegheny Ludlum
Allis-Chalmers
Amer. Bank Note
Amer. Bosch Arma
Amer. Distilling
Amer. Export
Amer. Metal P'd'cts
Amer. Smelting
Amer. Steel Foundries

Anaconda
Anderson-Prichard
Atlantic Coast Line

Bayuk Cigars
Bell Aircraft
Bliss & Laughlin
Bond Stores
Bridgeport Brass

Bristol-Myers
Brown & Sharpe
Brunswick-Balke
Bucyrus-Erie

Canada Iron F'dries
Canadian Pacific
Carborundum
Chic. G't Western

160

Chic. Rock Island
Chrysler
Clark Equipment
Cleveland-Cliffs
Clevite
Cluett, Peabody
Colorado Fuel
Consol. Foods

Daystrom
Delaware & Hudson
Distillers Corp.-S.
Dome Mines
Domin. Steel & Coal

Eagle-Picher
Elec. Auto-Lite
Emerson Electric

Fairbanks, Morse
Flintkote

Gen'l Cable
Gen'l R'lw'y Signal
Getty Oil
Glidden
Granite City Steel
G't Northern Paper
Green (H. L.)

Hammermill
Harshaw Chemical
Hoffman Electronics
Hollinger Consol.
Houdaille Ind'tr's
Hudson Bay M'ng

Illinois Central
Interchemical Corp.
Interlake Iron
Int'l Minerals

Interstate Dept.
Island Creek Coal

Jones & Laughlin
Joy M'f'g

Kaiser Aluminum
Kelsey-Hayes Co.
King-Seeley
Koppers

Lee Rubber & Tire
Lehn & Fink
Lerner Stores
Lockheed

Magnavox
Manhattan Shirt
Matson Navigation
McCord Corp.
McCrory-McLellan
McDonnell Aircraft
McIntyre Porc. Mines
McQuay-Norris
Mercantile Stores
Mergenthaler
Merritt-Chapman
Mesta Machine
Midland-Ross
Mission Development
Monarch Mach. Tool
Moore-McCormack
Mueller Brass

Neisner Bros.
Newberry (J. J.)
Northern Pacific

Pan American Airways
Paramount Pict.
Peabody Coal

Pennsalt Chem.
Pepsi-Cola
Pet Milk
Pitts. Forgings
Pittston
Plymouth Oil

Reading Company
Reed Roller Bit
Robertshaw-Fulton
Royal Crown Cola

St. Regis Paper
Scovill M'f'g
Sheller M'f'g
Simmons Co.
Singer M'f'g
S'th'n Pacific Co.
Sperry Rand
Stevens (J. P.)
Sunray Mid-Cont.

Texas Gulf Sulphur
Thatcher Glass
Tidewater Oil
Twentieth Cen.-Fox

United Engineering
United Fruit
United-Greenfield
U. S. Lines
U. S. Plywood

Warner Bros.
Warner & Swasey
Western Airlines
Western Md. R'lw'y
Western Pacific R. R.
Western Union
Westinghouse Air
Wheeling Steel
Whirlpool Corp.

Stocks with a Quality Grade of C+

ACF Industries
ASR Products
Amer. Motors
Amer.-Standard
Amer. Viscose
Archer-Daniels
Armour & Co.
Atlas Steels

Balt. & Ohio
Bath Iron Works
Bliss (E. W.)
Budd
Burlington Ind'tr's

Case (J. I.)
Celotex
Cerro de Pasco
Collins Radio

Columbia Pictures
Congoleum-Nairn
Consol. Electrodyn.
Consol. Mining
Cooper-Bessemer
Cornell Dubilier
Crane Company
Crown Cork
Crucible Steel
Curtis Publishing
Curtiss-Wright

Decca Records
Delta Airlines
Divco-Wayne
Dr. Pepper

Eastern Gas & Fuel
Emerson Radio

Fairchild Engine
Fedders Corp.
Fibreboard Paper
Fruehauf Trailer

Gen'l Precision Eq.
Georgia-Pacific
Gimbel Bros.
Glen Alden Corp.
Grumman
Gulf Mobile & O.

Homestake Mining

Industrial Rayon
Inspiration C. Cop'r

Kearney & Trecker

161

Loew's, Inc.
Loew's Theatres
Lone Star Steel
Lowenstein

Mack Trucks
Magma Copper
Martin Co.
Masonite
Massey-Ferguson
McCall
Miami Copper
Missouri Pacific
Morrell (John)
Motor Wheel
Murray Corp.

Nat'l Airlines
Nat'l Can
Nat'l Homes "A"

Nat'l Malleable
Nat'l Theatres
N. J. Zinc
N. Y. Air Brake
N. Y. Central
Newport N. Ship.
Northrop Corp.

Pennsylvania R. R.
Philco
Pitts. Coke & Chem.
Pitts. & W. Va.
Poor & Co.

Rayonier
Raytheon M'f'g
Republic Aviation
Rheem M'f'g
Rhodesian Sel'n Tr.
Royal McBee Corp.

St. Joseph Lead
Schenley Industries
Sharon Steel
Spencer Kellogg
Spiegel, Inc.
Sun Chemical

Truax-Traer Coal

United Air Lines
United Elec. Coal
United Merchants

Walworth
Wesson Oil
West Ky. Coal
Wilson & Co.

Young Spring & Wire

Stocks with a Quality Grade of C

Admiral Corp.
Alco Products
Alleghany Corp.
Avco M'f'g

Baldwin-Lima-Ham.
Barker Bros.
Bigelow-Sanford
Bohn Aluminum
Braniff Airways
Bullard

Capital Airlines
Celanese
Chic. Milwaukee
Chic. & N. W.
Collins & Aikman
Commercial Solv.
Conde Nast
Cont'l Motors

Cuban-Amer. Sugar
Cudahy Packing

Delaware, Lack.

Erie Railroad

Foster Wheeler

Holland Furnace
Howe Sound

Int'l Silver

Lehigh Valley R. R.
Libby, McNeill

Mohasco Industries

Northwest Airlines

Oliver Corp.

Pabst Brewing

St. Louis-San Fran. R.R.
Smith-Corona March.
So. Puerto Rico Sugar
Stokely-Van Camp

Technicolor
Trans World Airlines

Underwood
U. S. Industries
U. S. Smelting

Van Norman

West Indies Sugar

Stocks with a Quality Grade of C—

Dumont Lab's
Minneapolis-Moline

N. Y., N. Haven
Seaboard & Western

Studebaker-Packard
Va.-Carolina Chem.

NOTE: Due to mergers and substitutions, the number of stocks appearing in *The Value Line Investment Survey, Weekly Summary-Index*, may vary slightly from week to week, but changes are insignificant.

TABLE 3

Here is the order of all stocks in *The Value Line Investment Survey* according to estimated relative Market Performance in the Next 12 Months, as published May 11, 1959. Rank for Probable Market Performance in the Next 12 Months may change in the course of a year, as the subject stock's price position changes in relation to all other stocks, or as new evidence requires revision of the earnings and dividend estimates on which its Rating is based.

804 Stocks Reviewed by
The Value Line Investment Survey,
May 11, 1959, Ranked According to Probable Market
Performance in the Next 12 Months

Stocks Ranked I for Probable Market Performance in the Next 12 Months

Name of Stock	Recent Price [4/30/59]	Name of Stock	Recent Price [4/30/59]	Name of Stock	Recent Price [4/30/59]
ASR Products	12	Cleveland Electric	52	Ford Motor	64
Admiral Corp.	22	Collins & Aikman	24	Ford of Canada	140
Algoma Steel	37*	Columbia Br'c't'g	46	Foremost Dairies	20
Alleghany Corp.	13	Columbian Carbon	51		
Amerada Petroleum	92	Conn. L't & P'w'r	26	Girard Trust	56
Amer. Chicle	54	Cont'l Illinois	122	Glens Falls Ins.	40
Amer. Distilling	44	Cont'l Insurance	58	G't Northern Iron	30
Amer. Mach. & F'dry	88	Corn Products	55	Gulf Mobile & O.	29
Amer. Natural Gas	70	Crane Company	40		
Amer. Tobacco	105	Crucible Steel	28	Hanover Bank	52
Amer. Viscose	50	Cudahy Packing	14	Hartford Fire Ins.	187
Anaconda	66			Holland Furnace	14
Arkansas La. Gas	64	Delaware, Lack.	11	Hollinger Consol.	34
Atlas Corp.	7	Detroit Edison	44	Home Insurance	52
				Howe Sound	18
Balt. Gas & Elec.	46	Eastern Air Lines	41		
Balt. & Ohio	45	Eastman Kodak	88	Imperial Oil	45
Bank of America	48	Elec. Auto-Lite	44	Indianapolis P. & L't	40
Bankers Trust	80	Emerson Radio	22	Interprov'c'l Pipe	54*
Bigelow-Sanford	17	Erie Railroad	13	Irving Trust (N. Y.)	38
Boston Insurance	35	Ex-Cell-O	41		
Brooklyn Un. Gas	54			Kearney & Trecker	17
Buckeye Pipe Line	33	Falconbridge	27*	Kerr McGee Oil	65
Burlington Ind'tr's	19	Falstaff Brewing	24	King-Seeley	34
		Fedders Corp.	20	Kresge (S. S.)	34
Canada Cement	35*	Fidelity-Phenix Ins.	63		
Canadian Oil Cos.	30*	Fireman's Fund	58	Laclede Gas	20
Canadian Pacific	30	Firstamerica	22	Lehigh Valley R. R.	8¾
Capital Airlines	20	First Nat'l (Bos.)	86	Lincoln Nat'l Life	221
Celanese	32	First Nat'l (Chi.)	345	Long Island L't'g	35
Cen. Maine P'w'r	27	First Nat'l (St. L.)	78		
Chase Man. Bank	59	First Nat'l City	78	Magma Copper	63
Chemical Corn	62	Food Fair	38	Mallory (P. R.)	43

163

Name of Stock	Recent Price [4/30/59]	Name of Stock	Recent Price [4/30/59]	Name of Stock	Recent Price [4/30/59]
Manufacturers Trust	54	Page-Hersey Tubes	31*	Stand'd Oil (Cal.)	55
Marine Midland	25	Parke, Davis	44	Stanley Warner	24
Massey-Ferguson	15	Penney (J. C.)	112	Steel Co. of Canada	77*
Merck & Co.	85	Pennsylvania R. R.	18	Stone & Webster	59
Minneapolis-Moline	22	Peoples Gas L't & C'ke	58	Studebaker-Packard	12
Mission Corp.	45	Phila. Electric	52	Sun Oil	63
Missouri Pacific	48	Phila. Nat'l Bank	43		
Mohasco Industries	16	Philco	35	Technicolor	8⅞
Monsanto	49	Phoenix Insurance	85	Tenn. Gas Trans.	34
Montana-Dak. Util.	31	Pitts. Coke & Chem.	23	Texaco Canada, Ltd.	71*
Morgan Guaranty Tr.	95	Pitts. & Lake Erie	93	Texas Eastern Trans.	32
Morrell (John)	27	Pitts. & W. Va.	20	Texas Gulf Sulphur	21
Murphy (G. C.)	47	Plymouth Oil	29	Texas Utilities	67
		Puget Sound P. & L't	34	Torrington	30
Nat'l Bank (Detroit)	59			Trans World Airlines	20
Nat'l Dairy P'd'cts	52	Reading Company	22		
Nat'l Fuel Gas	23	Reliance Insurance	49	Underwood	27
Nat'l Lead	122	Rheem M'f'g	22	Union Carbide	134
Nat'l Theatres	11			United Corp.	9¼
N. J. Zinc	26	St. Louis-San Fran. R. R.	23	United Gas Corp.	42
N. Y. Air Brake	29	Scott Paper	82	United Gas Imp't	58
N. Y. Central	28	Security-First Nat'l	55	U. S. Fire Insurance	32
N. Y., N. Haven	8⅝	Smith, Kline & French	146	U. S. Plywood	52
New York Trust	92	Spencer Kellogg	19	U. S. Smelting	34
Noranda Mines	52*	Sperry Rand	26		
		Spiegel, Inc.	39	Warner Bros.	40
Olin Mathieson	49			Washington Gas L't	51
				Winn-Dixie Stores	41
Pabst Brewing	14				

Stocks Ranked II for Probable Market Performance in the Next 12 Months

Name	Price	Name	Price	Name	Price
Abbott Laboratories	80	Carrier	44	Dominion Stores	78*
Allied Chemical	112	Case (J. I.)	23	Dow Chemical	88
Amer. Brake Shoe	49	Cen. Hudson G. & E.	22	Duke Power	47
Amer. Broadc.-Par't	27	Cerro de Pasco	41	Du Pont	242
Amer. Elec. Power	51	Champlin Oil	24	Duquesne Light	25
Amer. Motors	38	Chic. G't Western	49		
Amer. Seating	40	Chic. Rock Island	37	Empire Dist. Elec.	25
Amer. Snuff	60	Chrysler	65	Equitable Gas	38
Amer. Tel. & Tel.	252	Cincinnati G. & Elec.	34		
Amer. Trust	58	Coca-Cola	132	Fansteel Metal.	57
Anderson-Prichard	35	Colorado Fuel	26	Freeport Sulphur	35
Anheuser-Busch	26	Columbia Gas	22		
Archer-Daniels	46	Commercial Solv.	17	Gen'l Baking	13
Armour & Co.	24	Commonwealth Ed.	61	Gen'l Dynamics	58
Arvin Industries	26	Community Pub. Ser.	24	Gen'l Foods	78
Ashland Oil	24	Conn. Gen'l Life	382	Gen'l Mills	108
Atlas Steels	27*	Consol. Edison	64	Gen'l Tel. & Electro.	71
		Consumers Power	54	Gerber Products	68
Bliss & Laughlin	27	Cont'l Assurance	144	Getty Oil	24
Bohn Aluminum	30	Curtis Publishing	12	Grant (W. T.)	45
Borden Company	79			G't Amer. Insur.	42
Boston Edison	61	Delaware P'w'r & L't	63	Greyhound	23
Braniff Airways	15	Delta Airlines	32	Gulf Oil	114
Brown & Sharpe	31	Diamond Alkali	54	Gulf States Util.	58
		Diamond Gardner	33		
Cannon Mills	66	Dome Mines	18	Hartford Elec. L't	71
Carborundum	43	Domin. F'dries & St.	49*	Hershey Chocolate	76

164

Name of Stock	Recent Price [4/30/59]	Name of Stock	Recent Price [4/30/59]	Name of Stock	Recent Price [4/30/59]
Hooker Chemical	40	Mission Development	27	San Diego G. & Elec.	29
Houston L't & P'w'r	72	Moore Corp.	112*	Sangamo Electric	49
				Seaboard & Western	12
Idaho Power	45	Nat'l Biscuit	52	Sears, Roebuck	43
Illinois Central	47	Nat'l Can	11	Signal Oil "A"	37
Illinois Power	41	Nat'l Malleable	37	Socony Mobil Oil	45
Industrial Rayon	23	N. Y., Chic. & St. L.	34	So. Carolina E. & Gas	36
Inspiration C. Cop'r	44	N. Y. State E. & Gas	57	S'th'n Calif. Edison	59
Interlake Iron	27	Newberry (J. J.)	40	S'th'n Nat. Gas	40
Int'l Business Mach.	392	Newmont Mining	89	Starrett (L. S.)	97
Int'l Minerals	35	Northern Nat. Gas	31		
Int'l Shoe	36			Texaco	85
Iowa P'w'r & L't	37	Owens-Corning	74	Transamerica	29
				Transcont'l Gas Pipe	23
Johnson & Johnson	50	Pacific G. & Elec.	64	Travelers Insurance	90
		Pacific Lighting	52	Tri-Continental	42
Kansas City P. & L't	54	Panhandle Eastern	49		
Kennecott Cop'r	114	Penick & Ford	55	Union Electric	34
		Pepsi-Cola	30	Union Pacific	35
Lerner Stores	21	Phelps Dodge	64	Union Tank Car	34
Libbey-Owens-Ford	57	Pitts. Forgings	16	United Aircraft	60
Liggett & Myers	97	Potomac Elec. P'w'r	29	U. S. Industries	13
Loew's Theatres	14	Public Ser. (Colo.)	51		
Lone Star Cement	33	Public Ser. (Indiana)	46	Warner & Swasey	31
Lone Star Gas	43	Public Ser. Elec. & Gas	41	Washington Water	45
Louisville G. & Elec.	42	Pure Oil	45	Western Pacific R. R.	79
				Westinghouse Air	36
Martin Co.	49	Radio Corp. Amer.	62	Westinghouse Elec.	86
Maryland Casualty	40	Raybestos Manh't'n	62	Wisconsin Elec. P'r	39
May Dept. Stores	49	Raytheon M'f'g	71	Wisconsin Pub. Ser.	26
McCord Corp.	38	Reynolds Tob.	57	Woolworth (F. W.)	54
Merritt-Chapman	20	Rohm & Haas	623	Wrigley (Wm.)	88
Miami Copper	44				
Middle South Util.	48				

Stocks Ranked III for Probable Market Performance in the Next 12 Months

ACF Industries	53	Barker Bros.	8	Cont'l Casualty	136
Adams Express	29	Beatrice Foods	50	Cornell Dubilier	27
Alco Products	21	Beneficial Finance	26	Curtiss-Wright	37
Allied Stores	59	Blaw-Knox	44		
Allis-Chalmers	29	Brown Shoe	67	Dana Corp.	68
Alpha Portland	35	Brunswick-Balke	92	Decca Records	19
Amer. Airlines	30	Budd	27	Denver & Rio Grande	20
Amer. Can	44			Dumont Lab's	8⅛
Amer. Export	32	Campbell Soup	51		
Amer. Home P'd'cts	149	Canada Iron F'dries	35*	El Paso Nat. Gas	33
Amer. Insurance	27	Carolina P'w'r & L't	37	Elec. Storage Bat.	32
Amer. Invest. (Ill.)	20	Cen. Illinois Light	36		
Amer. Metal-Climax	27	Cen. & South West	60	Federated Dep't St.	59
Amer. Optical	45	Chesapeake & Ohio	73	First Nat'l Stores	65
Amer.-Standard	18	Chic. Milwaukee	26		
Amer. Steel Foundries	57	Clevite	36	Gen'l Amer. Trans.	59
Arizona Pub. Ser.	41	Columbus & S. O. El.	37	Gen'l Electric	84
Arkansas Fuel Oil	33	Consol. Cigar	54	Gen'l Portland Cem.	39
Atchison, T. & S. F.	29	Consol. Nat. Gas	50	Gen'l Public Util.	51
Atlantic City Elec.	45	Cont'l Can	47	Gen'l Refractories	52

Name of Stock	Recent Price [4/30/59]	Name of Stock	Recent Price [4/30/59]	Name of Stock	Recent Price [4/30/59]
Genesco, Inc.	36	Nat'l Homes "A"	24	Simmons Co.	52
Goodrich	92	Nat'l Steel	79	Simonds Saw	91
Gould-National	37	Niagara Mohawk	40	Singer M'f'g	50
Grand Union	52	Norfolk & Western	99	Skelly Oil	66
Grumman	27	Northern Ind. P. Ser.	51	S'th'n Co.	39
		Northern Pacific	51	Southwest. Pub. Ser.	44
Harbison-Walker	49	Northern States P'w'r	25	Stand'd Oil (Ind.)	51
Harris-Intertype	49	Norwich Pharm.	74	Stand'd Oil (Ky.)	68
Homestake Mining	40			Stevens (J. P.)	29
Hudson Bay M'ng	58	Ohio Edison	65	Sun Chemical	13
		Oklahoma G. & Elec.	33	Sunbeam	55
Industrial Accept'ce	38*	Oklahoma Nat. Gas	29	Sunray Mid-Cont.	28
Int'l Harvester	42	Owens-Ill. Glass	89	Sunshine Biscuits	102
Int'l Nickel	92			Swift & Co.	36
Int'l Salt	147	Pacific Tel. & Tel.	164		
Int'l Silver	45	Peabody Coal	14	Tampa Electric	50
Iowa-Ill. G. & Elec.	38	Penn-Dixie Cement	34	Texas P'c'f'c C'l	
		Penn. P'w'r & L't	58	& Oil	30
Johns-Manville	60	Philip Morris	63	Toledo Edison	17
		Phillips Petroleum	51		
Kansas City South'n	82	Pitts. Plate Glass	76	United Carbon	84
Kansas G. & Elec.	43	Pittston	68	United-Greenfield	18
Kansas P'w'r & L't	32	Poor & Co.	28	United Merchants	20
		Procter & Gamble	79	United Shoe Mach.	47
Lehigh Portland	31	Public Ser. (N. H.)	21	U. S. Fidelity & G'ty	86
Link-Belt	62	Pullman	61	U. S. Playing Card	97
Loew's, Inc.	32			U. S. Steel	91
Louisville & Nash.	84	Quaker Oats	47	Utah Power & L't	34
Mack Trucks	42			Vanadium	36
Macy (R. H.)	41	Rayonier	26	Va.-Carolina Chem.	31
Madison Fund, Inc.	19	Rochester G. & Elec.	43	Va. Elec. & P'w'r	39
Manhattan Shirt	18	Rockwell M'f'g	38		
Melville Shoe	28	Rockwell-Standard	38	Wesson Oil	35
Mercantile Stores	33	Royal Dutch Petr.	44	West Penn Electric	37
Minnesota Mining	147			Wheeling Steel	57
Minnesota P. & L't	38	Safeway Stores	38	White Motor	48
Mississippi R. Fuel	40	St. Joseph Lead	36		
Monarch Mach. Tool	22	St. Paul Fire &		Yale & Towne	33
Montana Power	75	Marine	60	Young Spring & Wire	35
Montgomery Ward	48	Schering	63		
Motor Wheel	17	Seaboard Finance	28	Zenith Radio	107
Murray Corp.	27	Sealright-Oswego	42		

Stocks Ranked IV for Probable Market Performance in the Next 12 Months

Aetna Fire Ins.	75	Atlantic Coast Line	61	C.I.T. Financial	55
Allegheny Ludlum	46	Atlantic Refining	50	Calif. Packing	58
Allied Mills	43			Camden Fire Ins.	37
Amer. Agri. Chem.	106			Canada Dry	21
Amer. Bakeries	47	Baldwin-Lima-Ham.	15	Canadian Brew's	42
Amer. Chain	57	Bath Iron Works	60	Carnation	65
Amer. Crystal Sugar	41	Beech-Life Savers	40	Caterpillar Tractor	95
Amer. Cyanamid	56	Bendix Aviation	79	Cen. Aguirre Sugar	22
Amer. Metal P'd'cts	30	Best & Co.	39	Cen. Illinois P. S.	46
Amer. Molasses	15	Bliss (E. W.)	19	Chic. & N. W.	27
Amer. Potash	46	Borg-Warner	43	Cities Service	58
Amer. Stores	90	Bridgeport Brass	41	Cleveland-Cliffs	52
Amer. Sugar Ref'g	36	Briggs & Stratton	53	Colgate-Palmolive	121
Armstrong Cork	41	Burroughs	41	Columbia Pictures	20

166

Name of Stock	Recent Price [4/30/59]	Name of Stock	Recent Price [4/30/59]	Name of Stock	Recent Price [4/30/59]
Commercial Credit	60	Jewel Tea Co.	49	Pepperell M'f'g	65
Conde Nast	9⅝			Pet Milk	48
Consol. Mining	22	Kellogg	41	Pfizer (Chas.)	130
Cont'l Motors	13	Koppers	43		
		Kress (S. H.)	43	Rexall Drug & Chem.	44
Dayton P'w'r & L't	53	Kroger	29	Robertshaw-Fulton	46
Deere & Co.	59			Royal Crown Cola	20
Delaware & Hudson	30			Ruberoid	47
Distillers Corp.-S.	34	Lee Rubber & Tire	29		
Divco-Wayne	25	Lehman Corp.	31	Seaboard Air Line	
Dr. Pepper	15	Libby, McNeill	13	R. R.	39
Domin. Steel & Coal	19*	Lone Star Steel	33	Shamrock Oil	39
		Lorillard (P.)	40	Shell Oil	85
Eagle-Picher	48	Louisiana Land	60	Smith (A. O.)	57
Eastern Gas & Fuel	31	Lowenstein	17	So. Puerto Rico	
Eaton M'f'g	72			Sugar	26
Endicott Johnson	36	Marshall Field	46	Springfield Fire & M.	31
		Masonite	44	Stand'd Brands	66
Federal-Mogul	58	McCall	20	Stand'd Oil (N. J.)	53
Federal Paper B'd	50	McCrory-McLellan	15	Stand'd Oil (Ohio)	64
Fibreboard Paper	52	McDonnell Aircraft	43	Stokely-Van Camp	17
Florida Power	29	McGraw-Edison	42	Sutherland Paper	44
Florida P'w'r & L't	91	McIntyre Porc. Mines	86		
Food Machinery	45	McKesson & Robbins	86	Tennessee Corp.	77
		McQuay-Norris	22	Time, Inc.	71
Gen'l Amer. Invest.	33	Mesta Machine	59	Timken Roller	57
Gen'l Cigar	28	Midland-Ross	47	Truax-Traer Coal	23
Gen'l Motors	49	Minneapolis-H'w'll	135	Twentieth Cen.-Fox	39
Gimbel Bros.	44	Moore-McCormack	22		
Glidden	49	Motorola	94	United Elec. Coal	37
G't Northern R'lw'y	59	Mueller Brass	29	United Engineering	21
G't Western Sugar	28	Myers (F. E.)	40	United Fruit	39
				U. S. Lines	33
Halliburton Oil	63	Nat'l Acme	60	U. S. Pipe & F'dry	26
Hammermill	31	Nat'l Distillers	32	U. S. Tobacco	26
Harshaw Chemical	30	Nat'l Sugar Refining	38		
Heinz (H. J.)	68	Nat'l Tea	21	Victor Chemical	38
Hercules Powder	70	Neisner Bros.	14		
Holly Sugar	23	New England Elec.	21	Walworth	17
Houdaille Ind'tr's	22			Western Auto S'ply	31
Household Finance	32	Oliver Corp.	18	Western Md. R'lw'y	77
				Western Union	36
Ingersoll-Rand	102	Pan American		Weyerhaeuser	45
Insur. Co. N. Amer.	138	Airways	31	Whirlpool Corp.	36
Int'l Tel. & Tel.	42	Pennsalt Chem.	89		
Interstate Power	19	Peoples Drug Stores	49	Youngstown S. & T.	120
Island Creek Coal	40				

Stocks Ranked V for Probable Market Performance in the Next 12 Months

Name	Price	Name	Price	Name	Price
Abitibi Power & Paper	37*	Amer. Smelting	47	Babcock & Wilcox	33
Addressograph	111	Amer. Surety	20	Bayuk Cigars	38
Aetna Life Ins.	254	Amphenol-Borg	42	Bell Aircraft	20
Air Reduction	85	Anchor Hocking	35	Bethlehem Steel	51
Aluminium, Ltd.	28	Armco Steel	70	Black & Decker	64
Aluminum Co.	83	Assoc. Dry Goods	53	Boeing	39
Amer. Bank Note	35	Associates Invest.	73	Bond Stores	24
Amer. Bosch Arma	37	Atlas Powder	84	Bristol-Myers	103
Amer.-Marietta	55	Avco M'f'g	14	British Amer. Oil	41
				Bucyrus-Erie	34

167

Name of Stock	Recent Price [4/30/59]	Name of Stock	Recent Price [4/30/59]	Name of Stock	Recent Price [4/30/59]
Bullard	20	Granite City Steel	61	Reed Roller Bit	25
		G't Atl'c & P'c'f'c	41	Republic Aviation	22
Celotex	43	G't Northern Paper	51	Republic Steel	69
Chain Belt	59	Green (H. L.)	32	Revere Copper	48
Champion Paper	42			Reynolds Metals	86
Chemetron	31	Hoffman Electronics	74	Rhodesian Sel'n Tr.	2⅛
Chic. Pneu. Tool	29			Richfield Oil	90
Cincinnati Milling	44	Inland Steel	139	Royal McBee Corp.	19
Clark Equipment	70	Interchemical Corp.	33		
Cluett, Peabody	58	Int'l Paper	116	St. Regis Paper	50
Collins Radio	41	Interstate Dept.	33	Schenley Industries	37
Combustion Eng.	37			Scovill M'f'g	25
Congoleum-Nairn	14	Jones & Laughlin	69	Sharon Steel	35
Consol. Electrodyn.	41	Joy M'f'g	49	Sheller M'f'g	18
Consol. Foods	27			Sherwin-Williams	224
Consolidation Coal	33	Kaiser Aluminum	43	Sinclair Oil	63
Container Corp.	28	Kelsey-Hayes Co.	46	Smith-Corona March.	17
Cont'l Baking	49	Kimberly-Clark	63	S'th'n Pacific Co.	68
Cont'l Oil	62			S'th'n Railway	58
Cooper-Bessemer	42	Lehn & Fink	54	Square D	30
Corning Glass	125	Lily-Tulip Cup	102	Staley (A. E.)	41
Creole Petroleum	53	Lockheed	36	Sterling Drug	55
Crown Cork	32			Stewart-Warner	51
Crown Zellerbach	57	Magnavox	58		
Cuban-Amer. Sugar	27	Matson Navigation	45	Texas Gulf Pr'd'cing	30
Cutler-Hammer	84	Maytag	81	Thatcher Glass	31
		McGraw-Hill Publ.	59	Thompson Ramo	68
Daystrom	43	Mead Corp.	45	Tidewater Oil	26
Douglas Aircraft	53	Mead Johnson	77		
Dresser Industries	40	Mergenthaler	56	Union Bag-Camp	48
		Minnesota & Ont. P.	33	Union Oil (Cal.)	45
Emerson Electric	62			United Air Lines	38
		Nat'l Airlines	24	United Biscuit	24
Fairbanks, Morse	34	Nat'l Cash Register	70	U. S. Gypsum	114
Fairchild Engine	9	Nat'l Fire Insur.	140	U. S. Rubber	57
Family Finance	32	Nat'l Gypsum	69	Universal Leaf Tob.	53
Firestone Tire	143	Newport N. Ship.	43		
Flintkote	40	No. Amer. Aviation	46	Van Norman	12
Foster Wheeler	42	Northrop Corp.	40	Vick Chemical	134
Fruehauf Trailer	24	Northwest Airlines	40	Virginian R'lw'y	48
Gardner-Denver	52	Ohio Oil	40	Walgreen Co.	54
Gen'l Cable	42	Otis Elevator	71	Walker (Hiram)	35
Gen'l Precision Eq.	41			Warner-Lambert	110
Gen'l R'lw'y Signal	36	Pacific Finance	65	West Indies Sugar	47
Gen'l Tire	75	Paramount Pict.	45	West Ky. Coal	18
Georgia-Pacific	65	Pillsbury Co.	45	West Va. Pulp & P'p'r	46
Gillette	51	Pitney-Bowes	39	Western Airlines	35
Goodyear Tire	144			Wilson & Co.	35
Grace (W. R.)	45	Ralston Purina	54	Worthington	78

* Canadian Funds.

NOTE: Due to mergers and substitutions, the number of stocks appearing in *The Value Line Investment Survey, Weekly Summary-Index,* may vary slightly from week to week, but changes are insignificant.

TABLE 4

Here is the order of all stocks in *The Value Line Investment Survey* in terms of their relative Appreciation Potentiality over a period of 3 to 5 years, as published May 11, 1959. Ranks are subject to change as prices change relative to one another, or as evidence appears that requires revision of the estimates of future earnings and dividends in the hypothesized economic environment, in relation to which the appreciation potentialities are measured.

804 Stocks Reviewed by
The Value Line Investment Survey,
May 11, 1959, Ranked According to Appreciation
Potentiality to 1962–64

Stocks Ranked I for Appreciation
Potentiality to 1962–64

Name of Stock	Recent Price [4/30/59]	Name of Stock	Recent Price [4/30/59]	Name of Stock	Recent Price [4/30/59]
Admiral Corp.	22	Canadian Pacific	30	First Nat'l Stores	65
Allegheny Ludlum	46	Capital Airlines	20	Foremost Dairies	20
Allis-Chalmers	29	Carrier	44	Freeport Sulphur	35
Alpha Portland	35	Case (J. I.)	23		
Aluminium, Ltd.	28	Cerro de Pasco	41		
Aluminum Co.	83	Champlin Oil	24	Gen'l Baking	13
Amerada Petroleum	92	Chemetron	31	Gen'l Dynamics	58
Amer. Broadc.-Par't	27	Chic. & N. W.	27	Getty Oil	24
Amer. Can	44	Colorado Fuel	26	Gould-National	37
Amer. Insurance	27	Columbia Pictures	20	G't Northern Paper	51
Amer. Mach. & F'dry	88	Conn. Gen'l Life	382	Grumman	27
Amer. Potash	46	Consol. Mining	22	Gulf Oil	114
Amer. Smelting	47	Consolidation Coal	33		
Amer. Surety	20	Cornell Dubilier	27	Halliburton Oil	63
Anderson-Prichard	35	Crucible Steel	28	Hammermill	31
Arkansas Fuel Oil	33	Curtis Publishing	12	Holly Sugar	23
Atlas Corp.	7			Houdaille Ind'tr's	22
Atlas Steels	27*	Decca Records	19	Hudson Bay M'ng	58
		Diamond Gardner	33		
Baldwin-Lima-Ham.	15	Domin. Steel & Coal	19*	Illinois Central	47
Bell Aircraft	20	Douglas Aircraft	53	Imperial Oil	45
Boeing	39	Dumont Lab's	8⅛	Industrial Rayon	23
Boston Insurance	35			Int'l Minerals	35
British Amer. Oil	41	Eastern Air Lines	41	Int'l Nickel	92
Burroughs	41	Eastern Gas & Fuel	31	Int'l Paper	116
				Island Creek Coal	40
Canada Iron F'dries	35*	Falconbridge	27*		
Canadian Oil Cos.	30*	Fireman's Fund	58	Joy M'f'g	49

169

Name of Stock	Recent Price [4/30/59]	Name of Stock	Recent Price [4/30/59]	Name of Stock	Recent Price [4/30/59]
Kaiser Aluminum	43	Paramount Pict.	45	Stevens (J. P.)	29
Koppers	43	Peabody Coal	14	Stokely-Van Camp	17
		Penn-Dixie Cement	34	Sun Oil	63
Lehigh Portland	31	Pennsylvania R. R.	18	Sunbeam	55
Lehigh Valley R. R.	8¾	Phila. Nat'l Bank	43	Sunray Mid-Cont.	28
Libby, McNeill	13	Pitts. Coke & Chem.	23	Swift & Co.	36
Loew's, Inc.	32	Pitts. & W. Va.	20		
Lone Star Cement	33	Pitts. Forgings	16	Technicolor	8⅞
Lowenstein	17	Pittston	68	Texas Eastern Trans.	32
				Texas Gulf Pr'd'cing	30
Martin Co.	49	Reading Company	22	Texas Gulf Sulphur	21
McCall	20	Reed Roller Bit	25	Texas P'c'f'c C'l & Oil	30
McDonnell Aircraft	43	Republic Aviation	22	Tidewater Oil	26
Merritt-Chapman	20	Rheem M'f'g	22	Torrington	30
Mission Corp.	45	Rhodesian Sel'n Tr.	2⅛	Truax-Traer Coal	23
Mission Development	27	Royal Dutch Petr.	44	Twentieth Cen.-Fox	39
Missouri Pacific	48	Royal McBee Corp.	19		
Montana-Dak. Util.	31			Underwood	27
Mueller Brass	29	St. Joseph Lead	36	Union Oil (Cal.)	45
Myers (F. E.)	40	Scovill M'f'g	25	United Air Lines	38
		Sharon Steel	35	United Biscuit	24
Nat'l Can	11	Signal Oil "A"	37	United Fruit	39
Nat'l Theatres	11	Smith-Corona March.	17	U. S. Plywood	52
N. J. Zinc	26	Socony Mobil Oil	45	U. S. Smelting	34
N. Y. Central	28	So. Puerto Rico			
N. Y., N. Haven	8⅝	Sugar	26	Vanadium	36
Newmont Mining	89	S'th'n Nat. Gas	40	Va.-Carolina Chem.	31
Noranda Mines	52*	Sperry Rand	26		
Northern Pacific	51	Spiegel, Inc.	39	West Indies Sugar	47
		Springfield Fire & M.	31	Westinghouse Air	36
Page-Hersey Tubes	31*	Stanley Warner	24		
Panhandle Eastern	49	Steel Co. of Canada	77*	Youngstown S. & T.	120

Stocks Ranked II for Appreciation Potentiality to 1962–64

Name of Stock	Price	Name of Stock	Price	Name of Stock	Price
ACF Industries	53	Champion Paper	42	Fairbanks, Morse	34
Abitibi Power & Paper	37*	Chase Man. Bank	59	Falstaff Brewing	24
Aetna Fire Ins.	75	Chemical Corn	62	Fansteel Metal.	57
Alco Products	21	Chrysler	65	Federal Paper B'd	50
Algoma Steel	37*	Cities Service	58	Firstamerica	22
Amer. Bank Note	35	Collins & Aikman	24	First Nat'l (Bos.)	86
Amer. Crystal Sugar	41	Columbia Br'c't'g	46	Food Fair	38
Amer. Invest. (Ill.)	20	Columbia Gas	22		
Amer. Metal-Climax	27	Commercial Solv.	17	Gen'l Amer. Invest.	33
Amer. Metal P'd'cts	30	Consol. Electrodyn.	41	Gen'l Amer. Trans.	59
Amer.-Standard	18	Consol. Nat. Gas	50	Gen'l Cable	42
Amer. Viscose	50	Consumers Power	54	Gimbel Bros.	44
Amphenol-Borg	42	Cont'l Can	47	Girard Trust	56
Archer-Daniels	46	Cont'l Insurance	58	Grace (W. R.)	45
Arvin Industries	26	Cuban-Amer. Sugar	27	Grant (W. T.)	45
		Cudahy Packing	14	G't Amer. Insur.	42
Babcock & Wilcox	33			G't Northern Iron	30
Balt. & Ohio	45	Delaware, Lack.	11	G't Northern R'lw'y	59
Bankers Trust	80	Distillers Corp.-S.	34		
Barker Bros.	8	Dominion Stores	78*	Hanover Bank	52
Bigelow-Sanford	17			Harshaw Chemical	30
Bucyrus-Erie	34	Eagle-Picher	48	Hartford Fire Ins.	187
		El Paso Nat. Gas	33	Holland Furnace	14
Canada Cement	35*	Erie Railroad	13	Homestake Mining	40
Canada Dry	21	Ex-Cell-O	41	Hooker Chemical	40
				Howe Sound	18

Stocks Ranked III for Appreciation Potentiality to 1962–64

Name of Stock	Recent Price [4/30/59]	Name of Stock	Recent Price [4/30/59]	Name of Stock	Recent Price [4/30/59]
Empire Dist. Elec.	25	Lerner Stores	21	Raybestos Manh't'n	62
		Libby-Owens-Ford	57	Rayonier	26
Fidelity-Phenix Ins.	63	Lone Star Steel	33	Raytheon M'f'g	71
First Nat'l (Chi.)	345	Louisiana Land	60	Revere Copper	48
First Nat'l (St. L.)	78				
First Nat'l City	78	Macy (R. H.)	41	Safeway Stores	38
Flintkote	40	Masonite	44	Sangamo Electric	49
Florida Power	29	Massey-Ferguson	15	Seaboard Finance	28
Ford Motor	64	May Dept. Stores	49	Shell Oil	85
Ford of Canada	140	McGraw-Hill Publ.	59	S'th'n Calif. Edison	59
		McIntyre Porc. Mines	86	Spencer Kellogg	19
Gen'l Motors	49	Midland-Ross	47	Square D	30
Gen'l Portland Cem.	39	Mississippi R. Fuel	40	Stand'd Oil (Ky.)	68
Gen'l Precision Eq.	41	Monsanto	49	Sun Chemical	13
Gen'l Tire	75	Montgomery Ward	48	Sutherland Paper	44
Gillette	51	Moore Corp.	112*		
Glens Falls Ins.	40			Tampa Electric	50
Glidden	49	Nat'l Acme	60	Thatcher Glass	31
Grand Union	52	Nat'l Biscuit	52	Thompson Ramo	68
G't Atl'c & P'c'f'c	41	Nat'l Fuel Gas	23	Travelers Insurance	90
G't Western Sugar	28	Nat'l Lead	122		
		Nat'l Malleable	37	Union Carbide	134
Heinz (H. J.)	68	Nat'l Tea	21	Union Electric	34
Home Insurance	52	New York Trust	92	Union Pacific	35
Household Finance	32	Northern Nat. Gas	31	United Gas Corp.	42
Houston L't & P'w'r	72			U. S. Fidelity & G'ty	86
		Owens-Corning	74	U. S. Fire Insurance	32
Indianapolis P. & L't	40			U. S. Industries	13
Inspiration C. Cop'r	44	Pacific Lighting	52		
Int'l Salt	147	Peoples Drug Stores	49	Warner Bros.	40
Int'l Shoe	36	Phelps Dodge	64	Warner & Swasey	31
Interstate Power	19	Philco	35	West Ky. Coal	18
		Public Ser. (Colo.)	51	Western Union	36
Kansas P'w'r & L't	32	Public Ser. (Indiana)	46	Weyerhaeuser	45
Kimberly-Clark	63	Puget Sound P. & L't	34	Wisconsin Pub. Ser.	26
Kroger	29			Wrigley (Wm.)	88
		Quaker Oats	47	Zenith Radio	107
Laclede Gas	20				

Stocks Ranked IV for Appreciation Potentiality to 1962–64

Name of Stock	Price	Name of Stock	Price	Name of Stock	Price
ASR Products	12	Balt. Gas & Elec.	46	Columbian Carbon	51
Aetna Life Ins.	254	Beatrice Foods	50	Columbus & S. O. El.	37
Air Reduction	85	Bendix Aviation	79	Commonwealth Ed.	61
Allied Chemical	112	Bethlehem Steel	51	Community Pub. Ser.	24
Allied Stores	59	Borden Company	79	Cont'l Casualty	136
Amer. Airlines	30	Borg-Warner	43	Cont'l Illinois	122
Amer. Chain	57	Bridgeport Brass	41	Corn Products	55
Amer. Cyanamid	56	Budd	27	Curtiss-Wright	37
Amer. Elec. Power	51				
Amer.-Marietta	55	Calif. Packing	58	Dayton P'w'r & L't	53
Amer. Motors	38	Campbell Soup	51	Delaware P'w'r & L't	63
Amer. Seating	40	Carolina P'w'r & L't	37	Delta Airlines	32
Amer. Tel. & Tel.	252	Caterpillar Tractor	95	Domin. F'dries & St.	49*
Anchor Hocking	35	Celanese	32	Dow Chemical	88
Armour & Co.	24	Chic. Milwaukee	26	Du Pont	242
Armstrong Cork	41	Chic. Rock Island	37		
Ashland Oil	24	Cincinnati Milling	44	Eastman Kodak	88
Atlantic Coast Line	61	Colgate-Palmolive	121	Elec. Storage Bat.	42

Name of Stock	Recent Price [4/30/59]	Name of Stock	Recent Price [4/30/59]	Name of Stock	Recent Price [4/30/59]
Equitable Gas	38	Lone Star Gas	43	St. Regis Paper	50
		Louisville G. & Elec.	42	Scott Paper	82
Fedders Corp.	20			Seaboard Air Line R. R.	39
Fibreboard Paper	52	Magnavox	58	Sears, Roebuck	43
Firestone Tire	143	Marshall Field	46	Singer M'f'g	50
Florida P'w'r & L't	91	Melville Shoe	28	So. Carolina E. & Gas	36
Foster Wheeler	42	Middle South Util.	48	S'th'n Pacific Co.	68
		Minneapolis-H'w'll	135	S'th'n Railway	58
Gen'l Cigar	28	Minnesota P. & L't	38	Stand'd Brands	66
Gen'l Electric	84	Mohasco Industries	16	Stand'd Oil (N. J.)	53
Gen'l Foods	78	Monarch Mach. Tool	22	Stewart-Warner	51
Gen'l R'lw'y Signal	36			Sunshine Biscuits	102
Gen'l Refractories	52	Nat'l Steel	79		
Gerber Products	68	Nat'l Sugar Refining	38	Texaco	85
Goodrich	92	Neisner Bros.	14	Texas Utilities	67
Granite City Steel	61	N. Y., Chic. & St. L.	34	Toledo Edison	17
Green (H. L.)	32	N. Y. State E. & Gas	57		
Greyhound	23	Northern Ind. P. Ser.	51	United Carbon	84
Gulf Mobile & O.	29	Northern States P'w'r	25	United Corp.	9¼
Gulf States Util.	58			United Engineering	21
		Ohio Edison	65	U. S. Rubber	57
Hershey Chocolate	76			Utah Power & L't	34
Hollinger Consol.	34	Pacific G. & Elec.	64		
		Penney (J. C.)	112	Va. Elec. & P'w'r	39
Insur. Co. N. Amer.	138	Pennsalt Chem.	89	Virginian R'lw'y	48
Int'l Business Mach.	392	Peoples Gas L't & C'ke	58		
Int'l Silver	45	Philip Morris	63	Walker (Hiram)	35
Iowa P'w'r & L't	37	Phillips Petroleum	51	Washington Gas L't	51
		Pitts. & Lake Erie	93	Western Md. R'lw'y	77
Johns-Manville	60	Poor & Co.	28	Westinghouse Elec.	86
		Public Ser. (N. H.)	21	Whirlpool Corp.	36
Kennecott Cop'r	114	Public Ser. Elec. & Gas	41	Wilson & Co.	35
				Winn-Dixie Stores	41
Lee Rubber & Tire	29			Wisconsin Elec. P'r	39
Lincoln Nat'l Life	221	Rochester G. & Elec.	43		
Loew's Theatres	14	Rockwell M'f'g	38	Yale & Towne	33

Stocks Ranked V for Appreciation Potentiality to 1962–64

Name	Price	Name	Price	Name	Price
Abbott Laboratories	80	Briggs & Stratton	53	Container Corp.	28
Addressograph	111	Bristol-Myers	103	Cooper-Bessemer	42
Allied Mills	43	Brown Shoe	67	Corning Glass	125
Amer. Agri. Chem.	106	Buckeye Pipe Line	33	Crown Cork	32
Amer. Bakeries	47			Cutler-Hammer	84
Amer. Chicle	54	C.I.T. Financial	55		
Amer. Home P'd'cts	149	Camden Fire Ins.	37	Dana Corp.	68
Amer. Snuff	60	Carnation	65	Daystrom	43
Amer. Trust	58	Cen. Hudson G. & E.	22	Denver & Rio Grande	20
Arizona Pub. Ser.	41	Cen. Illinois Light	36	Dr. Pepper	15
Arkansas La. Gas	64	Cen. Illinois P. S.	46	Dome Mines	18
Armco Steel	70	Chain Belt	59	Duke Power	47
Assoc. Dry Goods	53	Chic. Pneu. Tool	29	Duquesne Light	25
Atlantic City Elec.	45	Clark Equipment	70		
Atlas Powder	84	Cleveland Electric	52	Eaton M'f'g	72
		Clevite	36	Emerson Electric	62
Bayuk Cigars	38	Collins Radio	41	Emerson Radio	22
Best & Co.	39	Combustion Eng.	37	Endicott Johnson	36
Black & Decker	64	Conde Nast	9⅝		
Bohn Aluminum	30	Congoleum-Nairn	14	Fairchild Engine	9
Bond Stores	24	Conn. L't & P'w'r	26	Family Finance	32
Boston Edison	61	Consol. Edison	64	Federal-Mogul	58

173

Name of Stock	Recent Price [4/30/59]	Name of Stock	Recent Price [4/30/59]	Name of Stock	Recent Price [4/30/59]
Federated Dep't St.	59	Mercantile Stores	33	Robertshaw-Fulton	46
Food Machinery	45	Merck & Co.	85	Rockwell-Standard	38
Fruehauf Trailer	24	Mergenthaler	56	Rohm & Haas	623
		Miami Copper	44	Royal Crown Cola	20
Gardner-Denver	52	Minnesota Mining	147	Ruberoid	47
Gen'l Mills	108	Montana Power	75		
Gen'l Public Util.	51	Motorola	94	San Diego G. & Elec.	29
Gen'l Tel. & Electro.	71			Schering	63
Genesco, Inc.	36	Nat'l Dairy P'd'cts	52	Sealright-Oswego	42
Georgia-Pacific	65	Nat'l Fire Insur.	140	Sherwin-Williams	224
Goodyear Tire	144	Nat'l Gypsum	69	Simonds Saw	91
		Nat'l Homes "A"	24	Smith (A. O.)	57
Harbison-Walker	49	New England Elec.	21	Smith, Kline &	
Harris-Intertype	49	Niagara Mohawk	40	French	146
Hartford Elec. L't	71	Norfolk & Western	99	S'th'n Co.	39
Hercules Powder	70	Northrop Corp.	40	Southwest. Pub. Ser.	44
Hoffman Electronics	74	Northwest Airlines	40	Staley (A. E.)	41
		Norwich Pharm.	74	Stand'd Oil (Ohio)	64
Illinois Power	41			Starrett (L. S.)	97
Ingersoll-Rand	102	Oklahoma G. & Elec.	33	Sterling Drug	55
Inland Steel	139	Oklahoma Nat. Gas	29	Studebaker-Packard	12
Interchemical Corp.	33	Otis Elevator	71		
Int'l Tel. & Tel.	42	Owens-Ill. Glass	89	Tennessee Corp.	77
				Timken Roller	57
Jewel Tea Co.	49	Pacific Finance	65		
Johnson & Johnson	50	Pacific Tel. & Tel.	164	Union Bag-Camp	48
Jones & Laughlin	69	Pan American		United Gas Imp't	58
		Airways	31	U. S. Gypsum	114
Kansas City P. & L't	54	Parke, Davis	44	U. S. Playing Card	97
Kansas G. & Elec.	43	Penick & Ford	55	U. S. Steel	91
Kearney & Trecker	17	Penn. P'w'r & L't	58	U. S. Tobacco	26
Kellogg	41	Pet Milk	48	Universal Leaf Tob.	53
		Pfizer (Chas.)	130		
Lehn & Fink	54	Phila. Electric	52	Van Norman	12
Liggett & Myers	97	Pillsbury Co.	45	Vick Chemical	134
Lily-Tulip Cup	102	Pitney-Bowes	39	Victor Chemical	38
Long Island L't'g	35	Potomac Elec. P'w'r	29		
Lorillard (P.)	40	Procter & Gamble	79	Walgreen Co.	54
				Warner-Lambert	110
Mack Trucks	42	Radio Corp. Amer.	62	West Penn Electric	37
Mallory (P. R.)	43	Ralston Purina	54	Western Airlines	35
Maytag	81	Republic Steel	69	Western Auto S'ply	31
McKesson & Robbins	86	Rexall Drug & Chem.	44	Western Pacific R. R.	79
McQuay-Norris	22	Reynolds Metals	86	White Motor	48
Mead Johnson	77	Reynolds Tob.	57	Worthington	78

* Canadian Funds.

NOTE: Due to mergers and substitutions, the number of stocks appearing in *The Value Line Investment Survey, Weekly Summary-Index,* may vary slightly from week to week, but changes are insignificant.

TABLE 5

Here is the order of all stocks in *The Value Line Investment Survey* in terms of magnitude of their yield expectancies in the next 12 months, as published May 11, 1959. Yield expectancies vary with the passage of time because prices change, or dividend estimates may be altered as the estimates go farther out in time and new evidence appears.

804 Stocks Reviewed by *The Value Line Investment Survey*, May 11, 1959, Listed in Order of Estimated Yield in the Next 12 Months

Name of Stock	Recent Price [4/30/59]	Est'd Yield Next 12 Months [Based on Price, 4/30/59]	Name of Stock	Recent Price [4/30/59]	Est'd Yield Next 12 Months [Based on Price, 4/30/59]
Missouri Pacific	48	5.9–**9.4**	N. Y., Chic. & St. L.	34	5.9–**6.5**
			Pitts. & Lake Erie	93	4.3–**6.5**
G't Northern Iron	30	**9.2–10.0** •			
			Cen. Aguirre Sugar	22	**6.4**
Miami Copper	44	**9.1**	Illinois Central	47	**6.4**–7.4
			Midland-Ross	47	**6.4**
Inspiration C. Cop'r	44	**8.5–9.1**	Seaboard Air Line		
			R. R.	39	5.1–**6.4**
Pitts. & W. Va.	20	6.0–**8.0**			
			Amer. Export	32	**6.3**
Cuban-Amer. Sugar	27	**7.8**	Amer. Motors	38	**6.3**
			Louisville & Nash.	84	6.0–**6.3**
Interlake Iron	27	5.2–**7.4**	Phelps Dodge	64	**6.3**–7.0
King-Seeley	34	5.9–**7.4**			
			Alco Products	21	5.2–**6.2**
Poor & Co.	28	6.3–**7.1**	Colorado Fuel	26	3.9–**6.2**
			Creole Petroleum	53	**6.2**–5.3
Merritt-Chapman	20	6.0–**7.0**	Gen'l Baking	13	5.8–**6.2**
Minnesota & Ont. P.	33	**7.0**			
Truax-Traer Coal	23	**7.0**	Kansas City South'n	82	**6.1**
			G't Western Sugar	28	**6.1**–5.4
Gulf Mobile & O.	29	**6.9**	Amer. Sugar Ref'g	36	**6.1**
Hudson Bay M'ng	58	5.2–**6.9**	Balt. & Ohio	45	4.4–**6.1**
			Kennecott Cop'r	114	**6.1**
ACF Industries	53	5.4–**6.8**	United-Greenfield	18	5.6–**6.1**
Anaconda	66	**6.8**	U. S. Lines	33	**6.1**
Curtiss-Wright	37	**6.8**–5.4			
Moore-McCormack	22	**6.8**	Raybestos Manh't'n	62	5.5–**6.0**
Reading Company	22	4.5–**6.8**	Simmons Co.	52	**6.0**
Stone & Webster	59	5.1–**6.8**	Torrington	30	**6.0**
			United Merchants	20	5.0–**6.0**
Bliss & Laughlin	27	5.9–**6.7**	Wheeling Steel	57	5.3–**6.0**
Delaware & Hudson	30	**6.7**			
			Amer. Steel Foundries	57	5.1–**5.9**
Pitts. Forgings	16	**6.6**–7.5	Kelsey-Hayes Co.	46	5.2–**5.9**

175

Name of Stock	Recent Price [4/30/59]	Est'd Yield Next 12 Months [Based on Price, 4/30/59]	Name of Stock	Recent Price [4/30/59]	Est'd Yield Next 12 Months [Based on Price, 4/30/59]
McCord Corp.	38	5.8–5.9	Island Creek Coal	40	5.0–5.3
Mesta Machine	59	5.9–5.1	Kresge (S. S.)	34	4.7–5.3
Mississippi R. Fuel	40	5.9–4.5	Marshall Field	46	4.9–5.3
Mueller Brass	29	4.8–5.9	McCrory-McLellan	15	5.3
Nat'l Sugar Refining	38	5.9–6.6	Myers (F. E.)	40	5.3
Nat'l Theatres	11	5.9–6.8	Stand'd Oil (Ky.)	68	5.1–5.3
Smith-Corona March.	17	5.9	Time, Inc.	71	4.9–5.3
			United Shoe Mach.	47	5.3
Canadian Pacific	30	5.0–5.8			
Chic. Milwaukee	26	5.8	Allied Mills	43	5.2
Pepperell M'f'g	65	5.4–5.8	Allis-Chalmers	29	5.2
			Archer-Daniels	46	4.3–5.2
Cen. Maine P'w'r	27	5.2–5.7 •	Bond Stores	24	5.2
Crucible Steel	28	5.0–5.7	Columbia Gas	22	4.5–5.2
Elec. Auto-Lite	44	4.5–5.7	Eastern Gas & Fuel	31	5.2‡
Lerner Stores	21	5.7	Empire Dist. Elec.	25	4.8–5.2
Neisner Bros.	14	5.7	Falconbridge	27*	4.4–5.2
Pullman	61	5.7–6.6	Holly Sugar	23	5.2
Texas Gulf Sulphur	21	5.0–5.7	Liggett & Myers	97	5.2
Young Spring & Wire	35	5.7	Nat'l Fuel Gas	23	4.8–5.2
			New England Elec.	21	4.8–5.2 •
Amer. Metal-Climax	27	4.4–5.6	Newport N. Ship.	43	4.7–5.2
Grumman	27	5.6	Simonds Saw	91	4.4–5.2
Manhattan Shirt	18	3.9–5.6	S'th'n Railway	58	4.8–5.2
Mercantile Stores	33	5.0–5.6	Stevens (J. P.)	29	5.2
Rhodesian Sel'n Tr.	2⅛	5.6	Sunray Mid-Cont.	28	5.0–5.2
Socony Mobil Oil	45	4.4–5.6	Thatcher Glass	31	4.5–5.2
Spiegel, Inc.	39	4.6–5.6	U. S. Playing Card	97	5.2
Swift & Co.	36	4.4–5.6			
			Amer. Bakeries	47	5.1–5.5
Atchison, T. & S. F.	29	5.2–5.5	Amer. Tobacco	105	5.0–5.1
Chesapeake & Ohio	73	5.5–5.8	Best & Co.	39	5.1–5.5
Diamond Gardner	33	4.5–5.5	Boston Insurance	35	5.1–4.3
Gould-National	37	5.4–5.5	Dana Corp.	68	4.4–5.1
Int'l Harvester	42	5.5–5.7	G't Northern R'lw'y	59	5.1–5.5
McQuay-Norris	22	5.5	Macy (R. H.)	41	4.9–5.1
Monarch Mach. Tool	22	5.5–4.5	Paramount Pict.	45	4.4–5.1
N. Y. Air Brake	29	5.5	Philip Morris	63	4.9–5.1
Newberry (J. J.)	40	5.5	Union Tank Car	34	5.0–5.1
Plymouth Oil	29	4.5–5.5	United Fruit	39	5.1
Sheller M'f'g	18	4.4–5.5	Western Md. R'lw'y	77	4.7–5.1
			Wrigley (Wm.)	88	5.1
Allied Stores	59	5.1–5.4			
Amer. Brake Shoe	49	5.4–5.9	Alpha Portland	35	4.3–5.0
Bath Iron Works	60	5.0–5.4	Amer. Agri. Chem.	106	4.5–5.0
Chic. Rock Island	37	4.9–5.4	Amer. Invest. (Ill.)	20	5.0
Int'l Shoe	36	5.0–5.4	Amer. Snuff	60	5.0
Laclede Gas	20	4.5–5.4	Amer.-Standard	18	4.4–5.0
Nat'l Malleable	37	5.4	Baldwin-Lima-Ham.	15	4.0–5.0
Pitts. Coke & Chem.	23	4.3–5.4	Barker Bros.	8	Nil–5.0
Rockwell-Standard	38	5.3–5.4‡	Canada Dry	21	5.0–5.5
St. Louis-San Fran. R. R.	23	4.3–5.4	Cleveland-Cliffs	52	4.0–5.0
Sun Chemical	13	5.4–6.2	Cont'l Motors	13	5.0
Wesson Oil	35	4.0–5.4	Denver & Rio Grande	20	5.0–5.3
			Distillers Corp. -S.	34	5.0
Amer. Metal P'd'cts	30	5.3	Dresser Industries	40	5.0
Burlington Ind'tr's	19	5.3	Falstaff Brewing	24	4.2–5.0
Cannon Mills	66	4.5–5.3	Family Finance	32	5.0
Decca Records	19	5.3	Fedders Corp.	20	5.0–5.8
Domin. Steel & Coal	19*	5.3	Foremost Dairies	20	5.0
			Green (H. L.)	32	5.0–3.8

176

Name of Stock	Recent Price [4/30/59]	Est'd Yield Next 12 Months [Based on Price, 4/30/59]	Name of Stock	Recent Price [4/30/59]	Est'd Yield Next 12 Months [Based on Price, 4/30/59]
Greyhound	23	4.3–**5.0**	Celotex	43	**4.7**–5.6
Holland Furnace	14	4.3–**5.0**	Columbian Carbon	51	**4.7**
Homestake Mining	40	**5.0**	Columbus & S. O. El.	37	4.3–**4.7**
Iowa-Ill. G. & Elec.	38	4.7–**5.0**	Commercial Credit	60	**4.7**
Lorillard (P.)	40	**5.0**	Douglas Aircraft	53	**4.7**–1.9
Nat'l Acme	60	4.2–**5.0**	Duquesne Light	25	4.4–**4.7**
Public Ser. (N. H.)	21	4.8–**5.0**•	Equitable Gas	38	4.6–**4.7**•
Sharon Steel	35	**5.0**–5.7	Ford Motor	64	3.8–**4.7**
S'th'n Nat. Gas	40	**5.0**	Hershey Chocolate	76	4.1–**4.7**
Stanley Warner	24	**5.0**	Houdaille Ind'tr's	22	**4.7**‡
Texas Eastern Trans.	32	4.4–**5.0**	Interstate Power	19	**4.7**
United Aircraft	60	**5.0**–4.2	Jones & Laughlin	69	4.0–**4.7**
Wisconsin Pub. Ser.	26	4.8–**5.0**	Koppers	43	3.7–**4.7**
Woolworth (F. W.)	54	4.6–**5.0**	Kress (S. H.)	43	**4.7**
Youngstown S. & T.	120	4.2–**5.0**	Lone Star Gas	43	4.2–**4.7**
			Lowenstein	17	3.5–**4.7**
Amer. Crystal Sugar	41	3.9–**4.9**	Massey-Ferguson	15	**4.7**–5.3
Bethlehem Steel	51	**4.9**–5.1	Mohasco Industries	16	2.8–**4.7**
Boston Edison	61	4.6–**4.9**	Montgomery Ward	48	4.2–**4.7**
Bridgeport Brass	41	3.7–**4.9**	Penn-Dixie Cement	34	4.1–**4.7**
Cont'l Baking	49	4.5–**4.9**	Public Ser. (Indiana)	46	**4.7**•
Detroit Edison	44	4.5–**4.9**•	Republic Steel	69	**4.7**–5.1
Eaton M'f'g	72	4.2–**4.9**	Ruberoid	47	4.5–**4.7**
Gen'l R'lw'y Signal	36	4.2–**4.9**	Starrett (L. S.)	97	4.1–**4.7**
Grant (W. T.)	45	**4.9**	Stokely-Van Camp	17	3.5–**4.7**‡
Iowa P'w'r & L't	37	**4.9**	Toledo Edison	17	**4.7**
May Dept. Stores	49	4.5–**4.9**	Union Electric	34	4.5–**4.7**•
Melville Shoe	28	4.6–**4.9**	United Elec. Coal	37	4.3–**4.7**
Public Ser. Elec. & Gas	41	4.5–**4.9**	Washington Water	45	4.4–**4.7**•
Sinclair Oil	63	4.8–**4.9**	Western Pacific R. R.	79	3.8–**4.7**
Union Pacific	35	4.6–**4.9**	Wisconsin Elec. P'r	39	4.5–**4.7**
ASR Products	12	4.2–**4.8**	Abitibi Power & Paper	37*	**4.6**
Allegheny Ludlum	46	4.3–**4.8**	Anheuser-Busch	26	**4.6**
Amer. Chain	57	4.4–**4.8**	Champlin Oil	24	4.2–**4.6**
Amer. Insurance	27	**4.8**	Chrysler	65	3.1–**4.6**
Amer. Smelting	47	4.3–**4.8**	Conn. L't & P'w'r	26	4.2–**4.6**•
Arvin Industries	26	**4.8**–5.8	Consol. Cigar	54	3.9–**4.6**
Ashland Oil	24	4.2–**4.8**	Divco-Wayne	25	4.0–**4.6**
Buckeye Pipe Line	33	4.2–**4.8**	Federal Mogul	58	4.1–**4.6**
Carrier	44	4.1–**4.8**	Gen'l Motors	49	4.1–**4.6**
Collins & Aikman	24	3.8–**4.8**	Gen'l Refractories	52	3.8–**4.6**
Consumers Power	54	4.4–**4.8**	Girard Trust	56	**4.6**
Eagle-Picher	48	**4.8**	Glidden	49	4.1–**4.6**
Elec. Storage Bat.	42	**4.8**	Int'l Minerals	35	**4.6**
Federal Paper B'd	50	4.4–**4.8**	Minnesota P. & L't	38	4.2–**4.6**
Gen'l Cable	42	**4.8**–5.2	Nat'l Biscuit	52	**4.6**
Hammermill	31	3.2–**4.8**	Pacific Lighting	52	**4.6**
Lee Rubber & Tire	29	4.1–**4.8**	Philco	35	2.9–**4.6**
Link-Belt	62	**4.8**	U. S. Pipe & F'dry	26	**4.6**
Mack Trucks	42	4.3–**4.8**	U. S. Tobacco	26	**4.6**
Murphy (G. C.)	47	**4.8**	Walker (Hiram)	35	4.0–**4.6**
So. Puerto Rico Sugar	26	3.8–**4.8**‡	Wilson & Co.	35	4.0–**4.6**
Transcont'l Gas Pipe	23	4.3–**4.8**•			
United Engineering	21	**4.8**	Admiral Corp.	22	3.4–**4.5**
U. S. Plywood	52	4.3–**4.8**	Amer. Can	44	**4.5**
Warner & Swasey	31	4.5–**4.8**	Amer. Distilling	44	3.6–**4.5**
			Armco Steel	70	4.3–**4.5**
Amer. Molasses	15	**4.7**‡	Canadian Brew's	42	3.6–**4.5**
Borg-Warner	43	**4.7**	Crane Company	40	3.0–**4.5**
C.I.T. Financial	55	**4.7**	Dayton P'w'r & L't	53	**4.5**–4.8

Name of Stock	Recent Price [4/30/59]	Est'd Yield Next 12 Months [Based on Price, 4/30/59]
Flintkote	40	4.5
Industrial Accept'ce	38*	4.2–4.5
Joy M'f'g	49	4.1–4.5
New York Trust	92	4.5–4.6
Niagara Mohawk	40	4.5–5.0•
Norfolk & Western	99	4.0–4.5
Northern Nat. Gas	31	4.5
Northern Pacific	51	4.5–5.4
Northrop Corp.	40	4.0–4.5
Peoples Drug Stores	49	4.1–4.5
Puget Sound P. & L't	34	4.2–4.5
Reliance Insurance	49	4.5
Republic Aviation	22	4.5–6.8
Stewart-Warner	51	4.1–4.5
Sutherland Paper	44	4.5
Washington Gas L't	51	4.4–4.5
Yale & Towne	33	4.5
Amer. Optical	45	4.4–5.3
Atlas Steels	27*	4.4
Beneficial Finance	26	3.8–4.4
Brooklyn Un. Gas	54	4.1–4.4
Budd	27	3.7–4.4
Cincinnati G. & Elec.	34	4.4
Community Pub. Ser.	24	4.2–4.4
Consol. Edison	64	4.4
Consol. Foods	27	3.7–4.4‡
Deere & Co.	59	4.4–4.7
Endicott Johnson	36	4.4
Gillette	51	4.4
Gimbel Bros.	44	4.1–4.4
Int'l Silver	45	3.3–4.4
Kansas P'w'r & L't	32	4.3–4.4
Marine Midland	25	4.3–4.4
N. Y. State E. & Gas	57	4.0–4.4
Northern States P'w'r	25	4.4–4.5
Oliver Corp.	18	3.9–4.4
Phila. Nat'l Bank	43	4.4–4.9
Pure Oil	45	3.8–4.4
Richfield Oil	90	3.9–4.4
Singer M'f'g	50	4.4–4.0
S'th'n Calif. Edison	59	4.4–4.6
S'th'n Pacific Co.	68	4.4–5.0
Amer. Seating	40	4.0–4.3
Assoc. Dry Goods	53	4.2–4.3
Balt. Gas & Elec.	46	3.9–4.3
Canada Iron F'dries	35*	4.3
Chase Man. Bank	59	4.3–4.4
Cluett, Peabody	58	3.9–4.3
Consol. Nat. Gas	50	4.2–4.3
Cont'l Can	47	3.8–4.3
Ford of Canada	140	3.6–4.3
Gen'l Public Util.	51	4.2–4.3
Genesco, Inc.	36	4.2–4.3
Indianapolis P. & L't	40	4.3
Irving Trust (N. Y.)	38	4.3
Maytag	81	3.5–4.3
Ohio Oil	40	4.0–4.3
Oklahoma Nat. Gas	29	4.3
Pacific Tel. & Tel.	164	4.3–4.9

Name of Stock	Recent Price [4/30/59]	Est'd Yield Next 12 Months [Based on Price, 4/30/59]
Peabody Coal	14	4.3
Penn. P'w'r & L't	58	4.3
Pepsi-Cola	30	4.3–4.7
Phila. Electric	52	4.3
Potomac Elec. P'w'r	29	4.3
Quaker Oats	47	4.3
Rockwell M'f'g	38	4.0–4.3‡
Royal Dutch Petr.	44	3.0–4.3
Sangamo Electric	49	3.9–4.3
Seaboard Finance	28	3.6–4.3‡
Stand'd Oil (Ohio)	64	3.9–4.3
Sunshine Biscuits	102	4.3
West Penn Electric	37	4.3
Bank of America	48	3.8–4.2
Briggs & Stratton	53	3.8–4.2
Cen. Illinois Light	36	3.9–4.2
Chic. G't Western	49	4.2–4.6
First Nat'l Stores	65	3.8–4.2
Hartford Elec. L't	71	4.2–4.4•
Home Insurance	52	3.8–4.2
Interprov'c'l Pipe	54*	4.2
Interstate Dept.	33	3.6–4.2
Lockheed	36	3.3–4.2
Lone Star Cement	33	3.6–4.2
Morgan Guaranty Tr.	95	4.2
Noranda Mines	52*	3.8–4.2
Northern Ind. P. Ser.	51	4.2
Ohio Edison	65	4.1–4.2
Penney (J. C.)	112	4.0–4.2
Pennsylvania R. R.	18	4.2
Rochester G. & Elec.	43	4.2–4.7
Spencer Kellogg	19	4.2–6.3
Stand'd Brands	66	3.9–4.2
Stand'd Oil (N. J.)	53	4.2–4.0
Technicolor	8⅞	4.2
Universal Leaf Tob.	53	4.2
Virginian R'lw'y	48	4.2–5.2
Western Auto S'ply	31	3.9–4.2
Westinghouse Air	36	3.3–4.2
Whirlpool Corp.	36	3.3–4.2
White Motor	48	3.6–4.2
Amer. Broadc.-Par't	27	3.7–4.1
Atlantic Coast Line	61	4.1–4.3
Borden Company	79	3.8–4.1
Chic. Pneu. Tool	29	4.1
Cities Service	58	4.1
Cornell Dubilier	27	3.0–4.1
Fairbanks, Morse	34	4.1
First Nat'l (Bos.)	86	4.1
First Nat'l (St. L.)	78	4.1
Gardner-Denver	52	3.8–4.1
Harbison-Walker	49	3.7–4.1
Harris-Intertype	49	4.1
Inland Steel	139	3.7–4.1
Int'l Nickel	92	3.3–4.1
Kansas City P. & L't	54	4.1
Manufacturers Trust	54	4.1–4.3
Pacific G. & Elec.	64	4.1–4.2•
Penick & Ford	55	4.1–4.4

Name of Stock	Recent Price [4/30/59]	Est'd Yield Next 12 Months [Based on Price, 4/30/59]	Name of Stock	Recent Price [4/30/59]	Est'd Yield Next 12 Months [Based on Price, 4/30/59]
Shamrock Oil	39	4.1	Gen'l Dynamics	58	3.4–3.8
Stand'd Oil (Ind.)	51	4.1	G't Amer. Insur.	42	3.6–3.8
Tenn. Gas Trans.	34	4.1•	Halliburton Oil	63	3.8
Twentieth Cen.-Fox	39	4.1–4.9	Household Finance	32	3.8‡
United Gas Imp't	58	4.1	Idaho Power	45	3.8•
U. S. Steel	91	4.1–4.4	Johns-Manville	60	3.3–3.8
			Libby, McNeill	13	3.1–3.8
Amer. Viscose	50	2.0–4.0	Nat'l Dairy P'd'cts	52	3.8
Anderson-Prichard	35	3.4–4.0	Nat'l Steel	79	3.8–5.1
Armstrong Cork	41	3.7–4.0	Nat'l Tea	21	3.3–3.8
Atlantic Refining	50	4.0	N. J. Zinc	26	2.3–3.8
Bankers Trust	80	4.0–4.1	Pacific Finance	65	3.7–3.8
Beatrice Foods	50	3.6–4.0	Peoples Gas L't & C'ke	58	3.4–3.8
Beech-Life Savers	40	4.0–4.3	Rayonier	26	1.5–3.8
Bell Aircraft	20	4.0–5.0	Sealright-Oswego	42	3.6–3.8
Braniff Airways	15	4.0	So. Carolina E. & Gas	36	3.8
Cen. Hudson G. & E.	22	4.0–4.1•	Square D	30	3.3–3.8
Chain Belt	59	4.0	Stand'd Oil (Cal.)	55	3.8–4.4
Chemical Corn	62	4.0–4.2	United Gas Corp.	42	3.6–3.8
Corn Products	55	3.6–4.0			
Dr. Pepper	15	4.0	Amer. Natural Gas	70	3.7
Firstamerica	22	3.6–4.0	Anchor Hocking	35	3.7
Lehigh Portland	31	3.2–4.0	Carborundum	43	3.7–4.0
Maryland Casualty	40	3.8–4.0	Ex-Cell-O	41	3.7
Mead Corp.	45	3.8–4.0	Granite City Steel	61	3.7–4.9
Middle South Util.	48	4.0	Int'l Salt	147	3.2–3.7
Royal Crown Cola	20	4.0‡	Kansas G. & Elec.	43	3.7
San Diego G. & Elec.	29	3.6–4.0	Lehn & Fink	54	3.3–3.7
Texas P'c'f'c C'l & Oil	30	3.3–4.0	Long Island L't'g	35	3.4–3.7
			Martin Co.	49	3.3–3.7‡
Amer. Chicle	54	3.7–3.9	Morrell (John)	27	2.2–3.7
Amer. Surety	20	3.9	Panhandle Eastern	49	3.7
Amer. Tel. & Tel.	252	3.9	Public Ser. (Colo.)	51	3.7–3.8
Brown & Sharpe	31	3.9	Reynolds Tob.	57	3.7–3.8
Carolina P'w'r & L't	37	3.9			
Cerro de Pasco	41	2.9–3.9	Associates Invest.	73	3.6
Dome Mines	18	3.9	Babcock & Wilcox	33	3.0–3.6‡
El Paso Nat. Gas	33	3.9•	Black & Decker	64	3.1–3.6
First Nat'l City	78	3.9–4.1	Brown Shoe	67	3.3–3.6
Hanover Bank	52	3.9–4.1	Canada Cement	35*	2.9–3.6
Illinois Power	41	3.7–3.9	Cincinnati Milling	44	3.6–3.2
Ingersoll-Rand	102	3.9	Consol. Mining	22	3.6
Montana-Dak. Util.	31	3.2–3.9	Consolidation Coal	33	3.6
Page-Hersey Tubes	31*	2.9–3.9	Federated Dep't St.	59	3.4–3.6
Robertshaw-Fulton	46	3.3–3.9	Gen'l Amer. Trans.	59	3.4–3.6
Schenley Industries	37	2.8–3.9	Gen'l Portland Cem.	39	3.2–3.6
Timken Roller	57	3.5–3.9	Grace (W. R.)	45	3.6
Tri-Continental	42	3.9	Mallory (P. R.)	43	3.3–3.6
Utah Power & L't	34	3.8–3.9•	McGraw-Edison	42	3.3–3.6
Vanadium	36	2.8–3.9	Mergenthaler	56	3.6
Western Union	36	3.3–3.9	Minneapolis-Moline	22	2.7–3.6
			Pitts. Plate Glass	76	2.9–3.6
Calif. Packing	58	3.8–4.5‡	Rheem M'f'g	22	2.7–3.6
Celanese	32	3.1–3.8	Safeway Stores	38	3.2–3.6
Cen. Illinois P. S.	46	3.8	St. Joseph Lead	36	3.3–3.6
Cleveland Electric	52	3.5–3.8	Southwest. Pub. Ser.	44	3.6•
Coca-Cola	132	3.8–4.2			
Columbia Pictures	20	1.3–3.8	Aetna Fire Ins.	75	3.5–3.6
Cont'l Insurance	58	3.4–3.8	Amer. Elec. Power	51	2.9–3.5
Cooper-Bessemer	42	3.8–4.3	Blaw-Knox	44	3.3–3.5‡
Delta Airlines	32	3.8	Camden Fire Ins.	37	3.2–3.5

Name of Stock	Recent Price [4/30/59]	Est'd Yield Next 12 Months [Based on Price, 4/30/59]
Campbell Soup	51	3.1–3.5
Case (J. I.)	23	3.5
Clevite	36	3.2–3.5
Cont'l Illinois	122	3.4–3.5
Delaware P'w'r & L't	63	3.3–3.5
Fidelity-Phenix Ins.	63	3.2–3.5
Libby-Owens-Ford	57	3.5–4.0
McIntyre Porc. Mines	86	3.5
McKesson & Robbins	86	3.3–3.5
Motor Wheel	17	3.5–Nil
No. Amer. Aviation	46	3.5–4.3
Otis Elevator	71	3.4–3.5
Phoenix Insurance	85	3.5
Smith (A. O.)	57	2.8–3.5
S'th'n Co.	39	3.5
Sunbeam	55	3.0–3.5
U. S. Rubber	57	3.5
Walworth	17	3.5–2.6
West Va. Pulp & P'p'r	46	2.6–3.5
Worthington	78	3.3–3.5
Amer. Bank Note	35	3.4–3.7
Bendix Aviation	79	3.0–3.4
Freeport Sulphur	35	3.4
Gulf States Util.	58	3.4•
Interchemical Corp.	33	3.4
Madison Fund, Inc.	19	3.4
Magnavox	58	2.6–3.4
Masonite	44	3.0–3.4
Nat'l Bank (Detroit)	59	3.4
Nat'l Distillers	32	3.1–3.4
Newmont Mining	89	2.2–3.4
Owens-Ill. Glass	89	3.1–3.4
Phillips Petroleum	51	3.4
Tennessee Corp.	77	3.2–3.4
U. S. Fire Insurance	32	3.1–3.4
Warner Bros.	40	3.0–3.4
Weyerhaeuser	45	3.4
Air Reduction	85	2.9–3.3
Amer. Airlines	30	3.3
Amphenol-Borg	42	3.3
Armour & Co.	24	Nil–3.3
Atlantic City Elec.	45	3.3•
Bohn Aluminum	30	3.3
Canadian Oil Cos.	30*	2.7–3.3
Cen. & South West	60	3.0–3.3
Colgate-Palmolive	121	3.0–3.3
Commonwealth Ed.	61	3.3‡
Diamond Alkali	54	3.3‡
Fireman's Fund	58	3.1–3.3
Harshaw Chemical	30	3.3–3.8
Howe Sound	18	2.2–3.3
Louisville G. & Elec.	42	3.3
McCall	20	3.3–4.0
Security-First Nat'l	55	2.9–3.3
Staley (A. E.)	41	3.3–3.8‡
United Biscuit	24	3.3
Adams Express	29	3.2
Amer. Bosch Arma	37	3.2–3.5

Name of Stock	Recent Price [4/30/59]	Est'd Yield Next 12 Months [Based on Price, 4/30/59]
Avco M'f'g	14	2.9–3.2
Bliss (E. W.)	19	1.6–3.2
Boeing	39	2.7–3.2‡
Chemetron	31	3.2
Clark Equipment	70	3.2
Combustion Eng.	37	3.0–3.2
Container Corp.	28	3.6–3.2
Crown Zellerbach	57	3.2
Cudahy Packing	14	Nil–3.2
Duke Power	47	3.2–3.4
Gen'l Cigar	28	2.9–3.2
Gen'l Mills	108	3.0–3.2
Heinz (H. J.)	68	3.2–3.4
Kimberly-Clark	63	3.0–3.2
Kroger	29	3.2‡
Montana Power	75	3.2
Oklahoma G. & Elec.	33	3.0–3.2•
St. Regis Paper	50	2.8–3.2
Sears, Roebuck	43	2.9–3.2
Springfield Fire & M.	31	3.2
Texaco	85	2.8–3.2
Amer. Trust	58	2.8–3.1
Arizona Pub. Ser.	41	3.1–3.2
Daystrom	43	2.8–3.1
Gen'l Foods	78	3.1–3.2
Imperial Oil	45	3.0–3.1
Loew's, Inc.	32	3.1–4.7
Matson Navigation	45	2.7–3.1
McGraw-Hill Publ.	59	2.8–3.1
Mission Corp.	45	3.1
Nat'l Lead	122	2.7–3.1
Pillsbury Co.	45	3.1
Sperry Rand	26	3.1
Union Bag-Camp	48	3.1
Union Oil (Cal.)	45	2.2–3.1
Va. Elec. & P'w'r	39	3.1•
Algoma Steel	37*	3.0
Arkansas Fuel Oil	33	3.0
Brunswick-Balke	92	2.2–3.0
Cutler-Hammer	84	3.0
Gen'l Tel. & Electro.	71	2.8–3.0
Glens Falls Ins.	40	2.5–3.0
Parke, Davis	44	3.0
Procter & Gamble	79	2.8–3.0
Scovill M'f'g	25	Nil–3.0
Skelly Oil	66	3.0–3.3
Steel Co. of Canada	77*	2.5–3.0
Walgreen Co.	54	3.0
Amer. Cyanamid	56	2.9
Atlas Powder	84	2.9–3.2
Bucyrus-Erie	34	1.5–2.9
Burroughs	41	2.9–3.4
Champion Paper	42	2.9
Commercial Solv.	17	1.2–2.9
Curtis Publishing	12	2.9
Louisiana Land	60	2.5–2.9
McDonnell Aircraft	43	2.3–2.9‡
Nat'l Gypsum	69	2.9

Name of Stock	Recent Price [4/30/59]	Est'd Yield Next 12 Months [Based on Price, 4/30/59]	Name of Stock	Recent Price [4/30/59]	Est'd Yield Next 12 Months [Based on Price, 4/30/59]
Sherwin-Williams	224	2.6–**2.9**	British Amer. Oil	41	**2.4**
Sterling Drug	55	**2.9**–3.1	Domin. F'dries & St.	49*	**2.4**–2.7
Transamerica	29	2.8–**2.9**	Eastern Air Lines	41	**2.4**‡
U. S. Gypsum	114	2.6–**2.9**	G't Atl'c & P'c'f'c	41	4.4–**2.4**
Winn-Dixie Stores	41	2.6–**2.9**	Pittston	68	1.8–**2.4**‡
			Radio Corp. Amer.	62	**2.4**
Abbott Laboratories	80	2.5–**2.8**	Thompson Ramo	68	2.1–**2.4**
Allied Chemical	112	2.7–**2.8**‡	United Carbon	84	**2.4**
Amer. Mach. & F'dry	88	2.6–**2.8**			
Carnation	65	**2.8**–3.0	First Nat'l (Chi.)	345	**2.3**
Food Fair	38	2.6–**2.8**‡	Georgia-Pacific	65	1.9–**2.3**
Food Machinery	45	**2.8**	Texas Gulf Pr'd'cing	30	2.1–**2.3**
Hooker Chemical	40	2.5–**2.8**	Western Airlines	35	**2.3**‡
Jewel Tea Co.	49	2.4–**2.8**			
Kellogg	41	2.4–**2.8**	Amerada Petroleum	92	**2.2**
Shell Oil	85	2.6–**2.8**	Firestone Tire	143	1.8–**2.2**
Tampa Electric	50	**2.8**	Goodyear Tire	144	1.7–**2.2**
Texas Utilities	67	**2.8**	Insur. Co. N. Amer.	138	**2.2**
Union Carbide	134	2.7–**2.8**	Lily-Tulip Cup	102	2.0–**2.2**
Warner-Lambert	110	**2.8**‡	Murray Corp.	27	**2.2**–3.0
Westinghouse Elec.	86	2.3–**2.8**	Ralston Purina	54	**2.2**
			Smith, Kline & French	146	**2.2**
Amer. Home P'd'cts	149	**2.7**			
Amer. Stores	90	2.2–**2.7**	Merck & Co.	85	1.9–**2.1**
Bristol-Myers	103	2.3–**2.7**	Norwich Pharm.	74	1.9–**2.1**
Columbia Br'c't'g	46	2.6–**2.7**	Pabst Brewing	14	Nil–**2.1**
Cont'l Oil	62	2.6–**2.7**	Revere Copper	48	**2.1**–2.6
Du Pont	242	2.5–**2.7**	St. Paul Fire & Marine	60	**2.1**–2.2
Emerson Radio	22	**2.7**	Schering	63	2.1–2.2
Fibreboard Paper	52	2.3–**2.7**‡	West Indies Sugar	47	**2.1**§
Florida Power	29	**2.7**			
Gen'l Electric	84	2.5–**2.7**	Amer.-Marietta	55	**2.0**–2.1
Goodrich	92	2.4–**2.7**	Eastman Kodak	88	1.9–**2.0**
Int'l Paper	116	2.6–**2.7**	G't Northern Paper	51	1.2–**2.0**
Olin Mathieson	49	2.0–**2.7**	Hartford Fire Ins.	187	1.6–**2.0**
Pet Milk	48	**2.7**–3.1	Lehman Corp.	31	**2.0**
Scott Paper	82	2.4–**2.7**	Monsanto	49	**2.0**‡
United Corp.	9¼	**2.7**	Moore Corp.	112*	**2.0**–2.1
			Motorola	94	1.7–**2.0**
Amer. Potash	46	2.2–**2.6**	Northwest Airlines	40	**2.0**–3.0
Bayuk Cigars	38	**2.6**–3.0	Pfizer (Chas.)	130	1.8–**2.0**
Emerson Electric	62	**2.6**‡			
Gerber Products	68	**2.6**–2.8	Dominion Stores	78*	1.6–**1.9**
Gulf Oil	114	2.4–**2.6**	Florida P'w'r & L't	91	1.8–**1.9**
Industrial Rayon	23	Nil–**2.6**	Hercules Powder	70	1.8–**1.9**
Int'l Tel. & Tel.	42	2.4–**2.6**	Nat'l Cash Register	70	**1.9**–2.0
Kaiser Aluminum	43	2.1–**2.6**			
Pan American Airways	31	**2.6**	Aluminium, Ltd.	28	**1.8**
U. S. Fidelity & G'ty	86	2.3–**2.6**	Fansteel Metal	57	**1.8**–2.1‡
Victor Chemical	38	**2.6**	Gen'l Precision Eq.	41	**1.8**–2.4•
			Hoffman Electronics	74	1.4–**1.8**
Arkansas La. Gas	64	2.2–**2.5**	Hollinger Consol.	34	**1.8**–2.1
Caterpillar Tractor	95	**2.5**	Johnson & Johnson	50	1.6–**1.8**
Fruehauf Trailer	24	Nil–**2.5**	Kearney & Trecker	17	0.9–**1.8**
Houston L't & P'w'r	72	2.2–**2.5**	Kerr McGee Oil	65	1.2–**1.8**
Pennsalt Chem.	89	2.1–**2.5**	Mead Johnson	77	1.6–**1.8**
Raytheon M'f'g	71	Nil–**2.5**	N. Y. Central	28	**1.8**–3.6
Signal Oil "A"	37	2.2–**2.5**			
Texaco Canada, Ltd.	71*	2.3–**2.5**	Cont'l Casualty	136	1.4–**1.7**
Zenith Radio	107	1.9–**2.5**	Grand Union	52	**1.7**‡

181

Name of Stock	Recent Price [4/30/59]	Est'd Yield Next 12 Months [Based on Price, 4/30/59]	Name of Stock	Recent Price [4/30/59]	Est'd Yield Next 12 Months [Based on Price, 4/30/59]
Aluminum Co.	83	1.4–**1.6**	Conn. Gen'l Life	382	**0.7**
Gen'l Amer. Invest.	33	**1.6**			
Gen'l Tire	75	0.9–**1.6**	Int'l Business Mach.	392	0.5–**0.6**
Nat'l Fire Insur.	140	**1.6**–2.1			
Rexall Drug & Chem.	44	1.1–**1.6**	Rohm & Haas	623	0.3–**0.5**‡
Royal McBee Corp.	19	Nil–**1.6**			
Sun Oil	63	**1.6**	Getty Oil	24	Stk.
			Nat'l Airlines	24	Stk.
Addressograph	111	1.4–**1.5**	Nat'l Homes "A"	24	Stk.
Bigelow-Sanford	17	Nil–**1.5**	Seaboard & Western	12	Stk.
Minneapolis-H'w'll	135	1.4–**1.5**	Tidewater Oil	26	Stk.
Pitney-Bowes	39	**1.5**			
Vick Chemical	134	1.3–**1.5**‡	Alleghany Corp.	13	Nil
			Atlas Corp.	7	Nil
Aetna Life Ins.	254	**1.4**–1.5	Bullard	20	Nil
Dow Chemical	88	**1.4**–1.5‡	Capital Airlines	20	Nil
Loew's Theatres	14	Nil–**1.4**	Chic. & N. W.	27	Nil
Travelers Insurance	90	1.3–**1.4**	Congoleum-Nairn	14	Nil
			Delaware, Lack.	11	Nil
			Dumont Lab's	8⅛	Nil
Crown Cork	32	**1.3**–2.5	Erie Railroad	13	Nil
United Air Lines	38	**1.3**‡	Fairchild Engine	9	Nil
			Foster Wheeler	42	Nil
Corning Glass	125	1.2–1.3	Lehigh Valley R.R.	8¾	Nil
			Lone Star Steel	33	Nil
Minnesota Mining	147	1.0–**1.1**	Magma Copper	63	Nil
Owens-Corning	74	**1.1**–1.3	Mission Development	27	Nil
			N. Y., N. Haven	8⅝	Nil
Conde Nast	9⅝	**1.0**–3.1	Reed Roller Bit	25	Nil
Consol. Electrodyn.	41	**1.0**–1.2	Studebaker-Packard	12	Nil
Lincoln Nat'l Life	221	0.9–**1.0**	Trans World Airlines	20	Nil
Reynolds Metals	86	0.8–**1.0**‡	Underwood	27	Nil
			U. S. Industries	13	**Nil**–3.1
			U. S. Smelting	34	**Nil**–1.5
Collins Radio	41	**0.9**	Van Norman	12	Nil
Cont'l Assurance	144	0.8–**0.9**	Va.-Carolina Chem.	31	Nil
Nat'l Can	11	Stk.–**0.9**‡	West Ky. Coal	18	Nil

* Canadian Funds.
‡ Plus stock.
• Dividends believed partly exempt from ordinary income tax.
§ Plus possible distribution from sale of properties.

NOTE: Where the dividend estimate is a range, the figures are so presented as to indicate the probable direction of any change. The yield based on the more likely dividend is printed in bold-face type.

Due to mergers and substitutions, the number of stocks appearing in *The Value Line Investment Survey, Weekly Summary-Index*, may vary slightly from week to week, but changes are insignificant.